A July 2009 Indie Next Pick • *Seattle Magazine Editors' Gift Pick 2009*

Praise for
hungry monkey

"This book serves up a delicious story about one father's quest to raise a foodie. It provides inspiration for persisting with your fussy eater, plus over 50 delicious recipes to try."
— *Scholastic Parent & Child*

"Sheds a refreshing light on the trials and tribulations of feeding kids . . . [Amster-Burton] covers everything from baby mush to pre-schooler snack time . . . A great read for any new parent."
— Bucks County Food Examiner

"[*Hungry Monkey*] had me laughing out loud in recognition . . . You don't even have to have kids to get a kick out of it, so long as you remember what it's like to be one."
— All You Can Eat (*Seattle Times* online)

"A loving, anecdotal account . . . [an] honest, whimsical take on picky eaters." — Table Talk (*Atlanta Journal Constitution* online)

"One of . . . This hilarious book . . . is a great remind . . . d kids can equal fun." . . . online)

. . . ill love this book."
— Frantic Foodie (*Seattle . . . . . . ntelligencer* online)

"Amster-Burton is smart, funny, a terrific writer, a great cook and on track to be voted father-of-the-year every year for the next decade, at least. How lucky for Iris, a.k.a. Hungry Monkey, that she landed in the Amster-Burton family and how really lucky for us that we can tag along on their adventures — and learn how to make pretzels and pad Thai, too."
— Dorie Greenspan, author of *Baking: From My Home to Yours*

"This charming, funny book is full of great ideas for family meals. In a world of culinary pandering to kids, where vegetables in disguise pass for cuisine, Amster-Burton gets the recipe right."
— Neal Pollack, author of *Alternadad*

"With its incisive wit and hilarious stories about Iris, *Hungry Monkey* made me want to have a child — just so I could start feeding her."
— Shauna James Ahern, author of *Gluten-Free Girl*

"Amster-Burton cast some sort of enchantment over me as I read about his all-too-real-life culinary adventures with his daughter. The proof? I actually found myself thinking: if Matthew were my dad, I don't think I'd mind being a little girl . . . or even a sock monkey . . . if I got my share of every meal."
— John Thorne, author of *Outlaw Cook* and *Mouth Wide Open*

"Amster-Burton has written a wonderful book. It reads so well you won't be able to put it down . . . except when overcome by a need to rush to your kitchen and execute one or another of his winning recipes."
— Paula Wolfert, author of *The Slow Mediterranean Kitchen*

"One of my greatest fears is imagining my daughter insisting on nothing but crustless grilled cheese sandwiches and 'chicken' McNuggets. *Hungry Monkey* goes a long way to allaying that concern." — Anthony Bourdain, author of *Kitchen Confidential*

hungry monkey

A Food-Loving Father's
Quest to Raise an
Adventurous Eater

**Matthew
Amster-Burton**

MARINER BOOKS
HOUGHTON MIFFLIN HARCOURT
Boston · New York

To Laurie

First Mariner Books edition 2010
Copyright © 2009 by Matthew Amster-Burton

For information about permission to reproduce selections from this book,
write to Permissions, Houghton Mifflin Harcourt Publishing Company,
215 Park Avenue South, New York, New York 10003.

www.hmhbooks.com

Library of Congress Cataloging-in-Publication Data

Amster-Burton, Matthew.
    Hungry monkey : a food-loving father's quest to raise an adventurous
eater / Matthew Amster-Burton.
    p. cm.
    ISBN 978-0-15-101324-1
    1. Children — Nutrition. 2. Food preferences in children. 3. Food
journalists — Anecdotes. I. Title.
    RJ206.A57 2009
    618.92 — dc22   2008052947

    ISBN 978-0-547-33689-3 (pbk.)

Book design by Melissa Lotfy
Text is set in Arno.

PRINTED IN THE UNITED STATES OF AMERICA

DOC 10 9 8 7 6 5 4 3 2 1

Grateful acknowledgment is made to the following for permission to reprint recipes:
    "Cowboy Beans." Adapted from *Mexican Everyday* by Rick Bayless with Deann
Groen Bayless. Copyright © 2005 by Rick Bayless and Deann Groen Bayless. Used
by permission of W. W. Norton & Company, Inc.
    "Yeasted Waffles." Recipe for Raised Waffles from *A Real American Breakfast* by
Cheryl Alters Jamison and Bill Jamison. Copyright © 2002 by Cheryl Alters Jamison
and Bill Jamison. Reprinted by permission of HarperCollins Publishers.

contents

hungry monkey

introduction

Where Do Monkeys Come From?

MY DAUGHTER'S FIRST MEAL was supposed to be, oh, let's say local organic carrots pureed with homemade chicken broth in a hand-cranked food mill. That's what everyone wants for their kid, right? I swear I was totally planning a feast of that nature when fate intervened and a doughnut fell on her head.

Leaving the local doughnut shop while carrying three-month-old Iris in the baby sling, I was, as usual, too impatient to make it the whole four blocks home before digging into my Double Trouble (chocolate cake with chocolate glaze). As I took a bite, a large crumb dropped, landing within range of Iris's pointy tongue. She opened her mouth and slurped up the chunk with the same eagerness as, well, me. Uh-oh. You're not supposed to feed a three-month-old anything other than breast milk or formula, and definitely not a doughnut. Apparently the American Academy of Pediatrics doesn't have any three-month-olds on their committees.

There's no evidence that the doughnut caused permanent damage, but Iris, now four years old, does exhibit some peculiar tendencies. In her favorite video game, Chocolatier, she builds a worldwide chocolate empire. Her favorite foods are pizza and burgers, but also sushi and a spicy Szechuan noodle dish. And recently, she had a friend over to play, and after they'd made a mess of the dining room baking pretend cakes, they ran over to me crying out, "We need more garam masala!"

When my wife, Laurie, told me that she was pregnant, I was working the world's greatest job: restaurant critic for a daily newspaper. Every week I'd be off to some new or neglected restaurant — a dim sum parlor, a Korean hole in the wall, a red sauce Italian joint, a Turkish kebab house — all paid for by the Seattle Times. Laurie would usually come along, and we'd feast on great food, miserable food, and a lot in between. On nights off from restaurant reviewing I'd cook dinner: green papaya salad with tiny dried shrimp, beef bourguignon, Brussels sprouts with bacon.

So when I learned we were going to have a baby, my first thought was *Are we going to have to eat fifties rejects like sloppy joes for the next eighteen years? Or feed our kid food we'd never eat ourselves?* (Okay, my actual first thought was *Jeez, I hope it was one of the better sperm.*) All I knew about baby food was that it came in a jar and looked liked washed-out fingerpaints. And I could barely remember anything I ate when I was a kid beyond pepperoni pizza, burgers, steak, and roast chicken. I hated roast chicken. In sixth grade, a friend and I vowed never to eat foods other than pizza, burgers, and hot dogs — in retrospect, something of a drawn-out suicide pact.

Now, I still like pizza, burgers, and hot dogs, and I've even kind of come around on roast chicken, especially the *poulet rôti* served at Le Pichet near Pike Place Market. But, pact or no pact, I didn't want to be trapped into eating them in rotation, out of some sense of family solidarity, until our child left for college.

The words of John Allemang rang out in my head: "You don't have children?" writes Allemang in *The Importance of Lunch*. "You will never know what kind of gastronomic compromises you've been spared. Children don't just bring a jolt of reality to adult appetites. They remake reality, turning a sophisticated cook who used to smoke her own duck sausages into a desperado who will stop at nothing — not even packaged luncheon meat — to silence the complaints of the young."

I thought about the day my friend Matt and I spent making two kinds of Thai sausage, one with sticky rice and garlic (*sai krok*), the other with lemongrass, galangal, and chiles (*sai oua*). *Those days are over, pal,* Allemang seemed to be saying. And that doesn't only apply to sausage. Another friend had always emailed me MP3s of new bands I just *had* to listen to, until he had twins. "I just don't have time to keep track of music anymore," he confessed, and his bulletins abruptly stopped.

Not to spoil the ending of this book, but Allemang was wrong: Iris and I have spent plenty of time together making sausage. She'll drop any toy to run over and help me operate the meat grinder. He was also right: Iris takes supermarket deli ham to school in her lunch box at least once a week.

After Iris was born, I read a lot of books about feeding babies and young children. Most of them were vegetable-puree cookbooks, party food books (of the "English muffin pizzas that look like cat faces" variety), and dull, clinical books that read like a free pamphlet from the pediatrician's office. What I wanted were stories about real parents and real kids learning about food together — making discoveries, making mistakes, making cookies.

So I wrote my own. *Hungry Monkey* is the book I wish someone had handed me before Iris was born so I would have known that breastfeeding is challenging (even for dads), that there are two simple rules to take a lot of the stress out of feeding kids, and that it's okay to feed a baby sushi and spicy enchiladas. Most important, I would have been reassured that having kids doesn't require dumbing down your menu: if you love to eat, a new baby presents an opportunity to have more fun with food than ever before in your life.

And, yes, more frustration.

· · ·

Laurie and I were married for eight years before having a baby, and I sometimes wonder what exactly we were doing all that time. Not like, "How could we have waited so long?" I have no regrets about that. No, I mean, now we spend hours and hours every day looking after Iris — what did we do with those scads of free time for eight years? It seems like we should have been able to score a couple of Nobel Prizes, or at least build a huge, eccentric art installation.

Instead, we have a small, eccentric child. In most ways, Iris eats like a typical four-year-old. She prefers white food, takes her burger plain, and is skeptical of vegetables. But she's also picky about certain things that are clearly a result of her parents' food obsessions. One day I burst into Iris's room in the morning and said, "How would you like some pancakes and bacon?"

"Nueske's," said Iris. Nueske's is a very smoky and expensive artisan bacon from Wisconsin, which we don't always keep in stock, so I attempted to substitute the supermarket brand without telling her. At breakfast, Iris ate a whole pancake and nibbled two bites of bacon. "Dada, this bacon doesn't taste good," she said.

Later she made up a game called I'm Takin' Your Bacon, in which I sidle down the hall and she runs up behind me and snatches my imaginary bacon. "I know!" said Iris, grabbing her toy pirate ship. "We're playing I'm Takin' Your Bacon, level two: I'm Divin' Your Bacon Underwater."

Iris may be more of a bacon snob than I am, but I think we have the same overall philosophy about food:

Food is fun, and you get to enjoy it three times a day, plus snacks.

Hey, you do have to eat quite often, and food at its best can be enormously rewarding. With a little luck and a healthy serving of *Hungry Monkey*, having a child is a chance to have a second honeymoon with food. Or, if you've never given food much thought before, a first honeymoon, because now that you have a kid, you're going to be thinking about it *a lot*.

. . .

We live in the city, so we're lucky to have access to certain things that I think of as essentials of life: cheese shops, Asian grocery stores, farmers' markets, premium chocolate. This has certainly influenced my palate and my career, and it provides plenty of field trip opportunities for me and Iris. But this book is about finding the fun in food wherever you are and whoever you're sharing it with — though from experience I can say that sharing it with a kid is pretty hard to beat.

Besides, I'm not interested in being a smug city guy (well, at least not all the time). As much as I love our local Asian supermarket, Uwajimaya, I have to admit that I sometimes journey to a Korean chain supermarket in the suburbs, twenty-five miles away, where the prices are lower and they sell fifty kinds of kimchi. There are great ingredients *everywhere*. The average suburban Whole Foods sells more kinds of good chocolate than were available in all of Seattle ten years ago. That's why I don't hesitate to recommend ingredients like Korean hot sauce, Chinese rock sugar, or poblano chiles. If these things aren't on your supermarket shelves today, they will be soon. In the meantime, you can order online (and I don't hesitate to recommend substitutes, either). Anyway, now and then you can see the Seattle flannel peeking out from under my snob suit. I'm a fan of frozen hash brown potatoes and boxed macaroni and cheese.

In short, if your situation is different from ours, it doesn't mean you can't have fun sharing food with your baby or toddler. I don't believe, as you often read in the paper, that you must insist on a nightly family dinner or your kid will drop out of school to concentrate on her meth lab. I'm lucky to have the time to cook dinner six nights a week, but man, if I have to read one more sanctimonious essay about the power of family dinner, I am canceling ours and replacing it with beer and a *Melrose Place* DVD marathon.

No, I cook dinner because I enjoy it, I have time to do it, and taking Iris out to dinner means watching her turn into a pumpkin around seven p.m., and by "pumpkin" I mean "wailing, puking lunatic." Having a kid hasn't made me any more tolerant of screaming kids in restaurants, so we do our best not to contribute to the problem. You're welcome.

Even though I like to cook some complicated meals, there are a lot of days when I have to start making dinner at five-thirty p.m. and have it on the table at six, and in chapters 15 and 16 I reveal my strategies for making food fast without having it taste like fast food.

I've included over fifty of my family's favorite recipes — some that Iris loves now and some that she used to eat and her parents hope she will enjoy again someday. The recipes range from the extremely simple (the best way to cook hot dogs) to more complicated but very kid-friendly weekend fare (*bibimbap,* a Korean rice dish that is, in terms of tasting great and pleasing everyone, the savory equivalent of make-your-own sundaes). Every recipe includes prep time, and that means how long it takes a normal human to make it, not a chef. Many recipes are marked QUICK (under thirty minutes) or EASY (limited slicing and dicing). I've also offered ideas (LITTLE FINGERS) for letting kids help out with some of the recipes.

Part of the reason I enjoy cooking so much, I admit, is that it's a break from parenting. But yes, I'm a stay-at-home dad. I didn't plan to be one. Does life ever go according to plan? Iris says she is going to be a doctor, but on her days off she will work at a construction site. She will have two dogs, two cats, and a baby. The baby will be named Daffodil. She will live in the building across the street from us, which offers only studio apartments. Good luck with that, dear.

We live in a lively Seattle neighborhood that, for me, is like a support group, so I'm not really on board with the traditional stay-at-home-dad spiel about how my wife doesn't understand how hard I work and how I need to connect with other dads who really get me. Okay, I admit, I did attempt to find a weekly "night out with the guys" activity and somehow ended up on an otherwise all-female bar trivia team. "We decided to call our team Girls Town," said the team captain. "I hope you don't mind."

I hadn't even told them that I read magazines like *Parenting* and *Working Mother*. The main thing I've learned from these magazines is that moms feel guilty about everything. I seem to be immune to this. Here are some things I don't feel guilty about:

- Letting Iris watch TV while I wash dishes.
- Introducing her to Crunch Berries.
- The fact that she likes hardly any green vegetables.
- Having a job. (Or, as Iris calls it, "typing on the baby computer.")
- Teaching Iris to play Donkey Kong Country 3 on the Super Nintendo.
- Saying I'm too tired to tell a kitties vs. pirates story with her dolls.
- Serving frozen potstickers for lunch.

Although, gosh, when I look at it all together like that, maybe I should feel guilty.

But I don't. Feeding a young child is stressful and unpredictable, you do whatever it takes to make it work, and the job is never done. But you could say the same thing about snowboarding or touring with the Rolling Stones. "Stressful and unpredictable" doesn't preclude fun.

Enjoying food is how Iris and I get along. When it comes down to it, I don't have that much in common with a little girl. I will always get bored long before Iris when we play sidewalk chalk or Candy Land (the worst game of all time). But I never get tired of sharing food with Iris. No matter how picky she is on any given day, food always offers us something we can agree on. It could be in the form of Szechuan noodles, pizza, chicken enchiladas . . . or just a small crumb of doughnut.

1

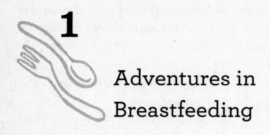

Adventures in Breastfeeding

AS LAURIE'S DUE DATE approached, I would frequently ask her, "Is my little buddy coming out today?" (Not *that* frequently, just three or six times a day.)

"Not today," she would always reply.

One morning, we woke up and I asked the usual question. "Not today," sighed Laurie. Then she made a face somewhere between relieved and horrified. "I think my water just broke," she said.

Excellent! So we took the bus to the hospital. When I mention this to people, they always think I am telling one of my funny jokes. Really, we took the bus. But we forgot to ask the driver for a third transfer for our extra passenger on the return trip.

True to every medical TV show, when we arrived at the hospital, there were some very helpful nurses and an intern who looked like he was sixteen. Laurie wasn't having any contractions. One of the nurses rooted around and said, "That doesn't feel like a head."

Shit! The baby has no head! was my first thought. Then our regular ob/gyn came in wheeling an ultrasound machine. "Your baby's butt-first," she said. "Let's go. C-section, right now." Our ob/gyn did not mess around.

I *highly* recommend the emergency C-section. I joked with the anesthesiologist for a while, and then a nurse handed me a baby. It was a girl with a distinctive pointy nose. We named her Iris. I did not instantly fall in love with the baby — it took about an hour, during which time Iris had her first taste of mother's milk.

She was not impressed.

Periodically there will be a minor furor when a parenting magazine prints a photo of an actual breast on the cover.

For example, when *BabyTalk* magazine kicked off the summer of 2006 with a nursing baby cover, readers went ballistic.

"I don't want my son or husband to accidentally see a breast they didn't want to see," said one woman in an AP interview. What did she do with the magazine? "I shredded it." Phew! Now her thirteen-year-old son will not develop an interest in breasts.

Personally, I have no problem with seeing a breast on the cover of a magazine, or inside a magazine, or . . . Sorry, what were we talking about? But I do have one complaint: seeing that happy baby latched on makes the process look easy.

The popular conception of breastfeeding goes something like this: the baby is delivered, the happy mom brings it to her breast, and baby is welcomed to the world with a slurp of sweet, delicious milk.

This is a terrible lie. For the first several days after delivery (and generally longer if it's a C-section), there is no milk. There is only colostrum. As English words go, *colostrum* is about as mellifluous as *smegma*. The colostrum lobby should hire one of those naming agencies to come up with a new name for it.

Here's what La Leche League says about colostrum:

> This special milk is yellow to orange in color and thick and sticky. It is low in fat, and high in carbohydrates, protein, and antibodies to help keep your baby healthy. Colostrum is extremely easy to digest, and is therefore the perfect first food for your baby.

This is all true. Here's what they don't say: *Babies fucking hate it.*

Ours did, at least. Iris reacted exactly as I would react if you brought me something orange, thick, and sticky, and told me to eat it because it's good for me. She didn't want to nurse. She would finish nursing and cry. She lost over half a pound, and she weighed less than seven pounds when she was born.

This went on for four days; it felt like four years. It was absolutely the worst experience of my life. Why we didn't supplement with formula at this point, I don't know. It's not like it would have meant a permanent switch away from breastfeeding. I hasten to add that I now know that this experience was completely normal, and that babies are supposed to lose weight after delivery, and they have plenty of stored energy and water to get them through the colostrum days. If you know someone expecting their first baby, could you please take them aside right now and explain this? Thanks.

Finally, Laurie woke up from a nap leaking milk all over the bed. Yes! I brought Iris over for some of the good stuff. She drank up and made the satisfied milk face we'd heard about.

Iris was delighted with milk, but that didn't mean it was a big milk party from that point on. Now she had a new problem: the milk was there, but she had trouble finding the nipple. Seriously, we would put her right there, half an inch away, and she would root around like we were pulling a trick. She was as bumbling as, well, a thirteen-year-old boy. We had to wait until she started screaming and then Laurie would shove a nipple into her mouth.

I will spare you the parts about sore nipples and sore backs and the part where I called the lactation consultant to come over. I should mention the nursing pillow recommended by the lactation consultant, which made a big difference. I will tell you the name of the product, and then I will never say these words again: My Brest Friend.

According to Laurie, on our first night home from the hospital I made one of our favorite dinners, salmon with cucumber salad. I have no memory of this, or much of anything from those first three months before Laurie went back to work. I remember Iris nursing almost constantly, day and night, and taking naps on our laps. She refused to be put down, ever, for twelve weeks. I'm not exaggerating for effect: we held her 24-7 for twelve weeks. I called her the Ice Princess, because she never smiled. Sometimes, when it had been twenty minutes since her last feeding and she was ready for the next one, I called her Hungry Monkey.

Laurie basically lived in an easy chair, drinking water from a pink plastic hospital pitcher ("It was like my best friend," she said recently), nursing the baby, and requesting snacks. I'd leave cheese and crackers and a pitcher of ice water before leaving for work. During pregnancy, Laurie's most powerful craving had been for cheeseburgers. That lessened after Iris was born. Somewhat. "I kept a stash of beef jerky at work while pregnant and nursing," she said, "which I had never done before and haven't since."

After a few weeks, Laurie pointed out that our very skinny baby had gotten kind of chubby. I started calling her Littlechubs. (Iris, that is.) Sometimes Chublets. Sometimes Sweet Chubs Alive. I will stop now. In fact, now that Iris is four years old and tall and slim, I should probably stop calling her Chublets altogether, but if she complains I'll explain that it's like how enormous guys are always nicknamed Tiny.

Iris ate nothing but breast milk for seven and a half months. I was in charge of parceling out the expressed breast milk. Every night while watching *Seinfeld* reruns, I'd have my little lab bench set up on a TV table, making the next day's bottles like a mad scientist dairy farmer. If this sounds weird, in retrospect maybe it was, but when you have a new baby, everything is weird.

Laurie is a public school librarian and has the summer off. This is awesome, because it supports my surfing habit. Okay, I'm lying —I don't actually spend the summer surfing, unless you count Web surfing. At the end of August, it was time for Laurie to go back to school. Iris would still breastfeed when Laurie was home, but we switched to formula the rest of the time. Every morning, Laurie would go into Iris's room and nurse her before leaving for work. This made me nervous. Ninety-five percent of the time, Iris went right back to sleep for another couple hours. The other five percent, she would be up and ready to roll at six a.m. It was Russian roulette with milk.

Stirring together the formula powder and water for the first time, I felt like a jerk. Not because I was worried about nutrition. I figured Iris was made out of breast milk and would continue to get it several times a day. No, I was worried about flavor. I took one taste of the formula and gagged. "She's not going to like this," I said, spitting.

"How do you know it's any different? Did you taste the breast milk?" asked Laurie, giving me a funny look.

"Of course. Didn't you?"

"No."

Breast milk mostly tastes like sugar, while formula tastes exactly like iron-fortified milk powder. But I was wrong — Iris gulped it down, oblivious that I had replaced her soul-satisfying human milk with Folger's — er, formula. Great, she was eating fine. On the other hand, this stuff was swill. It tasted worse than artificial coffee whitener. And my daughter had no problem with it? She'd inherited Laurie's blue eyes and my tendency to scream when I don't get what I want. Didn't she get any of our good taste in food?

Iris went to sleep at five-thirty p.m. during this time, so we'd put her to bed and then I'd make dinner for me and Laurie. (Don't hate me: Iris would then wake up at ten p.m. and several other times during the night.) It was baby, baby, baby all day and then we'd sit out on the balcony with TV tables and relax and watch the bus go by. It was summertime, high season in Seattle for tomatoes, shell beans, corn, peppers, sorrel. I was exhausted but cooked on auto-pilot — it's really easy to be a good cook in Seattle in the summer. Yes, as much as I love having Iris at the dinner table today, I'm a bit nostalgic for those kid-free meals, when we could discuss important matters without Iris breaking in by saying, "Excuse me RIGHT NOW."

At age one, babies can add cow's milk to their diet, and I was eager to offer some to Iris, since it's a lot cheaper and tastier than formula. I put some cold whole milk into her sippy cup. Rejected! I tried warm milk. Forget it.

We found the solution at a small local coffee chain called Starbucks. As a card-carrying hipster, I was embarrassed about taking my child to Starbucks — its patrons and employees are insufficiently pierced — so I called it Coffeebucks. We ordered steamed milk with almond syrup. Iris just called it "almond," and we still do. Not only did Coffeebucks sell steamed milk at a special kid's price, they would sell you a big bottle of their almond syrup for making almond at home. A few drops of almond syrup in each cup of milk turned Iris into a committed milk drinker and baby hipster.

One day Iris went out for a walk with my dad, who she calls Pops. "What did you and Pops do?" I asked. "Did you get some almond?"
"Yes."
"Where did you go? Coffeebucks?"
Iris shook her head. "No, STARbucks." Dad is *such* an idiot.

Serving almond at home meant keeping whole milk in the house. Parenting books tell you to start serving your kid low-fat dairy products when they turn two. The question is this: after two years of whole milk in the fridge, will *you* be ready to switch back to low-fat dairy?

I'm certainly not. Whole milk on my cereal is pretty much the most awesome part of having a kid. The other day I bought some skim milk for a recipe and was shocked at the color and consistency of the stuff. It was even worse than formula, yet adults buy it for themselves.

We didn't do all our almond-swilling at home and at Coffeebucks. We also supported our local independent coffeehouses, mainly Red Line. Red Line was a large, airy sandwich place down the street from us, and we took Iris there dozens of times. They had homemade cookies for fifty cents, and they always made Iris's almond just the right temperature. We even had a recurring bedtime song called "Goin' Down to Red Line."

The problem with frequenting your local independent coffeehouses is that they may go out of business, as Red Line did. This was exactly the kind of thing I didn't want Iris to have to learn about until she was an adult. As a food lover, having your favorite restaurant close down is like a death in the family, only worse. When your beloved grandmother dies, you don't have her stuffed and placed on a chair in the living room to remind you of her, whereas Red Line's space turned into one of those bad neighborhood pizza places that is constantly slipping menus under your door, and we have to ride past it on the bus all the time. We sing a teary round of "Goin' Down to Red Line" and pour a cup of almond on the ground in memory of our fallen homies.

Surely the warm corporate embrace of Coffeebucks would never let us down, I figured. Well, in 2008, Starbucks discontinued almond syrup in their stores, so it was back to Torani syrup for us. This was puzzling, since steamed milk with almond was the default drink not only for baby hipsters but also for the considerable population of non–coffee drinkers who love foam. Starbucks should start a separate chain of stores for young kids and their parents, sited next to existing locations and modeled after Gap Kids. Babybucks would specialize in almond, hot chocolate, and cookies, and everything would be caffeine-free. Because, after all, there really aren't enough Starbucks locations in the world.

Iris continued nursing before bedtime until just shy of her second birthday. A baby that can both nurse and talk is a comedian. First, she somehow decided that the word for *milk* would be *neh*. She would call for "NEH!" exactly like an old man saying, "Feh!"

One night, Iris finished nursing and said, "Ahhh. Dinner." Her first full sentence was "Iris would like some more milkies." You can't say no to that.

But eventually Laurie did say no, and we switched Iris over to a small bedtime cup of steamed milk with almond. What a hipster. Of course, I've been known to drink a small glass of port or Madeira before bed as if I'm a fusty nineteenth-century Englishman, so I can't really belittle other people's affectations.

2

Discovering the First Rule of Baby Food

THE TONGUE-THRUST REFLEX is not a professional wrestling move.

It's actually an instinctive protection against choking. If you put something other than a nipple into a young baby's mouth, they'll gag and push it out with their tongue. Most babies lose the tongue-thrust reflex before six months, but Iris was still doing it at six and a half months.

Fine with us, since the American Academy of Pediatrics recommends at least six months of exclusive breastfeeding. Other parents we knew seemed to be itching to start solids as early as possible. I don't know why. I assume they took a look at their chubby babies and said to themselves, "There's no way this hunk can survive on milk alone." There's also the old myth about solids and sleep: put a little rice cereal in the baby's bottle and he'll sleep through the night. This is dangerous and dumb, and I thought nobody believed it anymore until I overheard two moms talking about how they always spiked the bottles of their two-month-olds.

Solids are messy and complicated. I'm thirty-three years old and

I still dribble them on my shirt several times a week. But we had a seven-month-old milk-fed dairy queen, and she was very curious about food. Her eyes would trace the path of our forks to our mouths as we ate. But what should we feed her, exactly? We didn't know.

These were some options we rejected:

Baby cereal. Some people deplore baby cereal, saying it gives kids an appetite for bland carbohydrates. These people presumably hang out with the mom who thinks she can keep her son away from pictures of breasts. We had a much better reason for rejecting baby cereal: everyone else starts with baby cereal, and we didn't want to be like everyone else. I swear this sounded like a good reason at the time.

Meat. "When your baby's ready for her first food, you can make it almost anything — even meat," says *Parenting* magazine. Few people are allergic to meat, and it's very nutritious. More to the point, you can freak people out by telling them your baby's first food was meat. But we didn't end up actually doing it, mostly because jarred meat is especially gross and because I didn't know yet whether I could give her home-cooked meat without making her choke.

Lint. Nothing would have pleased Iris more than being allowed to eat lint off the floor. She'd been trying to get away with it for months. Every time she succeeded, Laurie or I would frantically pull the piece of lint out of her mouth and then Iris would cry at the injustice. We should have named her Roomba.

Finally, we decided on fruit. It was August, the height of farmers' market season in Seattle. Market stands were loaded with cherries, peaches, plums, berries, melons, and even kiwi fruits, which apparently grow in Washington. (Either that or we have a farmer with a sense of humor and a hefty FedEx bill.)

In the end, we selected an apricot. I don't like apricots, and I don't think Laurie likes apricots either. We certainly haven't bought any apricots since then. But I dutifully peeled and mashed the apricot and spooned a bit into Iris's mouth. Most of it dribbled down her chin. I couldn't swear that she swallowed any. It was a bit anticlimactic.

If this doesn't make a whole lot of sense (why did we feed her an apricot if I don't even like apricots?), I blame sleep deprivation. Mentally, I'm a pretty average guy. Most of my brainpower on a typical day is devoted to thinking about work, electronic gadgets, and sex. I'm pretty sure I never thought about any of those things during all of 2004, because I was thinking about sleep, Iris's and mine. I have a printout of emails I sent Laurie during that first year of parenting, and it all sounds exactly like this:

> April 26: "She's napping now, so if she takes a long nap she'll be up when you get home, but if she takes a short one she may need to start another before you get here."
> June 10: "Iris napped for two and a half hours! Boy is she chipper now."
> August 31: "I put her down for a nap at 9:10, and I'm not sure whether she's asleep yet. She did go back to sleep this morning until 7:30."
> October 7: "She is taking a good morning nap. I put her down about 10:10, and she talked for about fifteen minutes and then went to sleep, and she's still asleep at 11:35."

For another couple of months, Iris would mostly nibble at things we ate. A tiny chunk of meatball here, a soft crumb of bread there. For lunch, I came up with a couple of dishes that became Iris's early favorites; I called them Baby Creamed Spinach and Baby Chicken and Mushrooms.

Iris ate plenty of these finely minced delights, but it quickly became clear that she didn't want her own food. She wanted *our* food. It was hard to get her to eat Baby Chicken and Mushrooms if I wasn't eating it, too. But my first realization that feeding Iris was going to be different than I expected came in the form of a pirozhki.

There's a Russian bakery down our street that specializes in pirozhkis, meat or vegetable pies in a soft crust. You can think of them as Hot Pockets from the old country. One day I got my favorite beef, cabbage, and cheese pirozhki for lunch. The beef and cabbage are braised together until shreddably soft. Iris and I were playing on the floor and sharing the pirozhki, and I kept giving her bites until I realized that she had eaten more than half the pirozhki. I would have to start buying two pirozhkis. (Luckily, they had a club card.)

We'd been taking Iris to restaurants since she was a baby (a quiet, mostly sleeping one, I assure you), but it got a whole lot more fun once she could eat along with us. We brought her to a Chinese restaurant where she gobbled fish and tofu. At a Mexican place, she ate all the spicy shredded beef out of my burrito. We took her out for sushi, and she eviscerated the spicy tuna roll, scooping out the core of fish and rice and leaving us the seaweed. This was all before she turned one. Suddenly we had a baby who chose pad Thai instead of strained peas, Szechuan fish rather than pureed squash.

One night, I brought home some Thai takeout that was too complicated for Iris to chew (lots of bell peppers in the stir-fry, as I recall). She really wanted some, and she tried hard, but after a couple of bites she gave up, frustrated. "We need to start planning out things for dinner that we can all eat," said Laurie, and I agreed: we would invite Iris to share every meal. This proved to be not only safe and more fun than opening little jars, but also unexpectedly simple: we just had to smash, chop, or blend the food so our toothless little buddy could eat it.

Fortunately, babies have powerful gums. Iris and I used to play a game in which I leaned in closer and closer to her face until suddenly she clamped her gums onto my nose. This was fairly painful, but worth it because of the way it would make Iris laugh. After her first teeth came in, two little incisors with sharp edges that would have made the Gillette corporation envious, I made the mistake of volunteering for this game again. The result was like a scene from *When Animals Attack*.

We never asked Iris's pediatrician if it was safe to share our food with her. I figured she was eating a combination of the foods recommended in baby books, and I was vigilant about choking hazards and, well, semi-vigilant about allergens.

I did buy one jar of baby food — I think it was Gerber beef with sweet potatoes, which sounded tasty and reminded me of what Baby Gloria ate for dinner in *Bread and Jam for Frances*. Iris flat out rejected it. Her tastes were too global for this mush.

If I said we didn't use *any* commercial baby food, however, I'd be stretching the truth. We actually bought a lot of Gerber fruit purees and mixed them with plain yogurt. I highly recommend this, even if you don't have kids and your sudden purchase of baby food could freak out your significant other. Why didn't I make my own peach and pear purees? Because I tried it and the Gerber was tastier.

According to my mother, my favorite breakfast food when I was a kid was Dannon Prune Whip yogurt. For reasons that seem obvious, they don't make Prune Whip anymore. So I recreated it by mixing Gerber prune puree half-and-half with full-fat plain yogurt. Prune, pear, or peach whip with a side of Cheerios was our daily breakfast for months. Pear is the best, especially if you add a little cinnamon (or, as Iris calls it, "cimmanim"). I was proud when Iris took her first steps, but not as proud as I was when she successfully maneuvered a Cheerio into her mouth. Day after day I watched her pick up a Cheerio and angle it toward her face, only to miss her mouth by several inches. At such times I had to remind myself that Iris was perfectly smart and capable for her age, and it was okay that she would lose a battle of skill with a really slow adult, or even a Cheerio.

Soon, Laurie turned us on to something even better than whole-milk plain yogurt. ("Seriously?" I can hear you saying. "Better than plain yogurt?") Greek yogurt is made by taking regular yogurt and straining it through cheesecloth. It's sold in single-serving containers with a bit of honey or jam for mixing (the popular brand is Fage Total), or in pint tubs. It's impossibly smooth and rich. It's amazing that you can eat this stuff for breakfast without causing a scandal. It's pudding with active cultures.

Not to channel a sappy Peace Corps ad, but Iris taught me a lot more about breakfast than I ever taught her. Laurie had been telling me about Greek yogurt since before Iris was born, but I didn't listen, because I had naive views about the limits of yogurt. After my conversion to the fermented way, I came home from Trader Joe's with an assortment of their flavored Greek yogurts to try. Iris and I got completely addicted to their fig yogurt for a while. It has real fig puree in it, including seeds, which Iris called "bumps."

"Yogurt" was also one of Iris's first words, sort of. Laurie noticed at some point that whenever we served Iris yogurt, she made a noise like "eeeyoy-eeeyoy." Eventually she settled on "yoingyoing." So every morning I served up the yogurt and Iris bounced in her high chair, chanting, "Dada? Yoingyoing. Dada? Yoingyoing."

You know how TV chefs always have dazzling knife skills? How they can reduce a whole chicken to fryable parts in two minutes or chop an onion in seconds without shedding a tear? There are two ways to get skills like that: go to culinary school, or share all your food with a baby. Whatever we were having for dinner, I would reduce it to a chunky puree with my chef's knife.

Some things worked and some didn't, of course. We didn't eat any steak for a long time. I didn't want to put something on the table if Iris couldn't eat it, and chewy meat is a tricky item for babies, with or without teeth. (In terms of food, I guess Iris was growing up and we were regressing to childhood.) But anything reasonably soft — potatoes, braised meat, most vegetables, fruits, and basically any dessert — melted under my blade.

Never before had it been so important to keep my knife sharp. A sharp knife is key not only for baby food prep but for anything else you do in the kitchen. The platitude "a sharp knife is a safe knife" is true, but don't discount the potential for ninja self-defense moves, either.

There's a ton of misinformation about knife sharpening, and everyone will try to convince you that their method is "easy." You could buy a snazzy electric or manual sharpener costing up to two hundred dollars. You could learn to use a classic sharpening stone, which is inexpensive and *not* easy. You could, as I do, send your knives out to a professional, but not all professionals are created equal. A message board like eGullet or Chowhound can point you in the right direction. Of course, sending them away means you'll be knifeless for as long as two weeks.

But I have a revolutionary three-step knife-sharpening method that is absolutely foolproof, requires no skills other than shopping, and is not too expensive.

1. Buy a Forschner Victorinox chef's knife. This knife is widely used by professionals and frequently beats expensive German and Japanese knives in magazine ratings. You can find it for twenty-five dollars online and at many kitchen stores. It's available in sizes from six to ten inches. The eight-inch is right for most people.

2. Use the knife, steeling regularly, until it gets dull. Unless you use your knife to saw through tin cans like on a Ginsu commercial, it'll take at least a year to get dull. "Steeling" means running the knife against a long, thin sharpening steel like they do on TV. It doesn't actually sharpen the knife, but it does prolong the life of the edge. ("The Life of the Edge" would be a great name for a reality show, like *Flavor of Love* but with that guy from U2.)

3. Buy a new Forschner and give away the old one on Craigslist. Be up-front about the knife's dullness. Then

send me the name of the person you gave this dull knife to, so I can decline any invitations to their house.

You can buy an inexpensive baby food grinder (sort of like a big plastic peppermill), and if your baby likes smooth food, you may want to get one. From talking to parents, I've learned that some babies like extremely smooth pureed food and some like to live on the chunky side. (I guess this is no different from adults and their peanut butter preferences.) Iris was a chunk-style kid, so knife-chopped food was fine for her.

I didn't have to use the knife to chop Iris's food for very long. Nothing about a baby lasts as long as I think it will: I have, at various times, convinced myself that Iris would *never* have a good night's sleep or learn to use the potty. In fact, Iris is four now, and sometimes I still have to fight off the urge to mince up her dinner.

Iris continued slurping up everything we made for dinner. She loved endive gratin, salmon, pasta with arugula, barbecued ribs. After she grew teeth, we had to stop letting her gnaw meat off the ribs, because she could bite off actual chunks of bone. High in calcium, I guess.

She was eager and rarely threw food, but she did gag a lot. Nature is cruel: as soon as you get to stop worrying about SIDS, you have to start worrying about choking. Then it's playground injuries, driver's licenses, and stage-diving mishaps. (If you know a way to prevent any of these things, let's hear it.) It turns out all babies gag a lot when they're learning to eat, whether the food is chunky or smooth. It's not like we were giving her whole grapes or popcorn.

I was perhaps overly cautious about choking hazards. I recall cutting individual quills of penne pasta into four equal pieces. At one point I freaked out when my mom fed Iris whole black beans instead of chopping them first. Iris chewed and swallowed them without so much as a hiccup, and my mom gave me a look that meant *You may not believe this, but you did not personally invent child-rearing.* Years later I asked Laurie if she remembered this happening, and she said, "You did that to me every day. You were totally insane about it."

We were reassured in our feeding approach by Ellyn Satter's book *Child of Mine*. Satter is one of the first people the parenting magazines call when they're doing a story about picky eaters, and I was surprised when I read her book and found she advocated exactly the sharing-adult-food approach we were already using. She doesn't have a name for it, but I do: the First Rule of Baby Food.

The First Rule of Baby Food is that there's no such thing as baby food. Satter does recommend baby cereal as a first food (we didn't use it), but look what she says should be happening by eight to twelve months:

> Orchestrating special food for your child is getting the cart before the horse. The meals need to come first and your child's eating follows. Get the family meal on the table; then adapt that meal for your child.

Or take it from Jacques Pépin and his daughter Claudine:

> Except for very spicy food, she was served exactly what we ate from the time she was an infant. When she didn't like something, we barely acknowledged the fact. Conversely, when she ate spinach, broccoli, or chard, we never congratulated her because we didn't want her to feel that she had done something special.

In retrospect, I think I was gung-ho about sharing our food with Iris for the same reason people share food with each other everywhere: it's fun. It was the first opportunity for Iris and me to share an experience and enjoy it for the same reasons. I mean, I liked playing peek-a-boo (I called it "peekytoe") because it made Iris laugh, but it's not like it's something Laurie and I played before Iris was born — or, at least, I wouldn't admit to it. But I like enchiladas. Iris likes enchiladas. We can agree on enchiladas.

It was around this time that I started feeling like I should quit my job. Not my day job, which I'd already quit, but my night job reviewing restaurants. Whenever I went out at dinnertime I felt like I was missing the most exciting part of the day, like I was walking out on my dinner guest, abandoning our familial three-top. What cook would choose to go out instead of making dinner for someone who was always hungry and had never tried enchiladas, pad Thai, tomato sauce, corn, burgers, or ice cream? I could be the one to introduce Iris to all of these things. I'd be the chef and she'd be my VIP regular. She would learn to love all the food I love. She would be my Eliza Doolittle, with emphasis on the "little."

And my plan even worked, for a while.

BABY CREAMED SPINACH

! QUICK & EASY
 5 minutes

Aside from spooning this into a baby's mouth, it's good on crostini, sprinkled with salt. Frankly, I also like eating it out of the bowl.

Makes about ½ cup

    1 tablespoon butter
    6 ounces (1 package) baby spinach leaves
    2 tablespoons whole milk

Heat the butter in a skillet over medium heat until foaming. Add the spinach leaves and cook until wilted, about 3 minutes. Transfer to a blender, add the milk, and puree until smooth.

BABY CHICKEN and MUSHROOMS

! QUICK & EASY
 20 minutes

Serves several babies, or one adult and one baby for lunch

1 tablespoon butter
1 boneless, skinless chicken breast
  handful of sliced button mushrooms

Heat butter in a skillet. Add the chicken breast and sear on both sides until nicely browned and cooked through, about 4 minutes per side. Remove the chicken breast and add a handful of sliced button mushrooms. Cook until the mushroom liquid has evaporated and the mushrooms are lightly browned, 5 to 8 minutes. Finely mince the chicken and mushrooms together.

3

You Fed Your Baby WHAT?

WHEN IRIS WAS ONE, I was in a band called Fluffy Kittens with my friend Kenji, who has two sets of twin boys. While we practiced our songs, Iris would play with the four guys, and she quickly became attached to one of the older boys, Wressey. Not only did she want to play with him, but she wanted me and Laurie to tell stories about him whenever he wasn't around. "WRESSEYYYYYY STORYYYYYY," Iris would shriek, and I'd concoct increasingly elaborate adventure tales starring Wressey and Iris. (I wish I knew what Iris was picturing when I said they were down on the docks, fighting crime.) Eventually, for sanity's sake, we had to place a moratorium on Wressey stories during meals. "Wressey's on hiatus," I said when we sat down to dinner. The next day, as I strapped Iris into her high chair, she began to say, "Wress —" then shook her head sadly and whispered, "Hiatus." I guess now she's prepared for when Fox cancels her favorite show.

Then Wressey and his gang moved away and we didn't see them much anymore. Wressey became basically a fictional character. One day, Kenji called to say he and the boys were in town and wanted to meet up at the Seattle Aquarium. "Iris, do you want to go to the aquarium? With Wressey?" I asked. She nodded, speechless. This was better than going to the aquarium with Batman.

Iris trailed Wressey all over the aquarium until we were all exhausted and hungry. (Four boys, in case you are wondering, is *a lot of boys.*) We tumbled into the adjacent fish and chips place for lunch. I ordered a Sprite. Iris was curious. She was aquariumed out and on the verge of collapse. I let her drink some Sprite. She perked right up. It was time to head home. I popped her into the stroller with the giant cup of soda and wheeled her around, attempting to hide my face so that other parents would not see that I had turned into one of those people who gives a one-year-old a Big Gulp.

Since that day, Iris has never had soda again. Not because we've taken a hard line, but because she hates it. It's too fizzy. I recently offered her a *root beer float* and she didn't want any.

I was curious to see what America's most popular baby food book had to say on the subject of babies and Sprite, so I pulled *Super Baby Food* off the bookshelf and had a look:

> NEVER give your baby cola drinks or other sweet carbonated beverages, even when she's 21 years old.

Ruth Yaron's *Super Baby Food,* originally published in 1996, is a perennial bestseller, the finger-wagging grandmother of all the make-your-own-baby-food books (*Blender Baby Food, Top 100 Baby Purees,* and so on). When you're pregnant, people recommend *What to Expect When You're Expecting;* once you have the baby, it's *Super Baby Food* and its ice cube trays of puree. *SBF* reinforces the idea that babies need their own separate food and that you should spend a lot of time making it. I guess if there were a book telling you that babies don't need special food, it would have to be pretty short and consist mostly of jokes. (Uh-oh.)

Yaron recommends an organic vegetarian diet and credits it with keeping her own twin sons free of colds and the flu. If you are following *Super Baby Food,* you will make Super Porridge, Super Sprouts, and Awesome Orange Bread. "I keep kelp in a salt shaker," writes Yaron. "It's very convenient for sprinkling small amounts into foods." I'm sure it is.

I find an organic vegetarian diet impressive in the same way as a David Blaine stunt, but I'm betting that most people who buy *Super Baby Food* eat plenty of junk food themselves but want to give their baby a head start on something healthy.

Good luck with that. There was only a tiny window in which I could have possibly gotten away with serving Iris something other than what Laurie and I were eating, and it was long before the Sprite incident. Before Iris turned one, we used to take her to our favorite pizza place and, because she was unable to chew pizza, we'd bring along some buttered peas or some black beans and sweet potatoes and let her teethe on a pizza crust. I can't believe we *ever* got away with this. Just for old times' sake, I think I'll ask Iris if she wants to go out for pizza tonight, then only allow her to eat peas.

So there is something to that old anti-drug commercial — you know: "Dad, I learned it by watching you." You can only get away with separate "baby food" for so long: a few months, maybe a year at the very most. In Iris's case, it was about a month and a half. A baby's solid food intake during this entire period could fit in a Cheerios box. Most of their nutrition is still coming from milk. Breast milk is seriously nutritious and satisfying.

Yaron knows this. "The easiest way to feed your baby home-made food is to feed her along with the rest of the family," she writes in the introduction to *Super Baby Food*. "Take some of their unseasoned plain food, puree it, and feed it to her. However, if your house is like mine, the family sometimes doesn't eat together. Most of the time I end up feeding my baby with no one else around."

So did I, using a breakthrough foodstuff known as "leftovers." Not leftovers of "unseasoned, plain food," which sounds like torture. Just whatever we had eaten for dinner the night before. That's what Iris and I had for lunch pretty much every day: leftover enchiladas, salmon cakes, stew, all sorts of vegetables. Yaron's use of the word "feeding" here strikes me as all wrong. Yes, technically I was putting the spoon in Iris's mouth, but I wasn't *feeding* her so much as having a lunch date.

Sometimes Iris would go to the babysitter's at lunchtime and I'd send a salmon cake. They're highly portable and a delicious way to cook fresh salmon. I wish I had one with me right now.

This will totally blow my regular-guy image, but in 2007, a camera crew from the Food Network came to our house to shoot a three-minute segment called "Feeding Iris." They filmed me and Iris shopping at the Asian supermarket, cooking Ants on a Tree noodles, and eating lunch. On the voiceover I talk about the First Rule of Baby Food. (If you've seen the segment, you should know that the part at the end when Iris says, "You're doing a good job, Dada!" was totally staged.)

After the segment aired, I got an email from a mom who started out by saying, "You, sir, have blown my mind." (There is a point to this story other than that I'm an awesome TV star, I swear.) She said she liked my suggestion that she share food with her baby, but she was nervous because she wasn't a very good cook: she relied heavily on convenience products and ate things like canned chili.

I told her that Iris and I often had canned chili for lunch when she was a baby. I'd buy the habanero chili con carne with beans, and Iris would eat spicy kidney beans and beef chunks. We also had frozen Indian food and enchiladas sometimes. I don't think these things are as tasty or as nutritious as homemade, but they're certainly tastier and no less nutritious than baby food, super or otherwise. You don't have to be a good cook to share food with your baby. For that matter, I don't think being a good cook makes you a better person (just look at Gordon Ramsay), although it may help you get a date, which was probably not the foremost concern on my correspondent's mind.

Sharing food with Iris and sending her out into the world with leftovers instead of "baby food" required ignoring all sorts of warnings put forth by books like *Super Baby Food*. (My lawyer would like to remind you that none of the following constitutes advice, and you should never do anything described below. Nudge, nudge.)

Strong flavors scare babies.

"Bland is best for baby," writes Yaron. No, really, it isn't. Bland is best for people who grew up before "habanero" entered the popular discourse. Here's pediatrician Michel Cohen, from his book *The New Basics*:

> Don't be afraid to feed Lucy food that's spicy or strange. Try steak, fish, pasta, vegetables, salty foods, peppery foods, garlicky foods; all you need is a fork or a food processor and a little bit of imagination.

Iris was so into spicy foods as a baby, I wrote a whole chapter about it.

Don't put salt in your baby's food or you will ruin her kidneys.

"Most importantly, you should not add table salt to any of your baby's food or cooking water, either as a source of dietary sodium or as a flavor enhancer," says *Super Baby Food*.

Okay, she's right: babies don't need added salt in their diet. But most of the salt in our diets comes from processed food, which is made with a lot of salt as a preservative. If most of your food is home-cooked, however, it's unnecessary to make a no-added-salt portion for a baby. Compared to those salty processed foods, home cooking just can't compete in terms of milligrams of sodium. (Obviously, if you have someone with salt-sensitive hypertension in your house, you should ignore all of this, but you know that.)

Adding salt, as boring as it sounds, is one of the things about cooking I most enjoy. I have a cool little wooden salt dish with a lid that rotates on and off. I fill it with Diamond Crystal kosher salt.

Chefs and picky home cooks use kosher salt because, unlike table salt, kosher is easy to pick up with your fingers.

Measuring salt with your fingers is fun. Whenever I have some vegetables cooking in a skillet, which is most of the time, I'm tasting for salt and sprinkling a little here and there. Beans cooked with salt are much tastier than beans salted at the end of cooking, because they're seasoned throughout (and it's a myth that salt makes them tough). If you're a good cook, salting as you go, making a salt-free portion is a real pain.

I do have to admit that Iris is a total salt fiend. If you put her near an open salt dish, she will continue dipping her finger in until the salt is gone. "I'm just tasting," she will explain, reaching for a spoon. She does the same thing with soy sauce, only more so. "Why is soy sauce so salty?" she asked me the other day, finishing off the little dish of soy sauce I served alongside her potstickers.

"Because it's a condiment," I replied. "Not a beverage."

Never feed your baby sushi.

Super Baby Food, page 281: "WARNING: Never give sushi or other raw fish, meat, or poultry to babies or children."

Yaron gives no justification for this statement. Presumably she thinks it goes without saying that sushi is teeming with deadly parasites. I wrote a whole chapter about this one, too. The short version is this: sushi is delicious.

Never feed your baby nonorganic food.

Super Baby Food, page 39: "Only certified organic foods should be used to make food for your precious baby."

(If your baby's not particularly precious, you can just spike her bottle with Miracle-Gro.)

I'm being flip because I don't have a good response to this. Like many people, sometimes I buy organic and sometimes I don't. It depends on how much money I have in my pocket and how the produce looks. When I'm shopping at the supermarket, the organic produce is often inferior to the conventional — and I'm not talking about the kind of cosmetic blemishes that food writers like me tell you to overlook. (Nobody has to be told about the virtues of ugly tomatoes anymore, right?) I compared Italian parsley the other day and the organic wasn't just twice the price — it was yellow, which means old. Then again, maybe it got old because no one was buying it because it was twice the price, because of bad subsidies . . . My brain is starting to hurt.

If you wanted a detailed analysis of this issue, you'd be reading Michael Pollan rather than me, so I'll bring it back around to what I'd like to teach Iris. It's simple: your taste buds are smart. My tongue has been dragging me around all my life and I've learned to follow it. More often than not, what tastes good *is* good. A diet based on values other than taste is, to use the swear word of the moment, *unsustainable.*

Okay, maybe a lot of people follow this same philosophy straight to McDonald's. Like I said, I'm no Michael Pollan.

Don't let your baby drink beer.

Actually, this isn't covered in *Super Baby Food.* Maybe Yaron is pro-beer.

When I was a kid, my dad would always let me try a sip of his beer. I don't think this was some kind of strategy to teach me to drink responsibly; probably he just thought a child beer prodigy was funny. As I recall, my all-time favorite was Watney's Red Barrel. As an adult, it occurred to me to Google "Watney's Red Barrel," and I learned that (a) they don't make it anymore, and (b) this is just as well. Also, if my dad *was* trying to teach me about responsible drinking, I guess it worked, because my limit as an adult is two whole beers.

I have offered Iris beer several times, and she's just not interested. Whatever, kid. I think the availability of good beer is one of the best things about living in Seattle. They sell over two hundred different beers at my local supermarket, including dozens made in the Northwest. When Iris was two, I pushed her through this aisle in the stroller and she said, "Dada, we went through a beer tunnel." Hopefully "Through the Beer Tunnel" won't be the title of her recovery memoir.

Allow several days after introducing each new food to watch for signs of allergies.

"It is possible that your baby has one or more food allergies," writes Yaron. "Because of this, it is important that you wait several days after the introduction of any new food in order to see if that new food will trigger an allergic reaction."

A four- to seven-day wait after *every* new food? For how long? Yaron doesn't say. This advice, repeated everywhere, makes me break out in hives. Iris's first favorite food, chicken enchiladas, contains about a dozen ingredients — some of which practically nobody is allergic to, like cilantro. (Okay, I know cilantro tastes like soap to some people, but that's not an allergy, and those people are missing out on some really good salsa.) I could have made the enchiladas with just tortillas the first week, then tortillas and chicken the following week, then tortillas and chicken and onions, and so on for twelve weeks. Sounds like an interesting performance art project, but not much like dinner.

Laurie and I have no food allergies. If we did, I'm sure we would have been a lot more cautious. But this advice is so cautious, hardly anybody follows it.

Don't give your baby nuts, especially peanuts, until age three.

"Some experts recommend waiting until age three before introducing a baby to peanuts, peanut butter, peanut oil, or anything containing these foods," writes Yaron. She doesn't say whether she agrees with them; instead, she foists you off on your pediatrician.

Peanut allergies are not funny. Having a serious nut allergy is like living in a world full of shiny sharp objects that you can blunder into at any time — and being the parent of a nut-allergic child must be even harder.

But after a 2008 review, the American Academy of Pediatrics found no evidence that waiting to introduce potential allergens can prevent or lessen the severity of food allergies. Here's how they put it:

> Although solid foods should not be introduced before 4 to 6 months of age, there is no current convincing evidence that delaying their introduction beyond this period has a significant protective effect on the development of atopic disease . . . This includes delaying the introduction of foods that are considered to be highly allergic, such as fish, eggs, and foods containing peanut protein.

They did find, however, that in high-risk infants, four months of exclusive breastfeeding may help prevent allergies. And you shouldn't feed honey to babies under age one, because it can, in rare cases, cause infant botulism — not an allergy, but a potentially deadly form of food poisoning. Other than that, yes, the most prestigious group of pediatricians in America says it's okay to feed your baby oysters, eggs, and peanuts. If your child is allergic, you're better off knowing now. (Furthermore, they found no evidence that a pregnant or breastfeeding woman should avoid these foods if she isn't allergic to them.)

Here's what we did. There was a nice Thai restaurant down the street from us where the waitresses loved Iris, who was about eight months old at the time. We'd stop in for pad Thai, hold the peanuts (I was trying to follow the AAP's old recommendation), and Iris munched on the noodles. One time I forgot to tell them to leave the peanuts off, and Iris demanded her noodles. While she ate them, I kept my hand nervously on my cell phone. Nothing happened: Iris is among the 99 percent of kids who don't have peanut allergies.

As you can probably tell, I find food allergies intensely frustrating, even though I don't have any. They are indisputably real and dangerous, but they affect only a small number of people. I feel annoyed by having to leave peanut butter out of Iris's preschool lunch, and then I feel guilty about feeling annoyed. I hope someone comes up with a cure for the most serious food allergies, because I really love peanut oil, especially the fragrant Lion & Globe brand from Hong Kong, and want to share the delicious things I stir-fry in it with all the children of the world.

While I don't have firsthand experience with food allergies, I do have pretty good secondhand experience. Iris's favorite adult (yes, totally better than her parents) is Shauna James Ahern, author of the blog and book *Gluten-Free Girl*. Shauna has a major food allergy. She can't eat wheat, other grains related to wheat, or any of the jillions of products containing wheat-derived ingredients.

This hasn't gotten in the way of Shauna's hedonistic approach to food; in fact, it *sparked* her interest in food. If she was going to have to think about her food all the time anyway in order to avoid eating wheat and getting sick, she was going to make every mouthful fantastic. The first time we went to Shauna's house, she made the gingerbread cupcakes from chapter 9, but entirely without wheat flour, and they were great. I think Iris would be happy to move in with Shauna and her husband (a professional chef), give up gluten, and visit us on weekends. Shauna's backyard has a treehouse.

So if Iris does develop an allergy, which is certainly possible (Shauna's condition wasn't diagnosed until she was in her thirties), I hope I'm mature enough to do as Shauna did and turn it into an opportunity. Allergic to peanuts? Fine, make your house the most delicious peanut-free zone in town. After all, good olive oil and lard are just as tasty as peanut oil (not to mention gluten-free).

Sorry if I've been too hard on *Super Baby Food*. Let me say something I really like about the book, which is that the cover was designed by Maryrose Snopkowski. Isn't that an awesome name? Try saying it out loud and I promise it will ward off disease and make you feel great.

PAD THAI SAUCE

! QUICK & EASY

 15 minutes

Since this sauce can be refrigerated up to 1 week or frozen up to a month, there's no reason not to make enough for several batches of pad Thai, as specified here.

Tamarind paste, made from the fruit of a tropical bean tree, is sold in 1-pound blocks in Asian markets, or order online from importfood.com ("pure tamarind paste, seedless, 17.5 ounce jar"). Its tart, woody flavor is essential for pad Thai.

Makes about 1½ cups, enough for at least 12 servings

- 4 ounces tamarind paste
- 1½ cups boiling water
- ¼ cup peanut oil
- 6 tablespoons fish sauce
- 1 tablespoon rice vinegar
- ¼ cup (about 2 ounces) palm sugar, crushed (or substitute white sugar)

Place the tamarind paste in a bowl and pour the boiling water over it. Let sit 5 minutes, then stir gently, pressing the paste against the side of the bowl to break it up. Let sit another 5 minutes and stir again. Repeat until there are no remaining large chunks of paste, then strain through a sieve into a bowl, pressing gently on the tamarind paste and scraping the bottom of the sieve. Discard the contents of the sieve. Add the peanut oil, fish sauce, rice vinegar, and palm sugar to the tamarind liquid and stir until the sugar dissolves.

SIMPLE PAD THAI

! QUICK & EASY

"🕐" 30 minutes, mostly unattended

This recipe is gluten-free but loaded with peanuts, eggs, citrus, and fish: things you weren't supposed to feed babies in the old days. Consider throwing in garlic, shallots, tofu, or meat if you and your baby would enjoy them, but this is amazingly good just as is. For a baby, cut the noodles into short lengths before serving.

Serves 2 adults plus 1 baby as a light meal

- 4 ounces rice stick noodles, soaked in hot tap water 20 minutes and drained
- 2 teaspoons peanut oil
- 1 large egg
- ¼ cup pad Thai sauce (see recipe)
  - lime wedges, for serving
  - chopped peanuts, for serving

Heat the peanut oil over medium-high in a large nonstick skillet until shimmering. Add the egg and scramble vigorously until nearly cooked, about 15 seconds. Add the noodles and pad Thai sauce and cook, tossing with a spatula and a wooden spoon, until the sauce is nearly all absorbed and the noodles are tender and well coated, about 2 minutes. Serve immediately with chopped peanuts for sprinkling and lime wedges for squeezing.

4

Stew You Can Chew

IRIS HAS A SUBSCRIPTION to the children's version of *National Geographic*. Every issue has an exclusive cover story along the lines of "Elephants Exist — And They Have Trunks!" On the back page is a cute animal picture with a thought bubble to fill in. In the most recent issue, it was a bulldog facing down a rubber duck. According to Iris, the bulldog was thinking, *I want to eat roast duck leg.*

I can explain. When Iris was nine months old, you see, I was working on a newspaper article about duck legs.

The seared duck breast, cooked medium-rare and fanned out on the plate, is a staple of fine-dining restaurants from Seattle to Bangkok. It's relatively easy to recreate at home. It's also boring. Duck legs are better — meaty and flavorful, much cheaper, and easy to prepare with crispy skin and tender meat.

In the article, I included a recipe for duck ragu, long-simmered duck legs with tomatoes and vegetables, spiced with cloves. After cooking, you shred the duck meat and stir it back into what has become a rich, warming sauce, perfect to serve over pasta on a winter night. Unfortunately, I write for the Sunday magazine section of the newspaper, which means that unlike the pampered war and city council reporters who write a story one night and find themselves on A1 the next day, I have to turn my stories in months ahead of publication. So I was cooking quarts of warm and hearty duck ragu in the middle of August.

Iris didn't care. At one point, just before I finished the article, she and I ate duck ragu for lunch and dinner three days in a row. Sometimes we skipped the pasta and just ate the sauce. Thus began Iris's — and our family's — love affair with stew.

Stew is the ultimate in baby food. It's easy to make. It's easy to eat: you don't even need teeth. The variety is endless. It doesn't suffer from spending a couple days in the fridge — in fact, it gets better. The ingredients are cheap. You can make it on Sunday and reheat it after work, for several days in a row, if you want. You can convert leftovers into hash or pasta sauce. Other than vegetarians, everyone I know loves a good stew except my father, who would turn down a perfectly braised lamb shank and say, "Tastes like stewed meat to me."

We make stew almost every week. Sometimes I use a recipe and sometimes not. Sometimes I brown the meat first and sometimes I don't bother. Sometimes I use the pressure cooker, sometimes the oven, and sometimes the stovetop. It just doesn't matter. If you follow a few simple rules, it's hard to make a bad stew:

Choose cheap, tough, fatty meat. Duck legs, chicken thighs, beef chuck, pork butt (shoulder), lamb shoulder, lamb or veal shanks, beef short ribs, oxtails. Except for veal shanks, none of these are expensive, even if you get them from a good butcher or farmers' market stand. Oxtails, which sound scary, are actually a great cut for beginners, because you can't possibly overcook them. You could leave a pot of oxtails in the oven and go see *Harry Potter and the Deathly Hallows,* and (spoiler alert!) the oxtails would be fine when you got back. I often see stew recipes that call for things such as beef top round or pork tenderloin, which are too lean to stew well. Don't waste your time.

Use a heavy pot. For the longest time I made stews in a big, cheap stockpot. Then I got a blue Le Creuset Dutch oven for my birthday. It really does make better stew — the temperature inside stays more constant, and the lid has a tighter fit. Plus, it's the only pot I own that never disappears and turns up later in Iris's room, because it's too heavy for her to lift. The chefs I know have a thing for Staub brand pots, which are even heavier and have an alluring industrial look.

Don't undercook. If the meat is tough, keep cooking. Short ribs and oxtails can take four hours or more.

Reduce your broth. After tough meat, the most common stewing offense is flavorless broth. When your meat is tender, taste the liquid. If it's not rich, mouth-coating, and loaded with flavor, reduce it. Strain out the solids and boil the liquid until it's awesome. One night I got a late start making beef stew, and it was nowhere near done by dinnertime. So I reduced some of the broth and served it over polenta while the stew finished cooking. Nobody complained. When Iris was one she would demand spoonful after spoonful of broth, and we would get into arguments about whether it was called "broth" or "stock." Really. I assume I lost the argument, because I have no idea what the difference between stock and broth is anymore.

You don't have to keep the vegetables. Sometimes very soft stewed vegetables are great. But one of the best ways to enliven a dull stew is with a last-minute garnish of freshly cooked vegetables. This is how beef bourguignon and coq au vin are made: before serving, you sauté some mushrooms and pearl onions and toss them into the stew. You can use this strategy however you want, even if it means throwing out the vegetables that cooked with the stew. It's not wasteful. They've already done their duty, contributing their flavor to the broth. Or stock. Or whatever. One thing I love to do with beef stew in the winter is cut some carrots and parsnips into sticks, brown them in butter, then moisten them with some of the broth from the stew and cook until barely tender. Serve the vegetables alongside and see if you don't like them even better than the beef.

Don't be Eurocentric. Not every stew has to involve red wine and potatoes. Beef stewed with soy sauce is fantastic. Chili is a stew. Indian curries are stews. Red-cooked pork belly is stew. Having said this, European stews sure are great, aren't they? On New Year's Eve, the day after Iris turned one, we took her to a cassoulet party. Iris ate an adult-size portion of cassoulet, gorging on beans, sausage, duck confit, and pork.

Leftover braised meat of any kind is a special treat. It means I can make hash. Hash is basically the same as hash browns or home fries, but with stuff in it — stuff like meat, fish, onions, or mushrooms.

For a while I was in love with the idea of hash but frustrated by the results. Sometimes it would come out soggy and flavorful, sometimes crispy and dry, sometimes crispy and burned. I turned to the culinary geniuses at eGullet.org, who can answer any question about food. The moderator Sam Kinsey explained that there are two types of hash: wet and dry. A wet hash can take on the flavors of broth and cream but will never get crispy. A dry hash has individual pieces of browned meat and potato.

Now I make and enjoy both kinds, but the dry hash is my first love. My favorite meat for hash is duck. It's easy to cook some extra duck legs to have on hand for hash, and no meat goes better with potatoes. (No, not even beef.)

The traditional hash topping is poached eggs, but for an embarrassing reason (poached eggs are hard to make), I prefer fried. There are plenty of egg poaching gadgets, but they feel like cheating. Besides, fried eggs are great, and you can fry them in the hash pan right after the hash is done. When I was a kid, I would eat only the fully set white of a fried egg and leave the yolk, and most days Iris feels the same way, but sometimes she loves runny yolk and eats it with repeated dips of the fingertip.

The other embarrassing thing I have to admit: for wet hash,

Yukon gold potatoes are best, but for dry hash, I use frozen hash brown potatoes. They're already cooked, so they brown swiftly, and once they're bathed in butter and salt, they don't taste frozen anymore.

Say, don't these recipes have a lot of fat in them, and won't fat kill you?

Yes and no, respectively.

If there's one way food writers and chefs eat differently from the rest of the country, it's that we're not afraid of fat, and particularly not saturated fat. Witness the rise of pork belly on restaurant menus. Laurie and I went out for dinner recently and the crispy pork belly I ordered was so delicious that I asked the chef for his secret. "I braise it in pork fat," he explained, and I can't wait to try it at home. Iris is certainly excited, especially since she wasn't invited to dinner.

It's not just animal fat that gets me excited. I always keep canned coconut milk on hand for both sweet and savory applications — it's essential to great peanut sauce. (My favorite brands are Chaokoh and Mae Ploy.) I buy cold-pressed peanut oil from Hong Kong and olive oil from Spain, Italy, or (a recent find) Arizona.

Food writers go crazy for fat for two reasons.

First, fat is essential to good-tasting food. Not everything that tastes good is high in fat — peaches are fat-free — but many of the world's most delicious foods cannot be made successfully in a low-fat version. I'm thinking of the marbling on a good steak, sure, but also great vegetarian foods like butter-rich Indian curries or Tuscan white beans cooked with plenty of olive oil and anointed with more olive oil before serving.

Second, fat is our Hurricane Carter, our Claus von Bülow: wrongly convicted and still tainted even after its acquittal. The best evidence at this point says that dietary fat (with the exception of trans fat) is unrelated to heart disease and cancer risk, and also unrelated to weight gain, except for the studies that indicate that low-fat diets cause people to gain weight. Still, admit that you cook with lard and people will react like you keep a loaded gun in your kid's room.

Nutritionists recommend a high-fat diet for babies and toddlers under age two because it's known to be important for development. There's another, practical reason for it: for babies who are learning to eat, low-fat food is literally hard to swallow. (Frankly, it's not easy for this adult, either.) This is particularly true for nutritious, tasty, and challenging items such as whole grains, greens, and meat.

It made me sad when I read (in a quick cookbook called *Desperation Dinners*) that authentic French cassoulet "contain[s] enough cholesterol to give us a heart attack." The southwest of France — cassoulet country — has the lowest rate of heart disease in France and one of the lowest in the world, despite the enormous amount of saturated fat that people eat there.

My approach to nutrition: eat a variety of great-tasting food. The word *hedonism* has a bad Summer of Love connotation, but it precisely describes the way I approach food and the way I hope Iris will, too.

BEER-BRAISED SHORT RIBS with WHEAT BERRIES

! EASY

About 4 hours, mostly unattended

This stew freezes well for up to three months.

Serves 4 to 6

- 3–4 pounds beef short ribs (flanken or English-style)
  salt and pepper
- 3 tablespoons olive oil
- 2 cloves garlic, thinly sliced
- 1 large onion, diced

1 carrot, peeled and diced

1 celery stalk, diced

1 cup wheat berries (see note)

2¼ cups porter beer, such as Black Butte Porter

1 cup canned crushed tomatoes, not drained

1½ cups chicken stock

2 tablespoons minced parsley

1. Preheat oven to 450°F.

2. Season the ribs liberally with salt and pepper and place them on a foil-lined baking sheet (bone-side down if you're using English-style ribs). Roast 45 minutes or until they're nicely browned and have rendered plenty of fat. Reduce oven temperature to 275°F.

3. While the ribs are roasting, heat the olive oil in a Dutch oven or other large pot over medium heat. Add the garlic, onion, carrot, and celery. Cook until vegetables are limp but not browned, 5 to 10 minutes.

4. Add the wheat berries, beer, tomatoes, and chicken stock, and stir to mix. Add the browned ribs, raise the heat to medium-high, and cover. When the pot is boiling, transfer it to the oven (you did remember to turn it down to 275°F, right?). Braise for 2½ to 3 hours, or until meat is very tender. Season with additional salt and pepper to taste.

5. If serving immediately, remove the meat and strain the sauce, then skim off the fat with a spoon or gravy separator. Otherwise, cool to room temperature and refrigerate everything together, skimming off the solidified fat before reheating. Give each person one or two ribs (remove the bones before serving if you like), a ladleful of wheat berries and sauce, and a sprinkling of parsley.

NOTE Wheat berries are available in the bulk section at any health food store. Mine has sometimes managed to run out, so I've substituted pearl barley to good effect. Hard or soft wheat berries will work. For another variation, substitute French green lentils for the wheat berries.

DUCK RAGU

"⏰" About 3 hours, mostly unattended

This chunky, rustic sauce is not the kind that clings closely to pasta; what you'll end up with is more like an intense stew with pasta in it. It's also highly economical: it stretches two duck legs to serve four. This sauce is equally at home with short pastas such as rigatoni and long ones such as spaghetti. Increase the cayenne pepper to ¼ or even ½ teaspoon if you like spicy food. This sauce freezes for up to three months.

Serves 4 (enough for 1 pound pasta)

 2 duck legs
    salt and pepper
 1 teaspoon butter
 1 teaspoon extra virgin olive oil
 1 stalk celery, diced
 1 medium onion, diced
 1 medium carrot, diced
 2 cloves garlic, minced
 1 teaspoon brown sugar
 ¼ teaspoon ground cloves
 ⅛ teaspoon cayenne pepper
 1 cup dry Marsala
 1 cup canned diced tomatoes with juice

1. Trim the duck legs of excess fat (that is, trim off any skin that hangs over the edge of the meat) and season liberally with salt and pepper on both sides.

2. Preheat the oven to 300°F. In a medium saucepan, heat the butter and oil over medium heat. Place the duck legs in the pan, skin-side down, and cook until well browned, about 10 minutes. Flip the legs and cook 5 minutes longer. Remove the duck legs to a plate.

3. Pour off all but about a tablespoon of fat. Add the celery, onion, and carrot. Cook until lightly browned, about 5 minutes. Add the garlic, brown sugar, cloves, and cayenne, and cook until fragrant, stirring frequently, about 1 minute longer.

4. Add the Marsala and tomatoes and bring to a boil. Return the duck legs to the pan, cover, and place in the oven. Bake 1½ to 2 hours or until the duck is very tender — you should be able to stick a fork into the meat with little resistance.

5. Remove the duck to a plate and cool. Strip the duck meat from the bones and shred by hand or chop with a sharp knife. You may include the skin at your option (I usually toss it, I admit). Return the duck meat to the pan and simmer until slightly thickened, about 5 minutes. Serve over pasta.

CARNITAS

! EASY

"⏰" 3 hours, mostly unattended

Keep carnitas simple. It's easy to think of all kinds of tasty stuff to throw into the pot, but it ends up cooking down into sludge and burning at the end. Serve with corn tortillas, roasted poblano chile strips (rajas), shredded cabbage, hot sauce or salsa, and lime wedges. Guacamole or ripe avocado slices would also be welcome.

Serves 6

- 3 pounds boneless pork shoulder or country-style ribs, trimmed and cut into 1-inch cubes
- 1 large onion, diced
- 1 cup chicken broth
- ¼ cup tequila
- 2 tablespoons lime juice, from 1 lime
  salt to taste

1. Combine all the ingredients in a large saucepan and bring to a boil. Reduce heat to medium-low and simmer, uncovered, 2 to 3 hours until the meat is tender, the onions have melted into the stew, and the broth is evaporated. (If necessary, turn up the heat near the end of cooking to evaporate the rest of the broth.) At this point, you may optionally refrigerate the carnitas before continuing. They will keep several days in the fridge.

2. Heat a large nonstick skillet over medium-high heat. Add the carnitas and cook, stirring occasionally, until they are heated through and well browned, even burnt or crispy in places, about 10 minutes. Serve immediately with suggested accompaniments.

NOTE You can make a magnificent "salad" with leftover carnitas. Reheat them and toss with shredded cabbage, lime juice, and hot sauce. The pork fat and lime juice form a vinaigrette.

MEXICAN ROASTED PEPPER STRIPS (Rajas)

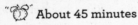 About 45 minutes

Heat a grill or broiler to maximum heat. Grill or broil fresh poblano chiles on all sides until well blackened, about 15 minutes total. Let cool, then slide the skins off. Cut the chiles open, remove the seeds and ribs, and slice the flesh into thin strips. Great with carnitas, but also in soups (especially tortilla soup or any chicken soup) and salads or as a garnish for grilled meats.

DUCK HASH

 35 minutes

If you don't have a leftover duck leg, you can make this with a leg of duck confit, which is fully cooked and — when you're not ordering it in a restaurant — quite inexpensive. Look for it at butcher shops, gourmet delis, and high-end natural foods stores, and expect to pay about five dollars per leg. Alternatively, take uncooked duck legs, season them with salt and pepper, and put them in the oven at 300°F for 90 minutes. You can, of course, substitute other proteins for the duck: consider corned beef, salmon, leftover turkey, chopped thick-cut bacon.

Serves 2 to 3

- 4 tablespoons butter or duck fat
- 1 pound frozen (diced) hash brown potatoes
- 1 cup leftover braised, roasted, or confit duck leg, diced
- 1 small onion, minced
  salt and pepper

1. Melt the butter or duck fat in a large nonstick or cast-iron skillet over medium-high heat. Add the potatoes, sprinkle with salt, and cook, stirring occasionally, until potatoes are golden brown on all sides, about 20 minutes. (This is a great place to develop or show off your professional skillet flipping skills.)

2. Add the duck and onion and continue cooking until everything is well browned, 5 to 10 minutes more, adding another tablespoon of butter if necessary. Season to taste with salt and pepper and serve with poached or fried eggs.

NOTE There are more stew recipes in chapter 15, about slow cookers.

5

Spice Girl

"**S**ORRY," I SAID to Laurie while tasting the chicken enchiladas one night. "I think I made these too spicy for the baby."

The baby, nine months old, proceeded to eat two entire enchiladas.

I love spicy food. If I don't eat anything spicy for a couple of days in a row, I get depressed. Laurie likes her food just as spicy as I do. Almost. Once we were at an Indian restaurant and ordered assorted pakoras. I surveyed the range of fried vegetables and chose one that I assumed was some kind of sweet pepper. It was no kind of sweet pepper. It was something much hotter than a jalapeño. I panted, gasped, and guzzled water. Then I leafed through the pakoras.

"What are you doing?" asked Laurie.

"I want another one of those."

My affinity for the hot stuff is cultural, to be sure, but it's also genetic. Clinically speaking, I'm a nontaster. I don't like to throw this term around, because I feel like they're going to take away my food writer's license, but nontasters lack the ability to taste a particular chemical known as PROP.

PROP is a thyroid medication. Decades ago, doctors noticed that some patients complained that their medicine was brutally bitter and some didn't. It turned out that the nontasters had fewer taste buds. Way fewer. (Personally, I have six taste buds, and four of them are devoted to chocolate.)

In the years since this initial discovery, researchers have learned more fun facts about nontasters, regular tasters, and supertasters. The supertasters live in an unfriendly world. If you've ever had your eyes dilated at the optometrist and then gone out into the sun, you understand how supertasters experience flavor.

Nontasters like me are able to tolerate spicy food without pain, and we also tend to like bitter foods, because they don't taste so bitter to us. That may be why I can inhale a big bowl of braised kale and why I enjoy bitter melon, the wrinkly Asian vegetable that is especially delicious when hollowed out and stuffed with seasoned ground pork. Actually, everything is delicious served that way.

So when Iris went on her enchilada binge, I figured I had a young nontaster on my hands. One time, Laurie and I were enjoying a big plate of *larb* and sharing bites of the spicy Thai chicken salad with Iris. She was sweating and panting — and asking for more. On a trip to Portland, we stopped at my favorite spice store, Penzeys, and bought a pound of their hottest chili powder. "My daughter loves this stuff," I bragged to the surprised clerk, and it was true.

I made spicy taco fillings, carnitas, and chili, and Iris gobbled them all. I made a fiery tomatillo salsa with five serrano chiles in it, and Iris would dip a chip into it, lick the salsa off, and dip again. (Double-dipping seems to be instinctive behavior. Once I went to a kids' birthday party and watched a pair of two-year-olds hanging out by the salsa bowl dipping and licking for twenty minutes without consuming a single chip.)

Around Iris's first birthday, we took her to a Szechuan restaurant called Seven Stars Pepper. She enjoyed the pork dumplings, of course, and the spicy fish, but her favorite dish was Ants on a

Tree, cellophane noodles (the trees) dotted with morsels of ground pork (the ants), red chile, and Szechuan peppercorns. It's become our whole family's number one favorite dinner, and the recipe is at the end of this chapter. (It's adapted from Terry Durack's wonderful book *Noodle*.)

One day, the usual roster of stuffed animals wasn't doing the trick and I was desperate for something to entertain Iris, so I poked around in a cupboard and found some cellophane bags of dried chiles. I dumped anchos, chipotles, and cascabels into a pot and let Iris have at it.

She held a chipotle to her nose. "Smoky," she declared. She picked up a cascabel and shook it, then made me open it to show her what was rattling inside. Even I was surprised at the sheer number of seeds, and we each tasted one. "Spicy!" said Iris, slightly shocked. Then she ate three more. Finally, she stirred the chiles in the pot and said, "Making chile soup." (Later I would learn that *cascabel* is Spanish for "little rattle.")

Unfortunately, I had to perform a toy recall on the dried chiles. One day I found Iris with a cayenne pepper in her hand and a horrified look on her face. "Iris's chin is spicy," she complained. But soon she forgot about the trauma as she tossed some chiles into a pot with a toy mushroom and said, "Making chipotle-mushroom stew."

Iris's spicy phase lasted for about a year. Then she started asking at dinner, "Is this not spicy? Because I don't like spicy things." For a while this was all talk. She'd still choose the spicy over the sweet Italian sausage and we still went through several tablespoons of hot chili powder per week. She continued to steal bites of tofu from my four-star spicy pad Thai.

Then it became clear that she really couldn't stand the heat and intended to get out of the kitchen. Recently we had a salad bar dinner. Laurie and I had salads of farm-fresh greens, cranberry beans, bacon, croutons, and caramelized shallot vinaigrette. Iris had a salad consisting of bacon and croutons. "This crouton has *pepper* on it," she lamented. Laurie and I were reduced to surgically removing flecks of black pepper from Iris's croutons so she could enjoy her "salad." Now I have to make a point of telling Iris that I am not putting pepper on things. Like, "This fish smells delicious. And there's no pepper on it." Never mind that she still loves being in charge of filling the pepper grinder because those little peppercorns are so cute. I'm thinking about filling the pepper grinder with white pepper to see if I can fool her.

Obviously, starting with the spicy stuff early won't turn your kid into a chile-head. But Iris still loves Ants on a Tree, even though I refuse to dumb it down into some bland P. F. Chang's spaghetti.

Not that I'm bitter or anything. I'm learning to serve dishes that can be made in simultaneous spicy and nonspicy versions with little extra work. My friend Fahmida tells me this is exactly what they do for children in her native country of Bangladesh, where the food is as wildly flavorful and spicy as that of neighboring India.

LARB GAI (Thai Chicken Salad)

! QUICK

"⏰" 30 minutes

🗁 Food processor, spice grinder

The traditional way to make larb is to poach the chicken in the dressing. In hopelessly American style, I like everything browned, so I make it this way.

Serves 4 as part of a Thai meal, fewer otherwise

- 1 pound boneless, skinless chicken thighs (or ground chicken, if you can get decent ground dark-meat chicken, like at a butcher shop or Whole Foods)
- ½ cup thinly sliced shallots

2 tablespoons sliced scallions

1 tablespoon peanut oil

2 tablespoons fish sauce

3 tablespoons lime juice from 1 to 2 limes

1 teaspoon crushed red chile flakes or 1 tablespoon minced fresh Thai or serrano chiles (more to taste)

2–3 tablespoons toasted rice powder (see recipe below)
cabbage leaves
sticky rice (see chapter 11)

1. If you're using chicken thighs, place them in the food processor and pulse them until well ground but not quite paste, about ten one-second pulses.

2. In a bowl, combine the ground chicken, shallots, and scallions. Heat the peanut oil in large nonstick skillet over medium-high. Add the chicken mixture and cook until no longer pink and just starting to brown, about 5 minutes. While the chicken cooks, stir together the fish sauce, lime juice, and chiles.

3. Turn the chicken mixture out into a large bowl. Stir in the dressing and rice powder (recipe follows) to taste. I like a lot of rice powder. Serve at room temperature, optionally with sticky rice and green cabbage. If using cabbage, cut the raw cabbage into large wedges and serve each person a cabbage wedge. Peel leaves off the outside of the wedge and wrap a small amount of larb in the cabbage leaf before eating. Substitute lettuce if that's what you have on hand.

NONSPICY VARIATION Keep the chiles separate from the rest of the dressing, divide the dressed salad into two bowls, and stir the chiles into one of the portions.

Toasted Rice Powder

⏰ 30 minutes (includes cooling time)

Makes about 3 tablespoons

Place a dry skillet (not nonstick) over medium heat. Add ¼ cup uncooked Thai white sticky rice (preferred) or jasmine rice. Toast the rice, stirring and shaking the pan occasionally, until the rice is golden brown and smoking slightly, about 10 minutes. Cool to room temperature and grind to a very fine powder in a spice grinder or coffee grinder (you can also use a heavy-duty mortar and pestle). It's great on any Thai salad, and Iris loves having a little pile of it on her plate for dipping any kind of meat or fish. Okay, so do I.

STACKED GREEN CHILE ENCHILADAS

 2 hours

4 rimmed soup plates (you *could* make this as a casserole by stacking the tortillas in a large baking dish, but you'd miss out on crunchy cheese, which would be a tragedy)

Serves 4

The beans and green chile sauce (recipe follows) may be made in advance. Assemble and broil the enchiladas just before serving.

Cowboy Beans

This is more beans than you'll need for the enchiladas; serve some on the side or save them for lunch. Pureed with a stick blender or food processor, these make fabulous bean dip.

Makes about 4 cups

- 4 slices bacon, diced
- 2 cloves garlic, minced
   half a 15-ounce can diced tomatoes, not drained (preferably Muir Glen Fire-Roasted)
- 2 15-ounce cans pinto beans, not drained
- 1 tablespoon minced canned pickled jalapeños, optional
- 2 tablespoons minced cilantro

1. In a large saucepan, cook the bacon over medium heat until crisp. Add the garlic and cook 30 seconds, stirring. Add the tomatoes and cook, stirring regularly, 4 minutes. Add the beans, bring to a simmer, and simmer uncovered 15 minutes over medium-low heat.

2. Add the jalapeños (if using) and cilantro. Taste for salt. Beans should be a little soupy.

Green Chile Sauce

☞ Blender or food processor

Anaheim chiles vary in heat. This sauce usually comes out fairly mild, but sometimes it's more like medium-hot. For the guaranteed nonspicy variation, see the note below.

Makes about 4 cups

- 1½ pounds fresh Anaheim chiles
- 12 ounces tomatillos, husked and rinsed
- 3 cups low-sodium chicken broth
- 1 teaspoon dried Mexican oregano
- 1 clove garlic, minced
- ¼ teaspoon salt
  ground black pepper to taste
- 2 tablespoons cornstarch, dissolved in 2 tablespoons water

1. Roast the chiles on a grill or under a broiler until well blackened. When cool, peel the chiles and slit them open to remove the core and seeds. Mince and set aside.

2. Meanwhile, bring a pot of water to the boil and add the tomatillos. Boil 5 minutes, stirring once or twice. Drain and puree in a blender or food processor.

3. Put the tomatillo puree in the empty saucepan with the chicken broth, chiles, oregano, garlic, salt, and pepper. Bring to a boil, reduce heat, and simmer uncovered 10 minutes.

4. Add the cornstarch, stir, and return to a simmer. Simmer an additional 5 to 10 minutes, until sauce is thickened and reduced to about 4 cups. Keep warm over lowest heat if you're making the enchiladas now.

NONSPICY VARIATION Substitute two 7-ounce cans of mild roasted green chiles for the Anaheims. Because they're already roasted and peeled, simply mince them and add them to the sauce in step 3. You may divide the sauce into two and add hot sauce or minced pickled jalapeños to one portion before assembling the enchiladas for those who prefer things spicy, or just pass hot sauce at the table.

Making the Enchiladas

Because these enchiladas are broiled, not baked, it's vital to have the beans, sauce, and bowls hot when you assemble them. You'll need four soup plates with rims. Unless you have a large oven, you'll probably need to broil two plates at a time; don't worry, the enchiladas will stay hot. I've made these as cheese enchiladas by simply omitting the chicken, and they were still great.

These are large portions, and the plates come out of the oven too hot to set in front of a child. I cut out a section of my enchiladas to serve to Iris, along with some (okay, most) of the crunchy cheese from the rim.

¼ cup corn oil, lard, or vegetable oil
12 corn tortillas
2 cups shredded cooked chicken (rotisserie chicken works great)
2 cups cowboy beans, hot
4 cups green chile sauce, hot
1 pound shredded Monterey jack cheese
4 broiler-proof ceramic soup plates with rims

1. Place an oven rack about 6 inches from the broiler element and preheat to 200°F. Place the bowls in the oven to warm them.

2. Heat the oil in a small skillet over medium-high. Working one at a time, fry each tortilla for 20 to 30 seconds on each side, until they're just beginning to brown and stiffen. Hold each tortilla over the oil with tongs to drain, and place it on a paper towel–lined baking sheet.

3. Remove the bowls from the oven and set the oven to broil. Ladle ½ cup cowboy beans into each bowl. Top each with a tortilla, followed by ¼ cup chicken and a generous ¼ cup green chile sauce. Scatter with a thin layer of cheese (about 2 tablespoons). Make another layer of tortilla, chicken, sauce, and cheese. Finish with a final tortilla, sauce, and a thick carpet of cheese (about ¾ cup) extending onto the rim of the bowl.

4. Broil 3 to 5 minutes, or until cheese is well browned and bubbling. Serve immediately.

ANTS ON A TREE

⏰ 40 minutes

LITTLE FINGERS: Kids can measure and stir together the marinade ingredients.

Szechuan peppercorns are a strange beast. They're not really spicy at all. Instead, when you bite down on one, it causes a Novocain-like numbness with a faint citrus haze. There's no way to make this sound appealing if you haven't tried them, but the same is true of hot peppers. Szechuan peppercorns are, in fact, the dried buds of a citrus tree, and they were banned in the United States for decades because of the threat of citrus canker, a parasite that can ruin citrus crops. (Contraband of varying quality was readily available, of course.) They're now legal again as long as they've been heat treated (that is, baked). I have a bottle of the heat-treated ones from Penzeys.com, and they're great. If this were not a family book, I would recommend that you also get baked before enjoying a dish with Szechuan peppercorns.

Serves about 3

- 8 ounces ground pork
- 2 tablespoons soy sauce
- 1 tablespoon sugar
- 1 tablespoon hot bean paste
- 1 teaspoon cornstarch
- 6–8 ounces cellophane noodles
- 2 tablespoons peanut oil
- 2 scallions, white and light green parts only, thinly sliced
- 1 red jalapeño or Fresno chile, seeded and minced
- ½ cup chicken stock
- 1 tablespoon dark soy sauce
- ¼ teaspoon ground Szechuan peppercorns (optional)

1. In a medium bowl, combine pork with regular soy sauce, sugar, hot bean paste, and cornstarch. Refrigerate 20 minutes.

2. Place noodles in a large bowl and pour boiling water over to cover. Soak 5 minutes, stirring occasionally, and drain in a colander.

3. Heat oil in a 12-inch nonstick skillet or a wok over medium-high heat. Add the scallions and jalapeño and cook 30 seconds, stirring frequently. Add the pork and stir-fry until no longer pink, breaking up any chunks, about 3 minutes.

4. Add the noodles, chicken stock, dark soy sauce, and Szechuan pepper. Cook, tossing the noodles with two wooden spoons, until the sauce is absorbed and pork is well distributed throughout the noodles. Transfer to a large platter and serve immediately.

NONSPICY VARIATION Not really practical, but the hot bean paste is not really that hot, and the jalapeño is optional. Even at the height of Iris's sensitivity to hot stuff, she never complained about Ants on a Tree.

Ground pork. To really get the ants to climb the tree, you need finely ground pork. You can take regular ground pork and pulse it a few times in the food processor, but I'm too lazy to bother; the flavor is great either way, and Iris likes big pork bites.

Hot bean paste. This is the stuff Iron Chef Chen was always reaching for. Available at Asian groceries and some supermarkets, it's sometimes called hot bean sauce, or spicy bean paste, or similar.

Cellophane noodles. Also called bean threads or saifun. Look for mung bean starch in the ingredients. Around here, they're sold in a 6-ounce package.

Dark soy sauce. Also called soy superior sauce or mushroom soy sauce. I buy Pearl River Bridge Mushroom Soy Sauce at my local Safeway.

THAI CATFISH CAKES

! QUICK
🕐 30 minutes
🍲 Food processor

With no binder other than egg, these are unusual and delicious fish cakes. Serve with steamed rice, Thai sweet chile dipping sauce (available in bottles in Asian groceries and many supermarkets; look for Mae Ploy brand), and lettuce or cabbage leaves for wrapping.

Makes about 16 small fish cakes

    1   pound catfish fillets
    ¼   cup minced shallot
    ¼   cup chopped cilantro
    1   large egg
    1   tablespoon fish sauce

1 tablespoon Thai red curry paste
peanut oil for frying

1. Cut the catfish into one-inch chunks and place in a food processor. Pulse until the fish is reduced to a coarse paste, about five one-second pulses.

2. Combine the shallot, cilantro, egg, fish sauce, and curry paste in a bowl, and stir well to mix. Add the fish paste and stir until well combined. It will be a loose mixture.

3. Heat several tablespoons peanut oil in a large nonstick skillet over medium-high. Form the fish mixture into two-inch patties, adding each fish cake to the pan as you form it. Fry the fish cakes until golden brown, about 2 minutes per side, and serve immediately. They don't hold or reheat well.

NONSPICY VARIATION Replace the red curry paste with 1 teaspoon minced lemongrass and 1 teaspoon minced fresh ginger.

6

Part of This Complete Breakfast

IRIS AND I WERE seated at the breakfast table having a serious conversation about her future.

IRIS: When I'm big I'm going to drive a big tractor. And I'll have metal cows at my house.

ME: Metal cows?

IRIS: You push a button on the back and they eat grass.

ME: Do they make milk?

IRIS: Yes, you press a button on the udder and milk comes out into the container.

ME: Are these robot cows?

IRIS: No, silly. They're real pretend animals.

Iris and I have most of our important talks at breakfast. Laurie leaves for work at six-thirty a.m., which is (thank God) before Iris wakes up. So it's just me and the little buddy and the issues of the day. We have plenty of time to talk, because preschoolers take forever to eat breakfast. Once, when Iris was a baby, we were visiting friends and I had a terrifying glimpse into my future. I went over to their house and met their toddler, Jordan, who was fourteen months old. "We'll get going right after Jordan eats his breakfast," promised his parents. Just two hours later, we were on the road.

Iris isn't that slow, but she's still pretty sluggish — I can finish two waffles in the time it takes her to eat two waffle strips. Have you noticed how, when you have a kid, the shape of food becomes absurdly important? Iris likes her toast and waffles in strips, but English muffins have to be cut down the middle into two half-moons so she can play Aliens on the Moon, a game involving sausage aliens.

Also, Iris must have the bottom half of the English muffin, otherwise she'll turn it over and point out, "You gave me the half without the farina!" (I had to check the ingredient list to determine that the little specks were called farina.) Once Iris and I were in the bulk food section and I got really excited on finding an entire bin full of farina. I think I'm the only person ever to get excited about this. Iris was like, *Whatever.* Turns out farina is the same as Cream of Wheat.

IRIS: When I grow up, I want to be a lady.
ME: You will, but that's not really a job, per se.
IRIS: I'll put on my suit and build my farm. Everything is going to be metal at my farm. The suit is going to be metal so I don't blow away.
ME: What crops will you grow?
IRIS: I'm going to grow ginger cookies with my wheat.
  (pause)
IRIS: Do ginger cookies come from wheat?

How many strips of bacon can one toddler eat? It depends on the brand of bacon.

I think a lot about bacon. It's become a foodie cliche, but there really isn't anything more delicious. Three bacon cookbooks have come out in the last few years: *The Bacon Cookbook, Everything*

Tastes Better with Bacon, and *Seduced by Bacon.* The last is a particularly apt title. I've known plenty of baco-vegetarians. My friend Liza used to say, "Oh, dear, how did this bacon get into my sandwich?" Then she added prosciutto to her diet. Now she has given up vegetarianism entirely. Seduced by bacon.

My friends Henry and Lorna invented a dish called Bacon-Wrapped Bacon. It starts with red-cooked pork belly, which is pork belly braised with soy sauce, sugar, rice wine, ginger, and star anise. Henry and Lorna are Chinese American, and they are always complaining about the quality of Chinese food available in Seattle. This would be obnoxious if not for the facts that (a) they really do cook better Chinese food than almost any place in Seattle, and (b) sometimes they invite me over.

To make Bacon-Wrapped Bacon, Henry and Lorna cut the pork belly into chunks, wrap each chunk in a thin slice of bacon, and roast it until the bacon begins to crisp. Then they serve it with a spoonful of the rich and salty reduced braising liquid. They made this recently for a cocktail party, and some of the guests took a bite and protested that it was too rich. I did not have this problem.

Iris has been eating bacon since before her first birthday. At first I would cut the cooked bacon into bits. Then she graduated to half a slice. Now she eats two slices, but she is fanatical about texture. It has to be crispy but not into crunchy territory. And, as you know, it should be Nueske's.

The first time we tried Nueske's was after reading about it in the *New York Times,* and we ordered a couple pounds from Nueskes .com, which cost a bundle. The bacon was astonishingly smoky. For a lot of people, it would be too much, but we like big flavors.

We served it at a party once. "Good bacon, huh?" I said. "I got it on the Internet!" This is not a good way to impress people. Internet dating has become socially acceptable; Internet bacon, not so much.

Then they started selling Nueske's at a supermarket fifteen minutes from our house. This should have been life changing, but mostly I'm too lazy to go and get any, and it's often out of stock. I'm guilty of this a lot: I convince myself that some new noodle shop or frozen yogurt place is going to permanently rock my world, and then I go there a couple of times and forget about it.

Iris has little patience for my short attention span. She got a pirate ship toy in December 2006 and has played with it every single day since then. Every time I serve bacon, she asks, "Is it Nueske's?" If I admit it isn't, she gives me a look like, *Why would you mess around with bacon that isn't Nueske's? What's the point?* A few days ago, after letting our supply run dry for too long, I brought home a pound of the stuff. "I'm so glad they're back," Iris sighed.

"That what are back?"

"The Nueskes."

If you find instant oatmeal as sludgy and unappealing as I do, you might be tempted to write off the whole hot cereal section. But there's a family favorite hanging out among the packets: steel-cut oats. This is an old-school breakfast. The most common brand is McCann's Irish Oats, in a white can with a pry-off lid. McCann's motto is: "Certificate of Award: Uniformity of Granulation." Its motto *should* be "Fuck you, instant oatmeal." It takes more than half an hour to make Irish oats, and they're still chewy when you're done — wonderfully chewy and toasty, the granules popping between your teeth like caviar. (When Iris was a baby, I'd whiz her oats with the stick blender until smooth, which was probably unnecessary.)

Steel-cut oats are one of those foods that once marked you as poor and now prove that you're a member of the leisure class, because who else has thirty-five minutes to make oatmeal? Also, the can costs like nine dollars, although you can get steel-cut oats for much less in the bulk bins at a natural foods store. Quaker makes them now, too. "Steel-cut oats" is the generic term, but I like calling them "Irish oats" because Iris thinks I'm saying "Iris oats" and says, "So . . . those are my oats?" They sure are, especially when I add bacon to them in the recipe below.

Like many families, we have a sacred Sunday morning ritual. I'm talking about French toast.

The French toast I serve today is, like other popular Sunday morning activities, a synthesis of the ancient and modern. I use the same kind of bread that my mother used when I was growing up. But my batter is the opposite of hers. (I say "my batter," but it's actually from *Cook's Illustrated* magazine, and you can find the recipe in their book *The Best Recipe.*) Mom's French toast batter consists mainly of half-and-half and eggs. Mine uses low-fat milk and just one egg. Iris frequently eats French toast for lunch at my mother's house, so she has learned to navigate seamlessly between the two traditions.

Until shortly before Iris was born, Laurie and I made our French toast using challah, in a tip of the hat to my forebears. We bought the challah on Fridays at a local bagel shop. The bread was just stale enough by Sunday to survive a dip in batter. Then the bagel shop abruptly changed their challah formula. I remember precisely when this happened, because it was on April 1, and I was trying to figure out whether limp, under-risen bread could be someone's idea of an April Fool's joke.

I scouted around for a different challah. I found a store brand that worked well. They discontinued it. I tried another bagel shop where you had to special-order the challah. With great anticipation (how bad could something be if you had to special-order it?), I strode into the bagel shop and took the challah into my arms. It was a heavy, gritty, whole-wheat abomination, a disgrace to the Jews.

At one point I tried baking my own challah. It came out reasonably well, but I wasn't going to do it every week, although it would certainly have given me something to talk about with my grandmother.

Then, walking down the street one day, I spied a garishly yellow bag in the back of a bread delivery truck. TEXAS TOAST, it read. It was nothing more than regular white sandwich bread, thick-sliced, and (for reasons I can't explain) artificially colored yellow. This was the bread that made the French toast of my youth.

Now, a few words about syrup.

I would like to tell you about my adventures tracking down the ultimate in maple syrup. There are two common grades of maple syrup, A and B. This isn't like the system you're used to from high school or fresh eggs. Many food geeks consider grade B maple syrup superior: it's darker, richer, and more flavorful.

That is the theory, at least. Over here in real life, I prefer fake maple syrup, such as Mrs. Butterworth's, to any grade of real maple syrup. I felt guilty about buying the fake syrup until my sister-in-law Wendy, who has lived in Italy, admitted that she sometimes prefers Chef Boyardee ravioli to actual Italian ravioli.

As I thought more about this, though, visions of a steaming Vermont sugar shack filled my head, and I resolved to give maple syrup another try, if only for Iris's sake. I picked up a couple of bottles of organic Canadian maple syrup, one of each grade, and started substituting them for our usual store-brand sugar water on Sundays.

The experiment went undetected until I cracked open the grade B. "I don't care for this syrup," said Laurie. I have to admit, I liked its full-bodied caramel punch. Iris, no surprise, is fine with any syrup. I told her syrup is made from maple sap, so she kept dipping her finger in the Canadian stuff and yelling, "I love to eat sap!"

Next week, I guess I'll be clutching my flask of organic grade B while the rest of the family enjoys their high-fructose industrial runoff. Then, when the B runs out, I will balk at spending eleven dollars on another bottle of syrup. "Pass the sludge," I will say, and family harmony will reign again.

To Eggo is human, but homemade waffles are divine. The best are made with yeast. Just saying this, in my experience, is enough to drive many people off, but please read on. This is so easy and *so* worth it.

I've tried buttermilk waffles, sour cream waffles, and cornmeal-bacon waffles, and every time I stray, I end up saying, "That was pretty good, but I'd never choose it over plain yeasted waffles." That's right: yeasted waffles are better than *waffles with bacon in them*. Yeasted waffles brown better and are crispier and lighter than chemically leavened waffles.

Seattle has given the world many great things, such as Nirvana, Jimi Hendrix, and espresso. Okay, maybe espresso was invented in Italy, but Seattle definitely gave the world the caramel macchiato . . . Well, anyway, we also gave you Soundgarden.

At the 1962 World's Fair, Seattle also introduced to America a product that would have an unsavory effect on the nation's breakfast: the Belgian waffle. Now, I have no problem with Belgium. Belgian beer? Best in the world. Belgian pommes frites? Ditto.

But no Eurocrat is going to convince me that bigger indentations make a better waffle. Normally I don't look to Elvis Presley for food criticism — he's better known for gluttony than gourmandise. But the King knew a thing or two about waffles.

In 1963, Elvis starred in *It Happened at the World's Fair*. The plot involves Elvis and his pal hitchhiking to Seattle to make money to repair their cropduster, or something. The important part is when Elvis has to shepherd a little Chinese American girl named Sue-Lin around the 1962 World's Fair, and Sue-Lin has the appetite of — well, let's just say she wouldn't say no to a plate of fried peanut butter-and-banana sandwiches. After an eggroll fails to sate Sue-Lin's hunger, Elvis buys her a Belgian waffle with strawberries and whipped cream and watches with disgust as the girl plows her way through the international delicacy. Then, confirming Elvis's misgivings about foreign foods, Sue-Lin develops a stomachache and has to be escorted to the infirmary, where Elvis tries to stick his tongue down the throat of a foxy nurse (Joan O'Brien).

See, here's what Elvis and I understand, besides that Joan

O'Brien was quite a dish: a crunchy waffle is all about surface area, and for that, American-style waffle irons rule. Ours is the Toastmaster Family Waffler; it makes four waffles at a time and cost twenty dollars.

The waffle recipe calls for instant yeast; you could substitute active dry yeast, but you should be buying instant anyway (it's cheaper and doesn't need to be proofed in warm water). It's also called bread machine yeast or RapidRise yeast.

We make these for dinner as often as breakfast; I mix up the batter in the morning before Iris wakes up. What's better than breakfast for dinner? (Answer: pizza for breakfast.)

So, to sum up our morning repartee, when Iris grows up she's going to wear a metal jumpsuit, eat cookies, drive a tractor, and milk robot cows. This sounds awesome. I hope she invites me for breakfast.

IRISH OATS with CANDIED BACON

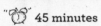 45 minutes

The McCann's website has some tips for making your Irish oats cook faster, such as presoaking them the night before. To me, this misses the point: they taste so good because you have to wait forever and get really hungry. The company also makes two different types of quick-cooking oats, both of which I find predictably inferior to the original. (Insufficient uniformity of granulation.)

I thought I had invented the idea of bacon on oatmeal and would be immortalized as a culinary genius, but then my friend Lucian told me he's been doing it for years.

Serves 3 to 4

FOR THE OATS
   1 tablespoon butter
   1 cup low-fat milk

    3 cups water
    1 cup steel-cut oats
    ¼ teaspoon salt

FOR THE CANDIED BACON
    8 slices thick-cut bacon, preferably double-smoked
    ½ cup light brown sugar

1. Preheat the oven to 375°F. Combine the butter, milk, and water in a saucepan. Bring to a boil over medium-high heat. Add the oats, reduce heat to low, and simmer, uncovered, 20 minutes. (Traditionally, you don't stir during this time, stirring later with a stick called a *spurtle* so as to make the oatmeal chunkier, but I've never found this to make much of a difference.)

2. Meanwhile, make the candied bacon. Take a baking sheet and *completely wrap it in heavy-duty foil.* Put the bacon on the foil-wrapped sheet and sprinkle it with ¼ cup brown sugar. Bake 8 minutes. Flip the bacon strips and sprinkle the other side with the remaining ¼ cup brown sugar. Bake an additional 8 minutes or until firm and lacquered. Cool briefly and cut into dice.

3. Stir the salt into the bubbling oatmeal and continue to simmer, stirring occasionally, until the oats are thick but not pasty, 5 to 10 minutes. Let the oatmeal rest for a few minutes in the pot, then serve topped with bacon, plus additional brown sugar and milk if desired.

YEASTED WAFFLES

Overnight, plus 15 minutes

Waffle iron, hand mixer (recommended for whipping egg whites)

Makes about 16 small waffles, serving 4

    10 ounces all-purpose flour
     1 tablespoon sugar

1 teaspoon instant yeast
¾ teaspoon salt
1 stick unsalted butter, melted and cooled until warm
2 cups warm milk (whole, low-fat, and skim are all fine)
1 teaspoon vanilla extract
2 large eggs, separated

1. The night before your morning wafflepalooza, mix the flour, sugar, yeast, and salt in a large bowl. Add the butter and stir until well combined. Stir in the milk and vanilla, leaving a few lumps; cover with foil or plastic wrap and leave overnight at room temperature.

2. By the morning, the batter will have developed a creamy head like a pint of Guinness. Stir in the egg yolks. Whip the egg whites to stiff peaks and fold gently into the batter with a spatula.

3. Pour an appropriate amount of batter onto a scrupulously preheated and greased waffle iron. This batter expands more than most, so err on the side of too little batter. With practice, you'll be able to get a fully realized waffle with minimal leakage. Cook 5 minutes or so, depending on the strength of your waffler.

7

Snacktime

SNACKTIME IS TRICKY.

Eating a snack is easy. Keeping it rolling, day after day, sometimes on the go, is hard. And as Iris gets older and more opinionated, it gets harder.

Actual snacks, age one: A bowl of buttered peas. Leftover mashed sweet potatoes. Black beans.

Actual snack, age three: Two sugar cookies and a meatball.

Once upon a time, we placed a plate of green beans in front of Iris at snacktime, and she Hoovered so many into her mouth that she couldn't chew them and gagged. Now Iris is perfectly toothy and capable of eating a bowl of green beans but has no interest in doing so.

Eating five or six small meals a day is popular diet advice, but for a baby or toddler, it's not a lifestyle choice — it's absolutely necessary, because they have tiny stomachs and seem to digest food as fast as garbage disposals. "Snack" quickly becomes an official meal, as vital as lunch.

Actually, I guess I'm like this, too. If I miss my three p.m. snack or make the mistake of eating a few tortilla chips and thinking this constitutes snack, I get sulky before dinner. Iris is always teaching me valuable lessons like this. Like, who knew that I needed a nap every day at one p.m.? Unfortunately, once Iris turned two and a half, she stopped taking naps, whereas I still start to fall asleep around one p.m. I would happily pay Iris five dollars to take a nap, but kids today just don't understand the value of money.

For a while, every afternoon featured almond and Booty. Almond is warm milk with almond syrup. Booty is Veggie Booty, a snack food made by Robert's American Gourmet and the primary form of sustenance for millions of toddlers. It's puffed rice and corn in popcorn-size chunks, dusted with a green powder consisting of dehydrated spinach and kale. Children who don't eat vegetables will eat Veggie Booty, which is why it's so popular. (It certainly isn't because of the taste, as it tastes like dehydrated spinach and kale.) I didn't feel great about letting Iris eat a bag of these green Cheetos every week, but they couldn't actually be *harmful,* right?

Wrong. In mid-2007, Veggie Booty was recalled. A batch of the green powder, which came from a Chinese factory, was contaminated with salmonella, sending a bunch of kids to the hospital. Thankfully, no one died in this outbreak, unlike the previous year's *E. coli* spinach disaster, in which a toddler died when his mother blended raw spinach into his smoothie. Note to self: health food can totally kill you. I had to throw away a half-eaten bag of Booty and resist the urge to rush Iris to the hospital just to make sure she didn't have salmonella poisoning.

This was the second time a recall had hit home. The first time, Iris's toy cell phone was recalled because the antenna could break off and present a choking hazard. We contacted the company, and they promptly sent a replacement. By this time, however, Iris was three years old, too old to choke on a busted cell phone, so we just kept both toys. This was probably unethical of us, but we got our karmic payback: two toy cell phones are *twice as loud* as one. I complained to Iris that she was making an infernal racket, and thereafter she would come to me, waving the two phones, and say, "Hey, Dada, you want to play Infernal Racket?"

Iris took it pretty well when I explained that they don't make Booty anymore. In fact, Iris seems to deal with disappointment better, in general, than I do. Recently I was boasting loudly about how I was going to make one of her favorite foods, sticky rice, with dinner, and then our bag of sticky rice turned out to be infested with flies. I wanted to cry. I wanted sticky rice. "That's okay!" said Iris cheerily, and asked to see the flies. She also says "That's okay!" if I forget my jacket in the rain, or even if I forget her jacket. When she does get upset, it's more likely to be about something like my refusing to pick up the balloon that is three feet away from her. ("But I'm really busy sitting on the couch!" wailed Iris.)

In case I felt smug about not being a Booty-eater (cue sophomoric giggle), the FDA also banned one of my favorite snacks on the same day: eel from China. On trips to the Asian grocery, I'd frequently pick up a package of frozen barbecued eel, the same stuff that sits atop *unagi* sushi. It makes a simple lunch or snack: Cook some rice in the rice cooker or on the stovetop. When the rice is done, toss an eel fillet, still frozen, on top, cover the pot, and let it sit another five minutes. Eat. You can get the same thing at most Japanese restaurants in Seattle for about fourteen dollars.

I did this often until eel imports from China were banned because the fish was contaminated with a quartet of illegal antibiotics. Basically all of the eel sold in the United States comes from China, which is weird, since a lot of eel is caught in the southeastern United States and shipped to Japan. There's a wonderful book about the American eel industry, *Consider the Eel,* by Richard Schweid. At one point, the author talks to a bunch of eel fishermen and asks how they like to cook their eel. They all say eel is gross and they don't understand why anyone eats it. But eel is one of the most delicious fish I know. The Chinese eel ban has done nothing to take Chinese eel off the shelves at the supermarkets I frequent, but now I'm too scared to eat it. There is a fish market in Seattle's Chinatown that sells live eel. When you clean a live eel, it keeps twitching even after you cut it up. My eel cravings are not that strong. Yet.

This federal intervention wasn't helping my snack problem, obviously. One insight that did help was realizing that afternoon snack is a good time for dessert. Obviously I'm not anti-dessert, but if Iris knows dessert is coming after dinner, she's likely to say, "Okay, I'm full," after two bites of enchilada. I find this puzzling, because as much as I like sweets, I crave salty and fatty things even more, and I would never pass up another enchilada no matter how alluring the siren song of tartlets in the oven.

I could try to make dessert a surprise and admit its existence only after the enchiladas are depleted, but it's hard to fool a four-year-old. So we have dessert in the afternoon. If we bake cookies, brownies, or cupcakes, it gives us something to do after lunch besides watching TV. Often we'll do milk shakes or malts, which are even nutritious, since they're full of milk. Berries and whipped cream are always a hit, although fresh berries make a painfully brief appearance each summer in Seattle — especially strawberries, which are good for a month at best. I won't buy strawberries from California, not because I'm a dogmatic locavore but because strawberries from California suck.

Some days Iris likes salami for snack and some days she doesn't. At the moment, she is really into Fra'Mani soppressata, made by Paul Bertolli in Oakland. She's always happy with ham, especially smoky Black Forest ham. For a recent afternoon snack we sampled *jamón ibérico,* a long-aged Spanish ham made from a special breed of free-range pigs. Ibérico was only recently approved for import to the United States, and many people call it the best ham in the world. I love prosciutto and serrano, but Iris finds the chewiness of the fat annoying. She had no problem with ibérico: its fat has a delectable melting texture and its flavor is similar to those of other hams.

"That was some *good* ham," said Iris. I would be delighted to make jamón ibérico a standard on our snack table except that it costs ninety-eight dollars a pound.

When Iris was a baby and first starting to eat a regular snack, I thought I had it all sewn up. The problem with a lot of snacks — cereal, crackers, low-fat yogurt — is that they're too low in protein or fat to be satisfying. One food that never has that problem is cheese (unless you count fat-free cheese, which is not actually a food but a form of chemical weapon). Laurie and I are crazy for cheese. We enjoy goat's, sheep's, and cow's milk cheeses, soft and hard cheeses, moldy and stinky cheeses. One of the best gifts we ever received was a four-pound hunk of Parmigiano-Reggiano from my mother. It did not last very long.

We love the blue cheeses made by Rogue Creamery in southern Oregon (especially the one smoked over smoldering hazelnut shells). We are big fans of Beecher's Raw Milk Flagship, made right in the middle of Pike Place Market. Our fridge often contains both Tillamook sharp Cheddar and Montgomery farmhouse Cheddar from England. Frequently I'll taste a cheese and it will become my favorite cheese for a few weeks; like an addict, I'll get nervous when my stash has shrunk to a bit of rind.

You get the idea. I figured Iris and I could make a daily snack of cheese. It's nutritious — it's just milk, after all. It's filling. It goes with crackers. The variety is endless.

Naturally, Iris hates cheese and has hated it since day one. Oh, she likes melted mozzarella on pizza, and she eats several grilled cheese sandwiches per week. But anything resembling the texture of non-melted cheese, forget it. Once she ate a stick of string cheese and then refused to ever do so again.

Stubbornly, I was determined to press on with this cheese boondoggle. Noting that Iris stole all of the crunchy baked-on cheese morsels from the top of my plate of stacked green chile enchiladas (see chapter 5), I wondered: What about a snack made entirely of baked crunchy cheese?

Score! *Frico* are Italian cheese wafers, but you can make them with almost any mix of cheeses as long as one of the cheeses melts well. I tend to mix Cheddar and Parmesan, because we always have those on hand, but you could try mozzarella, jack, pecorino Romano, or anything from the world of blue cheese.

A few months into the post-Booty era, Iris came home from preschool and I asked her what she had for snack. "Veggie Booty," she said. I went online and found the company's website. "The booty is back!" it declared. Of course, a lot of the websites I visit say that.

CORN PANCAKES with PUMPKIN BUTTER

! QUICK & EASY

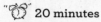 20 minutes

LITTLE FINGERS: These pancakes are relatively fragile and therefore not great for spatula practice. For a more kid-friendly spatula experience, try the Blueberry-Buckwheat Pancakes on page 170.

Pumpkin butter is available at Trader Joe's and most natural foods stores. Feel free to substitute apple butter, other fruit sauces and jams, syrup, or Nutella.

Makes about 12 pancakes

> 1 8.5-ounce box corn muffin mix
> 1 egg
> ¾ cup milk, plus more if necessary
>   butter
>   pumpkin butter

Whisk the muffin mix, egg, and milk together in a liquid measuring cup with a pour spout. Heat a nonstick skillet over medium heat and melt 1 tablespoon butter. Make pancakes as you normally would. The batter will thicken between batches and may need to be loosened with additional milk. Spread each pancake with pumpkin butter before serving.

BANANA-NUTELLA PANINI

! QUICK & EASY

"⏰" 15 minutes

🍳 Panini grill

🕺 LITTLE FINGERS: Kids can butter the bread and slice bananas with a butter knife.

My favorite panini grill is made by Krups, but you can certainly use a Foreman grill. Iris called Nutella "Nutelly" until recently, which is very cute.

Serves 2

    2 tablespoons butter, melted
    4 thin slices rustic bread
    1 ripe banana, cut into ½-inch slices
    2 tablespoons Nutella

Preheat the panini grill. Brush one side of each slice of bread with butter. Make 2 sandwiches, each with half the Nutella and banana slices, and with the buttered sides of the bread on the outside. Grill until golden brown.

FRICO (Crunchy Cheese Wafers)

! QUICK & EASY

"⏰" 30 minutes

🕺 LITTLE FINGERS: Kids can sprinkle cheese, nuts, and herbs.

Some nut and herb combos that work well: walnut and rosemary, hazelnut and oregano, pecan and thyme.

Makes about 24 crisps

  2 ounces Parmigiano-Reggiano, shredded
  2 ounces Cheddar, shredded
  ¼ cup finely chopped nuts (optional)
  2 tablespoons minced fresh herbs (optional)

1. Preheat oven to 400°F. Line a baking sheet with parchment paper.

2. Sprinkle the cheese in heaping teaspoonfuls on the parchment, spacing the piles about 1 inch apart. Flatten each pile gently with the back of a spoon and top each with a pinch of optional nuts or herbs. Bake 5 to 6 minutes, or until the cheese is bubbly and browning around the edge. It takes a bit of practice to find the perfect baking time; underbaked frico don't crunch, and overbaked frico are worse than burnt toast.

3. Let cool on the baking sheet for several minutes, then slide off with a spatula. Cool on paper towels to absorb grease. Serve at room temperature. Frico can be made in advance and stored up to one day in an airtight container.

8

Vegging Out

IRIS HAS A BOOK called *Let's Grow a Garden,* by Gyo Fujikawa. It was published in 1975 and has hippie written all over it. In the book, some young and unsupervised children decide to plant some vegetables. "Hurry, hurry, we must pick them now!" cries the narrator at the end of summer, and then the kids give away bushels of produce for free. Down with The Man!

My favorite part of the book is on the last page, where a girl is cradling a turnip the same way Lenny held a mouse in *Of Mice and Men.* I informed Iris that this girl is saying, "I love you, turnip," which Iris now dutifully repeats in a comical voice whenever we read the book. Sometimes she makes me hand her a turnip at the supermarket so she can gaze lovingly at it and deliver the punch line.

This doesn't, however, mean that Iris actually loves turnips. One day I handed her an issue of *Fine Cooking* magazine, flipped open to a drool-inducing photo montage of a dozen different roasted vegetables. "Which one of these would you like?" I asked. Turnips? Cauliflower? Beets? Carrots? Fennel?

"Just these," said Iris, pointing at the potatoes. Okay, I like roasted potatoes, too, especially when they're crunchy and salty enough to be a substitute for French fries. But I love all the other vegetables just as well. So does Laurie. Did you know that two vegetable-loving parents who serve vegetables at every meal can have a kid who only likes potatoes, and only if they're crunchy?

Actually, there are a couple of non-potato vegetables that Iris will eat, liberally sauced with caveats and qualifiers. (When we took Iris for her four-year-old checkup, her pediatrician asked, "So, Iris, do you like any vegetables?" and Iris replied, "Hmm. Beans and tomato chunks." Okay, I guess beans count. I have to give her credit for advanced weaseling skills.)

I write a taste-test column called *Chef Test* for a local magazine. Every month I recruit a chef to taste various brands of a particular ingredient and pick a winner. I did a canned tomato taste test with an amiably gruff Italian restaurant chef, and our runaway favorite was Del Monte Organic. I attempted to make it my house brand. I made an *amatriciana*-style sauce with bacon, olive oil, and lots of tomato chunks.

"I don't like these tomatoes," declared Iris.

"But they won a chef test!" I protested.

"Not with me!"

Iris's favorite canned tomatoes — today, at least — are Muir Glen Fire-Roasted.

She will tolerate spinach only if it's inside cheese ravioli or blended into a meatball (see chapter 12). In the same category, Iris likes bok choy if it's inside a dumpling.

Why vegetables? Why would someone reject every member of such a varied category?

Maybe Iris doesn't like vegetables because she knows Laurie and I like them and is declaring her independence. Possibly, but why vegetables and not, say, fish? Besides, I think we're good at serving everything, including vegetables, without making a big deal about it (more on this in chapter 10).

Maybe Iris doesn't like vegetables because they have flavors that irritate children's taste buds. This is almost certainly true of some vegetables, like leafy greens: they taste bitter, and bitter things are often poisonous. It's not true of carrots or corn niblets.

Here's my guess, and it's only a guess, not a scientific pronouncement. The age (around age two) at which kids start rejecting vegetables corresponds to when they start to get really good at sorting things into categories. Many children this age would rather sort a pile of M&M's into colors than eat them. Iris is four now and she still, after a game of Uno, says, "Let's play Sorting Uno!" which consists of sorting the cards into piles of the same color. Sorting Uno is the only game less fun than Candy Land.

So, a kid hits a certain age and begins to realize that these green things don't taste so good. She also realizes that the green things come in a category, vegetables, that includes things that aren't green. She can use her new categorizing skills to determine what's in and what's out. Then she can summarily reject the whole enchilada, assuming it's a vegetable enchilada. This may also have something to do with why most children prefer their food not to touch, and why Iris was so delighted when she was given a divided plate for a gift.

I realize not every child defines the vegetable category quite as broadly as Iris does. But that's the point. Children lump things differently, but they all love to lump.

What about dumplings? Crispy fried things? Well, those are different categories. I put plenty of bok choy in Iris's dumplings, but I'm not being sneaky about it; she helps me make them. So, Iris, how about stir-fried bok choy with the same flavorings of garlic, ginger, scallions, soy sauce, oyster sauce, and sesame oil? Forget it. That's a vegetable, and *I don't like vegetables.* You can almost see the cognitive dissonance waves steaming off her.

You'll notice there's one hypothesis I didn't entertain: maybe my vegetable dishes are lousy. In all modesty, I don't *think* so.

A substantial percentage of kids will reject even well-prepared vegetables, which are sadly hard to come by. In several years as an omnivorous critic, I never once came across a restaurant that did vegetables well and neglected the meat. That's partly because so many customers don't eat the vegetables, but also because meat is easy. You don't need to do anything special to coax out its flavor; just don't overcook it and everybody is happy. (Well, except people who like overcooked meat.)

Vegetables aren't exactly difficult, but with the exception of a few classics like corn on the cob and baked potatoes, they're not *automatic*. As John Allemang puts it, "What vegetables need is more of a helping hand." ("Helping hand," he promptly reveals, is a polite way of saying "fat.")

Cooking is something I know a few things about. Gardening is not. Often when we're out for a walk, Iris will ask me, "What kind of flower is that?" and I, despite having taken a botany class, will have no idea. (Sometimes I know the scientific name, which sort of appeases her.)

Plenty of people I know take great pleasure in spending time in the garden. But every time I read something about gardening, especially about all the things that can go wrong — avoid a dozen common tomato diseases! — it sounds suspiciously like taking on a bunch of extra children. (I was pleased to learn from the same article that "tomato diseases are rarely fatal." To whom?)

There's a community garden near our farmers' market, and Iris likes to trudge up and down the aisles and see what's growing. Often there's an improbably huge sunflower by the end of summer. I'm always amazed at the things my neighbors coax out of the ground: peppers, greens, onions, bushels of tomatoes.

Once Iris and I went for a walk to the garden and saw a beautiful patch of Swiss chard, and when we got home, Iris asked Laurie, "Do you know a plant called chard?" This is one of my favorite things Iris has ever said, so now whenever I mention chard (which is often, since it's one of my favorite vegetables), I turn to Laurie and say, "Do you know a plant called chard?"

"Why do you keep saying that?" asked Iris, exasperated. Four years old, and she's already getting tired of my shtick. The other day we walked past some chard growing in someone's yard and Iris said, "Hey, Dada, do you know a plant called chard? Good one, huh?"

Given Iris's interest in vegetables coming out of the ground (as long as they didn't go into her mouth), it was inevitable that we would try to grow *something,* so I suggested to Iris that we try planting some herbs. We went to the store and spent fifteen minutes staring at seed packets, of which they had several hundred varieties. "And I want to grow corn, and potatoes, and flowers, and watermelons . . ." began Iris.

"Let's start small," I suggested. "How about cilantro?" Iris doesn't particularly like cilantro, but it's my favorite herb, and a bountiful free supply sounded like a treat. Somehow I got her to agree, and we brought home the cilantro seed and a bag of potting soil. Dirt, in a bag, that you have to pay for!

We had a couple of plant pots on the balcony already from some previous failed experiment. One of them was sporting an astonishing weed, something viny and two feet long. I pulled the weed (Iris didn't want to touch it) and left it on the balcony. For several days thereafter, Iris would walk past the balcony door, peek out, and say, "That was a seriously big weed."

Iris hefted the big bag of dirt and poured, and some of it even got into the pots. When we opened the packet of cilantro seeds, I said, "Hey, these look just like coriander seeds . . . oh, right. Never mind." We scattered the seeds in the pots and poked them down with our fingers, ignoring the instructions from Ed Hume to plant them in rows twelve inches apart.

Then we waited. I'm sure we didn't actually crouch over the plant pots until the cilantro sprouted, but that's how I remember it. It took about nine days before anything happened. (It rained every day, so we didn't have to water them. Welcome to Seattle.) Then, a tiny green shoot! The next day, five more. Iris started getting proprietary. "Could you go out and water my cilantro?" she asked.

We marveled at the way some of the shoots still had seed casings attached.

I spotted the first ruffled leaf. "Iris, come quick!" I yelled. "It looks like real cilantro!" We peered into the pots. When a few more leaves appeared, we couldn't resist pulling one off and tasting it. Yes, *Iris ate a green leaf.* "In just a couple more weeks I think we'll be putting this on our quesadillas," I said.

"It will smell and taste SO good," said Iris, watering her cilantro pot. This was so much more fun than my old laboratory job, growing *E. coli.*

A few days later, the cilantro was bushy enough that we could see it from the sidewalk. It was time, according to the seed packet, to thin the plants out. I wanted to thin them right onto a quesadilla.

A great quesadilla means a lot to me. I don't have any quesadilla secrets. A hot pan greased with lard, name-brand Cheddar or jack cheese, and fresh cilantro; that's about it. The microwave is not involved. When I want to get a little fancier, I slice a sautéed chicken breast, toss the chicken with garlic and lime juice, and add that to the quesadilla. But for our homemade cilantro, simple was the way to go.

We didn't have any actual strategy for thinning the cilantro — we just reached into the pots and started pulling green stuff out until it didn't look too crowded. "Those ones are too close together," said Iris, giving a tug. She ate about twelve leaves while we were picking. I put her in charge of pulling leaves off the stems and inserting them into quesadillas. Then we heated up Iris's electric frying pan. Nobody got burned.

During lunch, Iris complained that there *wasn't enough cilantro* in her quesadilla. I had to find a small cross-section with an especially large amount of the herb stuffed inside. "Aww, that is so cute," said Iris when I put the sliver on her plate. "Now I'm definitely tasting some cilantro."

Now, if we can just grow tomatillos, chard, fennel, corn, and cheese — and avoid contracting verticillium wilt — my diabolical plan will be complete.

Our upstairs neighbor, Brenda, has a green thumb, and her balcony is ringed with flowerpots, all growing prodigiously. Sometimes she comes out to chat with Iris and check the progress of our cilantro. This is like having Frank Gehry size up your tree house. Luckily, Brenda is mostly interested in talking to Iris. I'm rarely prouder than when Iris says something like "Brenda, my dad is making enchiladas for dinner. With crunchy cheese!" Have I mentioned that I like living in an apartment?

One day, Brenda said, "Hey, Iris, I put something for you outside your door." Iris went to check, and it was a cherry tomato plant. This felt to me like a dare ("Sure, you can grow something easy like cilantro, but what about a real vegetable? I mean, fruit?"). But Iris was thrilled. We transplanted the tomato plant into a big plastic pot. I throw around the term "transplanted" like I know what I'm talking about, when really I'm just hoping we didn't kill the poor thing. "You have to put a stake in the pot," advised Brenda.

"A steak?" said Iris. "Really?"

Three weeks after our cilantro came up, it started to get weird. Iris and I went out on the balcony and noticed that some of the leaves were mottled and droopy. I'm not sure whether we've contracted a cilantro disease or whether this is part of the natural lifecycle of the plant. In any case, Iris looked up at me and said, in her most pathetic voice, "Maybe we could have just one more cilantro quesadilla before it dies?"

If anything, gardening with Iris is more fun than cooking with her. This is because we're both rank newbies. When I'm teaching Iris to cook, sometimes I sound a lot like my dad when he was teaching me to drive. Out on the balcony, however, we're equals in everything but height. I can't tell Iris she's planting too deep or overwatering, because I know exactly jack shit about gardening.

I felt confident enough to check out *Gardening for Dummies* from the library. It was the scariest book I've ever read. "Why are you returning that book to the library already?" asked Iris. "You barely even had time to read it."

"Well, gardening sounds pretty complicated," I replied. You have to decide what kind of containers to use. When to plant. When to transplant. How to deal with pests and infections. First, let's see if we get a tomato. If we do, when Iris is a little older she can be the family gardener. If she produces a steady stream of fresh, organic produce, then maybe, *maybe,* she can get a cat.

CORN with SCALLIONS, JALAPEÑO, and LIME

! QUICK

🕑 30 minutes

This recipe doesn't work well with canned or frozen corn. Sorry. Don't try substituting olive oil, margarine, or any other fat for the butter, either.

Serves 4 as a side dish

- 3 tablespoons butter
- 3 ears fresh corn
- 2 scallions, thinly sliced
- 1 jalapeño pepper, seeds removed if desired, minced
- 2 tablespoons water
  salt
- 1 tablespoon freshly squeezed lime juice

1. Cut the corn off the cob. I've tried various gadgets for this, but I keep coming back to this method: Stand the corn up in a large, shallow bowl. With a sharp knife, slice the kernels off the top half of the ear. (You won't be able to reach the bottom half because the bowl is in the way.) Turn the ear over and repeat to get the rest of the kernels.

2. Heat the butter in a large skillet over medium-high until bubbling. Add the corn, scallions, and jalapeño. Cook until the corn begins to brown and stick to the bottom of the pan, about 10 minutes, lowering the heat if necessary. Add water and scrub the bottom of the pan with the spatula to dislodge the extremely delicious brown bits. When the water has boiled off, add salt to taste. Off the heat, add lime juice and serve immediately.

BROWNED and BRAISED
BRUSSELS SPROUTS

!   QUICK & EASY

"🕰" 20 minutes

I'm not joking when I say Brussels sprouts are my favorite vegetable. We eat them at least once a week. The secret is that frozen are usually better than fresh. You don't have to tell your guests. Thaw frozen Brussels sprouts in the microwave on high for about 2 minutes, stirring after the first minute. If some are still partially frozen, it's no problem; continue with the recipe.

Serves 2

- 1½ tablespoons olive oil
- 1½ tablespoons butter
- 2 cups frozen Brussels sprouts, thawed and halved lengthwise
- salt and pepper
- ½ cup water

In a large skillet, heat the butter and oil over medium-high until the butter foams. Add the Brussels sprouts and cook until lightly browned, turning once or twice and sprinkling with salt and pepper, about 5 minutes. Add the water, cover, and reduce heat to medium-low. Cook 10 minutes or until sprouts are tender but not mushy. Uncover, boil off any remaining water, and serve.

PENNE with BRUSSELS SPROUTS and BACON

! QUICK

⏰ 30 minutes

Sure, the list of things that go well with bacon is a long one, but Brussels sprouts have got to be near the top. Cutting raw bacon is a little tricky — freezing it for 15 minutes or so makes it easier, as does a very sharp knife. The lemon juice is a nice accent, but if you don't have a lemon in the house or don't want to cut into one for a single teaspoon of juice, by all means make this anyway.

Serves 2 to 3

- 10 ounces penne rigate
- 2 tablespoons olive oil
- 4 slices thick-cut bacon, cut crosswise into ½-inch pieces
- ½ pound (about 2 cups) frozen (thawed) or fresh Brussels sprouts, trimmed and halved lengthwise if small, quartered lengthwise if large

  salt and pepper
- ½ cup chicken broth
- 1½ ounces (½ cup lightly packed) grated Parmigiano-Reggiano, plus more for serving
- 1 teaspoon lemon juice (optional)

1. In a large skillet, cook the bacon in the olive oil until crisp. Remove to a paper towel–lined plate, reserving the fat in the pan. Raise heat to medium-high and add the Brussels sprouts. Sprinkle with salt and pepper to taste and cook until lightly browned, 3 to 5 minutes. Add the chicken broth, reduce heat to medium-low, cover, and simmer 10 minutes or until sprouts are tender, stirring occasionally.

2. Meanwhile, cook the penne. Drain and add to the Brussels sprouts along with the bacon, Parmigiano, and optional lemon juice. Season with additional salt and pepper to taste, top with additional Parmigiano, and serve immediately.

ROASTED PARSNIPS

! QUICK & EASY

"⏰" 15 minutes (not including preheating time)

Farmers' market parsnips in season (late fall to spring) are so much better than supermarket parsnips that I never buy supermarket parsnips anymore. Come to think of it, does anybody buy supermarket parsnips? They're always on the shelf, but I never see anyone take any. Maybe there's a shadowy and powerful parsnip commission buying up shelf space.

Good fresh parsnips don't need to be peeled, and small ones don't have woody cores. Roast them, and they're as good as French fries. Really. Almost really.

> small parsnips, scrubbed and trimmed (cut the greens down to an inch or so)
> olive oil
> salt

Preheat the oven to 450°F. Rub the parsnips liberally with olive oil and salt and place on a foil-lined baking sheet. Roast 10 to 15 minutes or until the parsnips are golden brown and the tips are dark and crunchy.

CUMIN-GINGER CARROT COINS

! QUICK

"⏰" 20 minutes

These were, at one time, Iris's favorite food. With their culturally ambiguous spicing, they're a versatile companion to almost any main dish.

Serves 4 as a side dish

- 2 tablespoons butter
- 1 pound carrots, peeled and sliced into ⅛-inch coins
- ½ teaspoon ground cumin
- ½ teaspoon ground ginger
  salt and pepper
- ¼ cup water

Heat the butter in a large skillet over medium-high until bubbling. Add the carrots and cook, stirring occasionally, until the pieces are beginning to brown. Add the cumin, ginger, and salt to taste, and stir until fragrant, about 30 seconds. Add the water, reduce heat to low, and cover. Cook 5 to 10 minutes, or until the carrots are as tender as you'd like. Uncover, add pepper and more salt if necessary, and serve.

LEMONY CHARD and ESCAROLE

! QUICK & EASY

 20 minutes

I think I'm a centrist when it comes to greens. As much as I like the supple greens (lettuce, spinach) and the hardy ones (collards, kale), my favorites are the middle-of-the-road ones like chard and escarole that are at their best with just a bit of cooking. This is a great side dish for steak or for spaghetti and meatballs.

Because you start out with a large volume of greens, cook them in two batches or in two skillets simultaneously. The greens will cook down to a reasonable amount.

Serves 4 as a side dish

- 2 tablespoons olive oil
- 2 tablespoons butter
- 1 bunch chard, leaves chopped coarsely, stems discarded or reserved for another use

1 bunch escarole, leaves chopped coarsely

2 cloves garlic, minced

salt and pepper

1 tablespoon lemon juice

Toss the chard and escarole together in a bowl. Heat 1 tablespoon olive oil and 1 tablespoon butter in a large skillet over medium-high. Add half the chard-escarole mix and half the garlic and cook, stirring frequently, until wilted and beginning to brown, about 5 minutes. Cover, reduce heat to medium, and cook 1 minute. Uncover and season to taste with salt and pepper. Transfer greens to a bowl. Repeat with remaining ingredients. Stir in lemon juice and serve.

MINI-FRITTATAS with MUSHROOMS

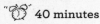 40 minutes

Nonstick muffin pan

WARNING: I tend to scoff when a recipe says I have to use a piece of nonstick cookware, but here, I am dead serious. If you don't use a nonstick muffin pan, it will be ruined. During morel season in the spring, I substitute ½ pound fresh morels for the creminis and porcinis. For other variations, try any combination of spinach, leeks, tomatoes — any pre-cooked or soft vegetable, really — and different kinds of cheese.

Makes 12 mini-frittatas, serving 4 with toast and fruit

½ ounce dried porcini mushrooms, rinsed

6 large eggs

¼ cup milk

¼ cup cream

1 ounce (⅓ cup) grated Parmigiano-Reggiano

¼ teaspoon salt

pepper

1 tablespoon butter

½ pound cremini mushrooms, diced small

¼ cup diced shallots

1. Pour boiling water over the dried porcinis and let sit 20 minutes to reconstitute. Drain and finely chop the porcinis.

2. Preheat the oven to 350°F. Whisk together the eggs, milk, cream, Parmigiano-Reggiano, salt, and pepper to taste in a Pyrex measuring cup.

3. Melt the butter in a skillet over medium-high heat. Add the mushrooms and shallots and cook, stirring frequently, until the mushrooms are golden brown and their liquid has evaporated, about 5 minutes.

4. Spray a 12-cup nonstick muffin pan with cooking spray. Spoon a generous tablespoon of the mushroom mixture into each cup and top with 2 to 3 tablespoons of the egg mixture. Each cup will be about two-thirds full. Bake 20 minutes. Using a spoon, turn the frittatas out of the pan and serve immediately with toast.

9

Sugar Makes
Parents Hyper

WHEN SHE WAS about to turn two, Iris became
obsessed with the *Martha Stewart Holiday Cook-*
ies magazine, a special issue with more than a hundred cookie recipes (now available in expanded form as the book *Martha Stewart's*
Cookies). Iris's favorite part was the table of contents, which featured a small photo of each cookie. She memorized as many as her
brain could handle and would flip open the magazine, point to each
cookie in turn, and announce its name. For her, the different cookies were no less salient as categories than the Things That Go in
a Richard Scarry book. Why is it any more important for a kid to
know the difference between a submarine and an RV than to correctly identify Peanut Butter Whoopie Pies, Blueberry Bonanza
Bars, and madeleines?

In fact, a madeleine from Espresso Vivace was the first thing
Iris managed to eat by taking bites rather than having me cut it up
for her. Ignoring the NO CELL PHONES WHILE IN LINE sign, I
called Laurie at work and said, "Iris ate a whole cookie! By herself!"
She's used to this kind of call from me.

Sugar seems to cause more parental neuroses than any other

food. We fear that, given free rein, kids would eat nothing but dessert, with grievous dental and other physical consequences. And as much as I enjoy playing the iconoclast, I can't advocate turning kids loose on the dessert cabinet. (Okay, I don't have a dessert cabinet. I want one now, though, because it sounds awesome.)

But I'm not trying to keep Iris away from sweets, either. I enjoy something sweet on a daily basis, and I see no reason she shouldn't do the same. As the nutritionist Ellyn Satter puts it, "If you give your child his serving of dessert with meals, have cookies for snacks now and then, bring home an occasional candy bar, and look the other way on Halloween, your child will get about the right amount of sugar."

Overly restricting sugar is mean. It turns kids into schemers who think only about sugar and how to get their hands on some. It encourages parents to use sugar as a reward or withhold it as a punishment. I can't think of a more effective way to take the fun out of eating. I don't want food to turn into a bargaining chip or a battleground. That way, I can feel free to put my foot down on other issues ("Four *SpongeBob* episodes in a row is enough!") and know that Iris and I always have food left as a point of agreement.

One utterly unscientific indication that we've struck the right balance with sugar is that Iris's food fantasies tend to involve sweet and savory foods in equal measure. Often we'll set up chairs in the hall to play Car, and she'll drive us to her favorite Chinese restaurant for noodles and dumplings; other times she'll run an ice cream stand in the bathtub. Sample game of Ice Cream Stand: "Dada, what kind of ice cream you like?" "Lemon verbena." "Uh, we don't have that. How about chocolate?"

Parents also withhold sugar because they're afraid it will make their kids hyperactive. This hypothesis has been amply studied, and it's wrong. "Many carefully controlled studies have been conducted to test this idea and failed to find any effect of sugar consumption on children's behavior," says Dr. Barbara Strupp, professor of nutrition and psychology at Cornell.

One such study, done at the Menninger Clinic in Kansas in 1994 and published in the *Journal of Abnormal Child Psychology*, recruited mothers who described their sons as "sugar sensitive." They were split into two groups. Half the moms were told that their boys had just drunk a super-sugary soda. The other half were told that the soda contained only aspartame. Actually, all of the kids got the sugar-free soda, but the moms who thought their kids had been drinking the hard stuff rated them as "significantly more hyperactive."

This is, as Strupp says, one of many studies that have found the same result. Some have been done in the lab, others in real-world settings. The link between sugar and hyperactivity has been debunked so many times that pediatric researchers probably smack themselves in the head and run away whenever it comes up.

More recently, a 2007 study in England suggested that the preservatives and artificial colors in junk food might be responsible for making kids loopy. I am skeptical of this result and wouldn't be surprised to see it refuted, but if you need another excuse to concentrate on homemade junk food, there you go.

Having said that, after we made the chocolate malt sandwich cookies from that Martha Stewart cookie magazine, Iris rolled up her stuffed cat, Littlecat, in a sushi rolling mat and started chewing on his whiskers, running around, and shouting, "Littlecat sandwich!" Just something to chew on, so to speak.

Getting along with a preschooler isn't always easy, but I can always say, "Hey, let's take a step back and have a cookie," and things will usually look better after that to both of us. Cookies, however crumbly, are the unshakable common ground between child and adult.

One evening, before bedtime, Iris put a pillow on the couch and said, "I made you a pie."

"What kind of pie is it?" I asked. "Is it a rustic crostata with a lard crust?"

"Yes," replied Iris. "Mama, here's some pie."

"Thanks," said Laurie. "What kind of pie is it?"

"It's rustic pie."

"But what kind of fruit is in it?"

"Lard fruit. It turned into a cake!" She paused, mulling the transformation over. "It's okay if pies are cakes," she concluded.

Dessert is a ripe area for experimenting, because there's so little riding on the result. It's an awful feeling when dinnertime is ten minutes away and suddenly I realize this new recipe is not going to happen, or I've overcooked the fish, or I forgot to start boiling water for the pasta. "I am going to starve this helpless child," I fret to myself. But if a batch of cookies doesn't come out, who cares? That's why you keep a bag of Milanos (or, as Iris has been known to call them, Poblanos) on hand.

Also, it's easy for kids to get involved in making desserts. There is rarely much chopping involved, and the high-heat part is just slipping a pan into and out of the oven rather than tending a skillet on a hot stove — so no shooing the kids away. Two-year-olds can measure dry ingredients, mix, pour, and (most important) apply frosting and sprinkles.

Iris is very into sprinkles, in the same sense that Robert Downey Jr. was very into cocaine. Typically, if I ask her to help put sprinkles on something, one-third of the sprinkles will end up on the cake and two-thirds will end up in Iris's stomach. "I'm just tasting them," she'll say innocently. This is always good for a laugh but, I have advised her, will probably not work in court any better than it did for Robert Downey Jr.

Another reason to involve kids in dessert is that you get to introduce them to the good stuff. I tend to carry a Valrhona Le Noir Amer 70 percent chocolate bar with me wherever I go, and Iris loves "the special chocolate" as much as I do. This is not a sweet bar; it's bittersweet grown-up chocolate of the type that gets name-checked on restaurant menus. (I hear it's loaded with antioxidants or something, too.) I get a special thrill when Iris lets a square of Valrhona melt on her tongue. They grow up so fast!

All set to prove that my kid has a sophisticated palate, I proposed that Iris and I should do a chocolate tasting, pitting some fancy Valrhona against Hershey's. We did it, and her favorite was Hershey's milk chocolate. I am sticking with the 70 percent. But at least we agree that Hershey's Special Dark is unbelievably vile.

Other than a drop cloth the size of Wyoming, there's one special piece of equipment I'd recommend buying before getting your kids involved in baking: a digital kitchen scale. If your child, like mine, exhibits a little more mental than physical coordination, the scale is for you. You can just plunk a big bowl on top of the scale and let the kid scoop with abandon. If they put in a little too much flour, scoop some out. This is a lot trickier to do with volume measurements, since it's hard to figure out how much was put in.

Few recipes include measurements by weight (though that's changing), but knowing that a cup of all-purpose flour is five ounces and a cup of white or packed brown sugar is seven ounces will take you a long way. You can find a calculator for other common ingredients at http://recipes.egullet.org/ksm.php#estimation.

Iris's single favorite dessert item is undoubtedly cupcakes. When she's not eating cupcakes, she reads about them. If you've ever wondered what type of printed material most resembles porn without actually involving naked people, the answer is cupcake books.

There are two types of cupcake books: soft-core and hard-core. Soft-core, typified by Elinor Klivans's *Cupcakes!,* focuses on interesting flavor combinations (vanilla cheesecake crunch-top, pumpkin-ginger, and so on). Hard-core cupcake books are sadly more common. Iris's favorite is Clare Crespo's *Hey There, Cupcake!,* which has recipes for cupcakes in all kinds of unlikely forms: shark fins, little villages, koala bears.

Hard-core cupcake books are dangerous, because your attempts will look nothing like the pictures in the book. Laurie did make the shark fin cupcakes from *Hey There, Cupcake!* on two separate occasions, and they were great. Then we got the similarly titled competitor *Hello, Cupcake!,* which has its own shark cupcake recipe. In this one, whole shark heads (glazed and decorated Twinkies) emerge from the frosting sea. "I am *not* making those," said Laurie immediately. If *Hey There, Cupcake!* is *Playboy, Hello, Cupcake!* is *Hustler.*

Luckily, Iris is happy with any cupcake as long as she gets to snorkel up a quart of frosting. For example, the other day I brought home a treat for Laurie and Iris from Cupcake Royale, Seattle's local cupcake chain. "Mama, I'm ready for my cupcake!" called Iris.

"We can share one cupcake because they're big," said Laurie.

"Sure!" replied Iris. "I can have my frosting and you can have the bottom. Isn't that a good idea, Mama?"

For Iris's first birthday, Laurie made gingerbread cupcakes with lemon glaze. We chose gingerbread because this was at the height of Iris's infatuation with spicy foods. The first birthday was fun because Iris had absolutely no idea what was going on: for some reason, she was allowed to eat an entire cupcake after successfully putting out the fire on top of it.

By the following year she was already talking about how her birthday would be in "'cember," although she didn't really understand that this represented a month rather than a vault full of cupcakes to which she'd be given the key at the appointed time. We let her choose her birthday cupcake from the Klivans book. Naturally, she picked the one with a giant mound of white frosting and plowed through it face-first until I thought we were going to have to chip frosting off her with an icepick.

Some of our favorite desserts feature fresh sour cherries. Here in Washington, sour cherry season lasts about two weeks in June. These cherries are expensive (best-quality ones are often $7.50 a pound), fragile, and harder to pit than sweet cherries. So why did we drop more than forty bucks on them last summer?

Imagine you've never had a lemon. Somehow you made it to adulthood and just never happened to taste one. Then someone hands you a glass of fresh-squeezed lemonade, or a lemon tart. Can you imagine the extent to which this would knock you on your ass?

You can't erase your memory of lemons, *Eternal Sunshine*–style, but if you've never had a fresh sour cherry, you'll find that their effect on desserts is as novel, bracing, and indispensable as lemon.

While only the terminally weird eat plain lemons, Iris and I are happy to snack on sour cherries right off the stem. We discovered fresh sour cherries during Iris's second summer, when she was one and a half. For once, we got to give *each other* the look that means *I'm tasting something new and delicious, and life is going to be good as long as these things keep showing up every summer.* Plus, Iris loves shooting cherry pits across the room with the pitter.

We do, in fact, make sour cherries into a rustic crostata with a lard crust; the recipe can be found in David Lebovitz's *Room for Dessert.* But we also make them into an extremely simple milk shake.

Recently, after reaching the limits of the "one more drink of water" ploy for extending bedtime, Iris hit upon the cake hug.

"I'm fixing you up a hug," Iris told me. "It's a cake hug. I'm putting in the flour and sugar and, uh, what else?"

"Butter?" I offered.

"Butter."

"Baking powder? Milk? Eggs?"

Done. "Mixing it up. Bake bake bake. Ding! It's ready. Now I'm putting on the whipped cream frosting and raspberry swirl." Finally she toppled me over with a hug. "You didn't eat the cake!" said Iris. "It's on your left side."

And that is the simplest form of the cake hug. I tried to convince her to use cake mix in the cake hug, but she just doesn't bake like that. The night after a ten-minute Grim Reaper Cupcake hug rigmarole (licorice frosting!), I put my foot down. "Iris, tonight I want just a simple hug."

"Okay, Dada," she replied. "This one will be from *The Quick Recipe*." She made a chocolate malt sandwich cookie hug, but consented to use pre-made cookies.

....

GINGERBREAD CUPCAKES
with LEMON GLAZE

! EASY

⏰ 1 hour (including 40 minutes baking and cooling time)

🍲 Muffin pan, paper muffin cup liners

🧑 LITTLE FINGERS: Kids can measure and whisk together dry ingredients, stir together dry and wet ingredients, and spoon batter into cupcake cups.

Makes 12 cupcakes

- 1¾ cups (8.75 ounces) all-purpose flour
- ½ teaspoon baking soda
- ½ teaspoon salt
- 1 tablespoon ground ginger
- 2 teaspoons ground cinnamon
- 6 tablespoons (3 ounces) unsalted butter, melted
- ¾ cup (5.25 ounces) dark brown sugar
- 2 eggs
- ¾ cup buttermilk
- 6 tablespoons molasses

  chopped crystallized ginger or other sprinkles for garnish

1. Preheat oven to 375°F. Line a 12-cup muffin tin with papers. In a medium bowl, whisk together flour, baking soda, salt, ginger, and cinnamon. In a large bowl, whisk together butter, brown sugar, eggs, buttermilk, and molasses until combined. Stir the dry ingredients into the butter mixture in two additions, stirring until the dry ingredients are incorporated after each addition.

2. Fill each cup about three-quarters full with batter. Bake until tops feel firm and a toothpick inserted in the center comes out clean, 18–20 minutes. Place pan on a wire rack to cool for 10 minutes before removing cupcakes from pan and continuing to cool to room temperature.

3. Slice a thin layer off the top of each cupcake to provide a flat surface for the glaze (recipe below). Top each cupcake with a generous tablespoon of glaze, garnish with a sprinkle of crystallized ginger (or other sprinkles), and let sit until the glaze is set. (I actually prefer these cupcakes without the glaze, but Iris would not approve.)

Lemon Glaze

LITTLE FINGERS: Kids can measure powdered sugar and whisk the glaze together.

1¼ cups (6 ounces) powdered sugar, sifted
2   tablespoons freshly squeezed lemon juice

Combine powdered sugar and lemon juice in a medium bowl and whisk until smooth.

CHOCOLATE MALT

! QUICK & EASY
5 minutes
Blender

Malt powder isn't just a great cookie ingredient. It's key to one of our favorite beverages, malted milk shakes. Since discovering the existence of malt powder at an early age, I don't think I've ever had a craving for a nonmalted chocolate milk shake. Vanilla malts are also excellent and probably Iris's favorite — just substitute vanilla ice cream.

Makes about 1½ cups, enough for an adult and a small child to share

- 1¼ cups (6 ounces) premium chocolate ice cream (such as Green and Black's Organic or Häagen-Dazs)
- ½ cup milk
- ¼ cup (1 ounce) malt powder

Place ice cream, milk, and malt powder in a blender and blend until smooth. An immersion blender also works well. Pour into glasses and serve immediately. Malts taste better through a bendy straw.

SOUR CHERRY SHAKE

! QUICK & EASY

5 minutes if your cherries are already pitted, 30 minutes otherwise

Blender

LITTLE FINGERS: Kids enjoy operating a cherry pitter, if you don't mind them getting covered with cherry juice.

If you can't get fresh sour cherries, jarred or canned sour cherries (not pie filling!) make a fine substitute; the jarred morello cherries from Trader Joe's are my favorite.

Makes 4 12-ounce shakes

- 2 pounds sour cherries, stemmed and pitted, or 24 ounces canned or jarred cherries, drained
- 1 quart vanilla ice cream

Place the cherries in a blender or food processor (reserving a few for garnish) and blend into a smooth puree. Add the ice cream and continue to blend until smooth, rich, and pink. Pour into four glasses and serve.

10

Picky-Picky

WHEN IRIS WAS about nine months old, I bragged that she showed signs of being an adventurous eater. She packed away pad Thai and spicy enchiladas, spinach and Brussels sprouts. I did my best to imply that this was because of my skills in the kitchen and my no-compromises approach to child feeding.

The nonparents who heard my boasts were impressed. The parents were not, because they knew a secret: all two-year-olds are pickier than all one-year-olds, and three-year-olds are even worse. The average one-year-old is as discriminating as a goat, still drunk on the knowledge that there is a whole class of things she can put into her mouth without her parents screaming and yanking them back out.

Don't believe me? Listen to this. Just before Iris turned two, we took a family trip to Vancouver, British Columbia, and had dinner at Vij's Rangoli, an incredible Indian restaurant. We ordered spicy salmon cakes, pork curry, and vegetable pakoras. Iris gobbled everything with gusto.

We had so much fun in Vancouver that we went back a year later and rented an apartment with a kitchen. I got enough takeout from

Rangoli for three meals. There were chickpea curries, meat curries, spicy green beans, and dal. This, with basmati rice, was our Christmas dinner. I'd been looking forward to it for a year. Iris, now almost three, ate the rice and possibly half a chunk of pork.

This progression from omnivorous to "Ewww!" was not at all what I expected. I figured most kids started out picky and steadily learned to like new foods. I didn't realize Iris would gobble a huge plate of Brussels sprouts one day and then decide two days later that Brussels sprouts were grown in Hell and sent up via dumbwaiter to torment her.

It's hard not to take this personally, since Brussels sprouts are my favorite vegetable and I write about food for a living. There are, no doubt, some three-year-olds who are truly adventurous eaters. But I haven't met any. Children of chefs? Hardly. I talked to one acclaimed Seattle chef who admitted that his five-year-old son likes to eat Trader Joe's frozen cheese pizza, *still frozen*. Another chef said of his three-year-old, "Once in a while we can get him to eat a little bit of broccoli, but it's pretty hit and miss right now." The chef with the young broccoliphobe makes some of the best vegetable dishes in town. We took Iris to his restaurant one night, and while Laurie and I moaned over a creamy Swiss chard gratin, Iris ate some noodles and a bunch of chocolate madeleines.

Kids love ketchup, right? Not all kids. At age two, Iris suddenly stopped liking all condiments other than soy sauce — even syrup — and has only partially recovered. I must have passed down an anti-condiment gene, because the same thing happened to me at around the same age. I ate plain burgers for many years. Plain as in bun, meat, bun. I've come around, sort of: instead of ketchup or mustard, I prefer A1, barbecue, or HP sauce. (HP sauce is really just the English version of A1, but don't tell the English I said that.) There's something awfully toddlerish about this preference. Down with your mainstream condiments! Give me extremely similar condiments with different names! I'm in charge of this burger, not some parent or corporate goon.

One of my clearest memories from the early 1980s is of a Saturday-morning public service ad starring a tiny lifeguard who rescues a potato from drowning in too much sour cream and sings a jingle entitled "Don't Drown Your Food." Really, there was a TV commercial warning kids not to overuse condiments. Maybe I wasn't picky, just overly influenced by TV.

When I saw Iris slipping down the same long, lonely road I once traveled, I thought maybe I could fend off her condimentophobia by setting her loose on a choice of sauces. She was excited about HP sauce for about a week but has taken her burgers plain since then, disassembling them and eating the meat and bun separately. (I'm pretty sure this is how Takeru Kobayashi, the tiny Japanese guy who can eat fifty-three hot dogs in twelve minutes, eats *his* burgers.) Lately, we're seeing signs of progress: sometimes Iris requests a dot of sauce on her plate and eats it with her finger, making sure that none of it defiles the rest of the food. And the other day at a restaurant, I saw her dip her French fry in ketchup. She looked around to make sure no one was watching, extended her tongue, licked a tiny dot of ketchup, and smiled.

Here's the big question: What should I do about this?

Not a month goes by without an article about picky eating in one of the glossy parenting magazines. The advice hasn't changed since the days of canned peas:

1. Present new foods alongside old favorites.
2. Sneak vegetables into pasta sauce or other foods.
3. Threaten to withhold dessert.
4. Be persistent: It may take ten or twelve tries before they learn to like a new food. (Every time someone mentions this, the number seems to change; I've seen it as seven tries, fifteen tries. I haven't yet seen "seven hundred tries," but that's about how many times we've served Iris Brussels sprouts.)

Sometimes I wonder whether anyone associated with those magazines even has kids, because none of these things works. There is a solution to picky eating, but you may not like it: it's recognizing that it isn't a problem. Kids are not dropping dead of scurvy. Oh, I know what they say next: lifelong eating habits are formed at a young age. As I heard one mom (Georgia Orcutt, author of *How to Feed a Teenage Boy*) say on the radio, "When they turn twenty, they're not suddenly going to discover spinach and Brussels sprouts."

I discovered Brussels sprouts at a restaurant in my twenties and have been cooking them once a week ever since. For that matter, think of all the newly minted college vegetarians who will discover all-you-can-eat salad at the dining hall this fall.

The adult palate isn't simply made up of childhood preferences that have hardened into prejudices. I didn't grow up eating sushi. Once I was forced to try it on a fourth grade field trip and almost puked. (Yes, I went to a school so upper-crusty that it force-fed sushi to kids.)

Then, when I was in my early twenties, I noticed many of my friends speaking in near sexual terms about their experiences with a platter of raw fish. I got myself invited along on a sushi excursion and was hooked (sorry) immediately. Now I take Iris to a place where you pick your sushi from a conveyor belt. I choose the salmon skin roll, the mackerel, and the spicy tuna, while Iris takes the potstickers and the cream puff.

I didn't start liking sushi because I was won over by the ocean-fresh flavors. It was because I was won over by the idea, and I had to mull it over for a while before I worked up the guts to give it another try. I already knew I was going to like it before I tasted it. (Another possibility is that the fourth grade sushi gave me a brain parasite that slowly reprogrammed me into a sushi lover.)

Another way of saying this is, yeah, it's possible to know you won't like something when you haven't even tried it. The MIT professor Dan Ariely even performed an ingenious experiment that confirms this.

For the study, Ariely and his colleagues used a foodstuff popular among college students: beer. They had no trouble recruiting subjects. The subjects tasted two beers: one glass of Sam Adams and one of "MIT Brew," which was just Sam Adams adulterated with a few drops of balsamic vinegar.

Most subjects who were not told about the secret ingredient liked the MIT Brew better than the regular. When subjects were told about the vinegar before drinking, they thought the vinegar-spiked brew was gross. No surprise there.

But when subjects were told about the vinegar after drinking, few changed their minds about it. That is, they said they still liked the MIT Brew — who cares if it's made with vinegar? — and would drink it again.

I don't have to explain how this generalizes to kids and new foods, because Ariely's paper did it for me:

> Our mothers often used creative labeling to trick us into eating something they knew we would otherwise oppose (e.g., by calling crab cakes "sea hamburgers"). They knew such deception was required to gain our consent, but that they need not maintain the lie *after* we had consumed the foods, and would often debrief us afterward, with smug satisfaction ("By the way, son, in case you were wondering, 'sea' means 'crab.'")

Another way to put this: if you think you're not going to like a new food, that's a self-fulfilling prophecy. In my career as a food critic, I've had a few experiences where I thought I would like something and didn't (sea urchin comes to mind, although I intend to give it a few more chances), but I can't recall ever thinking I wasn't going to like something and then being pleasantly surprised. Seriously, have you ever seen a kid whine because he didn't want to try broccoli, then take a bite and say, "Hey, this is pretty good!" Have you ever seen the Easter Bunny? Cold fusion?

Iris knows that tastes change over time, or at least she knows how to placate me. When I served salmon for dinner one night, Iris pushed hers around on the plate and sighed, "Iris *can't* like that." She came around on salmon and now eats tons of it, which is a good thing, because otherwise the Seattle authorities were going to take her into custody. Another time, Iris peered into a bowl of tamarind dipping sauce and said, "That looks *good*. And I don't want any." Recently she told me, "When I'm bigger, I'm going to like spicy foods. Tomatillo sauce, pickled jalapeños . . . what else am I going to like?"

Like most four-year-olds, Iris spends a mind-boggling amount of time pretending to do things — perform surgery, cook dinner, drive a truck. (For a while, she was so into the truck-driving idea that when she was accepted to preschool and I told her, "Iris, you're going to go to school this fall!" she replied, "Truck-driving school?") And in her imagination, she eats plenty of things that would never actually pass her lips — even pickled jalapeños. She does this even when she's playing alone in her room and thinks I'm not listening.

I'm sure it would be possible to get Iris to choke down some vegetables through a regime of bribes, but that would be like insisting that she enjoy all my favorite bands. I admit it — it was a thrill when Iris gorged herself on that plate of Brussels sprouts. I had a similar shiver of victory when she became obsessed with the indie rocker John Vanderslice. But you can't hang your happiness on this kind of rare event. Sure enough, Brussels sprouts were just a phase, and while Iris can still handle indie rock, she prefers show tunes and songs like "Here We Go Round the Mulberry Bush" as performed by some kids who sound like eunuchs on Zoloft. (Now she's into the Shins. Is that cool or uncool?)

How we handle picky eating is so simple that I call it the Second Rule of Baby Food (not that I invented this one, either; Ellyn Satter calls it "the division of responsibility"). The rule is, when I put the food down in front of Iris, my job is done. I don't also hold myself responsible for making sure it gets into her mouth — no cajoling, no airplane game. I have been known to say things like, "Iris, this kale is awesome," but I say that to everyone.

The Second Rule is appealingly simple but hard to implement in practice. I find it difficult to keep my mouth shut, not because I'm worried about Iris's nutrition, but because I'm like chef Dan Barber of Blue Hill in New York.

That is, like Barber, I have my own farm upstate where I . . . Wait, that's not it. Like Barber, when I cook for someone, I want to see them eat with gusto, clean their plate, wipe the plate with a piece of bread or their finger to get every last morsel, unsnap their pants, and sigh contentedly. Or, as he puts it:

> Clean plates don't lie. That's what I say when waiters at my restaurant, Blue Hill, ask me why I insist on examining every plate that returns to the kitchen with the slightest bit of food on it. The waiters think I'm intrusive. They also think I'm neurotic and insecure, but like most neurotic and insecure chefs, I don't quite agree. I tell them that a clean plate is proof of a perfect meal.

Iris offers a different indication of a perfect meal. She winks one eye and gives a thumbs-up. I'm not sure where she learned this. But I'll take it.

Watching Iris pull all of the soft crumb out of her bread for dinner one night, I wondered: Could she possibly be getting all the nutrients she needs from what appears to be a very limited diet?

I relaxed after reading a 2000 article entitled "Revisiting the Picky Eater Phenomenon: Neophobic Behaviors of Young Children." As you might guess, this article did not appear in *Parenting* magazine; it was in the *Journal of the American College of Nutrition*. I only read it for the articles.

The authors, who are professors of nutrition at the University of Tennessee, followed seventy children from ages two to seven.

Based on questionnaires filled out by the children's mothers, researchers divided the kids into two groups: picky and nonpicky. (Even the "nonpicky" kids were still pickier than most one-year-olds or adults, I'd wager.) Then they did a long-term analysis of the children's diets. The moms were right: the picky eaters ate a smaller variety of foods and were much more resistant to trying new foods. Some of the phrases used by the mothers of picky eaters were:

- "Eats maybe ten things; all others she finds repulsive."
- "Won't eat anything green."
- "'Mommy, I don't like it' — she hasn't even tried it!"

Presumably this sounds familiar. But there's a punch line. A nutritional analysis found that the picky eaters got just as many nutrients from their diet as the nonpicky eaters, and there was no difference in height and weight between the two groups. In other words, picky eating may be annoying, but it's not a medical problem.

Now, forget the academics. For a personal perspective, I called up one of the world's foremost experts on picky eating: my mother, Judy Amster, who raised three exceedingly picky boys.

"You did all the classic things," Mom sighed. "You didn't like anything, and you had no appetite. And that went on for a long time."

So what *did* I eat?

"You ate dry Cheerios without milk. You ate macaroni and cheese, and you ate pizza. But everything had to be separate. We started using those portioned-out plastic dishes. And you really, really didn't ever want to try anything new. One of the only things that I could guarantee you would eat was cut up white meat chicken, in small pieces, not touching anything."

This went on for *seven years,* from age three to ten. (Neophobic behaviors of young children, indeed.) "It was torture sending lunch to school for you," said Mom. "By then, the only thing that you would eat besides cookies, which I did put in because I wanted you to not fall down starving, was a PB&J on white bread, cut in half vertically. Then you would take the sandwich apart, take one half-circle bite in each of them and put them back together, and not eat anything else because you didn't want to spoil the circle."

Apparently I was not just picky, but borderline OCD. So what broke the cycle? Yep, old-fashioned peer pressure. In fourth grade, I started at a new school and made a new friend, Alex, whose mother was Japanese. "When you went home with him for dinner," Mom remembered, "you came home every time and said, 'How come we never have fish?' And I would say, 'Matthew, you threatened to move out if I brought fish into the house.' 'How come you never make curry?' 'Matthew, you don't want anything touching, no sauces, no gravies.' This went on with about twelve different things."

Alex and his family also took me out to a (sadly defunct) Chinese restaurant in Portland called Potstickers & Sizzling Rice Soup. "And you came home and asked about potstickers, and I said, 'Matthew, when we've taken you to a Chinese restaurant, the only thing you would eat was rice.'"

See, your kid isn't as bad as I was. And just like the kids in the study, I was completely normal in terms of growth. I did not collapse on the playground. And now I'll eat *anything*. Well, not tuna salad or egg salad, because those things are nasty. But anything else.

So picky eating isn't a health problem. Big deal. It's still not a whole lot of fun to have dinner with a family member who'd rather throw peas than eat them. I don't want to soft-pedal this. I'm frequently frustrated when I want to make something for dinner that is hard to adapt to Iris's palate. The most annoying example is Thai curry. I love Thai curry and even have one of those green Thai mortar and pestles, as seen on Jamie Oliver's show, for making curry pastes. But the most important ingredient in Thai curry is lots of chiles. There's no way to make a good Thai curry that isn't spicy, and Iris isn't into spicy these days. So for now, I mostly eat Thai curry when I take myself out for lunch.

At the same time, I've learned to savor the rare appearances of Future Iris, the one who is partial to tomatillo sauce and other strange foods.

One night I made roasted stuffed trout for dinner. "And will the trout get very, very big when you stuff it?" Iris asked. She helped me stuff the trout with fennel, bacon, red onion, and fresh herbs.

Stuffed trout is easier to make than it is to eat, because you want to just cut off a hunk with stuffing sandwiched between two pieces of boneless fish, but there are many bones in the way of this noble intention. For this reason and because Iris is frequently more enthusiastic about cooking than eating, I figured she would forget about the trout by the time it hit the table and concentrate on the hash browns I served with it.

Wrong. Iris ate the fish, the bacon, the vegetables, the potatoes, and even, well . . .

To say that she was undeterred by the fact that the fish's head was there on the platter would be an understatement. "There's the head!" she exclaimed. I found a piece of cheek meat and ate it, and Iris said, "I want to eat some cheek."

I said okay and rooted around for another piece. "There's some cheek," Iris said, pointing.

"No, that's the eyeball."

"I want to eat the eyeball."

"Seriously?"

"Yes." She took a bite. "It's gooey! Why is it gooey?"

"Eyeballs are just like that," said Laurie.

Iris thought about this, then requested and ate *the other eyeball.*

In case you were wondering why there are no soup recipes in this book . . .

It's November. A week ago, Laurie sent me to the store with a sacred mission: bring back half a spiral-sliced ham. I agreed to lug home the nine-pound hunk of pork even though I'm not so crazy about ham, because I had a plan. First, though, we had to make it through the week. I made baked farfalle pasta with cauliflower and diced ham. Ham and eggs. Ham with grits and kale. Laurie and Iris took ham sandwiches to work and school, respectively.

Today, Saturday, I commandeered the remainder of the ham and the bone and made a rich ham stock. After a couple hours of simmering, the meat practically shredded itself, and the broth was perfectly rich, smoky, and salty. I cooked a bag of split peas in the ham stock and added some sautéed vegetables, potatoes, the shredded ham, and a dash of sherry vinegar. I lifted the spoon to my lips and tasted. It was so good I barely noticed that it was ham for dinner, again. Beaming, I set the soup on the table.

"Didn't I tell you I hate soup?" said Iris.

ROASTED TROUT with FENNEL, ONION, and CILANTRO

⏰ 45 minutes

LITTLE FINGERS:
Let them stuff!

Trout range in size from about 6 to 16 ounces. That's a big range. Buy a second fish if necessary. As for the vegetables, I find I want to eat far more of them than can fit inside a fish, so I serve extra on the side. I also found that I prefer bacon on the side rather than in the stuffing, so by all means crisp up a couple of slices and use the rendered fat for cooking. Bacon as a side dish with dinner is underrated, don't you think?

You may find rainbow or golden rainbow trout at your market; if you have a choice, I recommend the rainbow, since it usually costs less and isn't artificially colored. Either fish will work well in this recipe; they taste the same.

Serves 2 to 3

1 tablespoon bacon grease, lard, or butter
1 large bulb fennel, cored and sliced
1 small onion, sliced
    salt and pepper
2 tablespoons minced cilantro
1 large farmed trout (12 to 16 ounces)
    lime wedges for serving

1. Preheat the oven to 450°F. Heat the bacon grease in a large skillet over medium heat until shimmering. Add the fennel and onion, sprinkle with salt, and cook until nicely browned and tender, 8 to 10 minutes. Transfer to a bowl, season with pepper and additional salt to taste, and stir in the cilantro.

2. Place the trout on a greased and foil-lined baking sheet. Stuff the belly of the trout generously with the vegetable mixture. Roast 15 to 20 minutes, until just opaque throughout (check the thick part along the back of the fish). Bring the whole fish to the table, peel back the skin, and serve chunks of fish topped with some of the stuffing and a generous squeeze of lime juice.

11

Feeding the Carburetor

POTATOES, GRAINS, AND PIZZA

IN CASE IT'S NOT clear by this point, I've been unsuccessful in molding Iris into a mini-gourmand food prodigy. When I ask her what she'd like for dinner, it's pizza or hot dogs more often than not.

I like hot dogs and I love pizza, and they're a regular part of our dinner rotation. Before having Iris, however, I would have argued strenuously (not to mention pompously) that there's no reason children should automatically gravitate to these foods, and if they've become our culture's default child chow, it's only because they're easy to produce in quantity at a low price and are therefore the lazy choice of overworked parents.

Boy, was I a dumb jerk. Now I realize that if you took the cast of *Lord of the Flies* and gave them a deep fryer and a sack of potatoes, they'd invent French fries within an hour. (Don't ask where they'd get the cooking fat.)

Maybe *Super Baby Food*'s "bland is best for baby" was more accurate than I'd like to believe. There are a whole host of classic starch and meat dishes that, if you have a kid, you're *going* to end up eating. Instead of resisting them, I wanted to come up with a version of each dish that would please me, Laurie, and Iris (even at her pickiest) equally.

Paddy Cake

Iris, who is not otherwise known for her zenlike asceticism, has always considered an unadorned bowl of rice a completely satisfying meal. No matter where we go, we're never far from a bowl of rice, because chicken teriyaki is Seattle's favorite lunch. Sometimes I take Iris around the corner to Teriyaki Madness, where the lunch special is an extra-large serving of rice, grilled boneless chicken thighs, and cucumber salad. I squeeze on some spicy sriracha sauce while Iris starts in on the teriyaki-sauced rice. It's hard to overstate how many people in Seattle eat teriyaki on a given day. It's so ubiquitous that it's totally unhip. I like it.

Japanese-style medium-grain rice and Thai jasmine rice are acceptable, but Iris's favorite is Thai white sticky rice. Once she turned down a trip to a restaurant that serves strawberry shortcake in favor of a Thai place with sticky rice.

Sticky rice is the staple food of northern and northeastern Thailand. It's one of those foods that if you haven't been exposed to them before cause a predictable sequence of reactions: (1) This is weird. (2) That was okay, but I'm not sure I get the point. (3) I must have more of that immediately.

There are some accouterments associated with sticky rice, like a special cooking pot and individual serving containers for keeping the rice warm, but none of them is actually necessary for cooking it at home. The hardest part of cooking sticky rice is finding it; I've never seen it outside of an Asian grocery, where it's usually sold in five-pound bags that may be labeled sticky, sweet, or glutinous rice. It looks like long-grain jasmine rice, but the grains are bright white and opaque, like high-brightness printer paper.

The other downside to sticky rice is that you have to soak it before cooking. This is no Minute Rice. The delay is worth it, however, not just because sticky rice is tasty, but because it's impossible to overcook. And you don't have to worry about how much water to use, because it's steamed, not boiled. It's stress-free rice. Check it out.

Iris is my recipe guinea pig. If I try something out on her and she likes it, I know that either it's really good or it's a type of cookie. Maybe to make her a more useful cookie taster, I should make a cookie chart, something like the Snellen eye chart. You know, "Lens one or lens two?" Is this cookie better than an Oreo? Better than a Trader Joe's cat cookie?

The most successful recipe test came when I was working on a story about *bibimbap,* the Korean rice dish with egg and assorted toppings, often including *bulgogi.* Bulgogi is thin-sliced beef in a sweet-salty marinade — usually grilled, but I sear it in a skillet because we don't have a grill. I used a marinade created by Kristin Yamaguchi of Yokohama, Japan, a master home cook and a good person to mention when I want to imply that I have far-flung friends of all ethnicities, though she is actually a *gaijin* from the Midwest. The stories she tells about her kids' school lunches in Japan make me very jealous.

Anyway, I made some of Kristin's bulgogi for afternoon snack and tasted it before offering it to Iris. "Oh, man!" I exclaimed. The combination of beef, soy sauce, sugar, and lots of sesame seeds is classic for good reason.

Iris took a bite. "Oh, man!" she echoed. "Wait until Mama tries this. She's going to say, 'Oh man!'" (Iris was right.) We spread out a picnic blanket on the living room floor and ate a ton of bulgogi. I don't remember what we had for dinner, but I'm sure we didn't eat much of it. Periodically Iris will sidle up to me and say, "Dada, we should have a bulgogi picnic and say 'Oh, man.'"

Bibimbap is an inspired combination from an underappreciated cuisine. You take a big bowl of rice and put all sorts of tasty stuff on top: beef, vegetables, kimchi, egg, and lots of the tangy Korean hot sauce called *gochujang.* Iris has her rice and bulgogi; I like to pile on some of everything and stir it up. It is perfectly polite (and terribly convenient for kids) to eat bibimbap with a spoon. With all the toppings, it's no longer just white food. It's like the Korean version of taco night: everybody gets their favorite toppings and nobody complains.

There is a downside to Iris's love of rice that I feel compelled to reveal. A kid can turn the most innocuous of foods into a health threat. If allowed to do so, Iris will eat enough rice to make her sick. Sick at either end, even: I have seen her eat rice until she puked, and I've seen her eat rice until she was so constipated, she didn't poop for days. So I don't make rice as often as I'd like to, and when I do, I make a limited quantity. Iris has gotten wise to this, though, and will ask, "Why didn't you make more rice? You know I love rice." Probably I should try offering her brown rice, but I love white jasmine rice and sticky rice as much as Iris does.

Now try the delicious bibimbap recipe!

The Corny Stuff

I don't know if it's the name, the association with southern poverty, or what, but when you say "grits," a lot of people — mostly Yankees — say "ew." We're about as Yankee as you can get, but we love grits. I've even caught Iris singing a little grits song, vaguely to the tune of "Twinkle, Twinkle, Little Star." ("Gritsy, gritsy, gritsy grits . . .")

Grits are coarse-ground dried field corn. How is that different from polenta? You can find plenty of conflicting answers to this question. Sometimes grits are called "hominy grits," but they're rarely made from hominy, which is corn soaked in lime water to dissolve the hulls before drying. Grits are often made from a different type of field corn (dent corn) than polenta (flint corn), but not always, and I'm not convinced anyone could tell the difference anyway. Grits are usually white and polenta is usually yellow, but you can find exceptions. Grits are often more coarsely ground than polenta. But again, not always.

It comes down to the flavoring, I think. If you're finishing your cornmeal with butter and Parmigiano-Reggiano and serving it with something Italian, it's polenta. If you're serving shrimp and gravy on top, that's grits. If you're not making something Italian or southern, call it whatever you want. Because, really, it's just corn.

We mail-order our grits from Anson Mills (whose products are sometimes found in specialty stores, but not in our area), where they're called white antebellum coarse grits. (If the words *white* and *antebellum* in close company make you nervous, join the club.) These are hard-core grits. You have to soak them in water and skim the inedible chaff and hulls off before cooking, and then you have to cook them for ninety minutes or so. The reward is grits unparalleled in texture and loaded with corn flavor. But Quaker quick (not instant) grits from the supermarket are pretty good, too.

The best way to cook grits or polenta is in the oven, a method I learned from one of those *Best American Recipes* books. Here's how it's done: Preheat the oven to 350°F. In a saucepan, whisk together 1 cup of grits or polenta and 4 cups of water, and throw in 1 tablespoon of butter. Bake uncovered 45 minutes. Stir and continue baking until it reaches the desired consistency, about 15 more minutes. Add salt to taste, additional butter, and optional Parmigiano-Reggiano.

I resisted this method for a long time because it seemed like cheating — how could it be real polenta if your arm doesn't fall off by dinnertime? But it works.

"What grows together goes together" is an old proverb about cooking. I don't know how it applies to one of my favorite foods, shrimp and grits. Shrimp do not, as far as I know, eat corn or live in cornfields, but one taste and there's no denying that shrimp and grits is one of those meant-to-be combinations like bacon and eggs, pork and beans, Boris and Natasha. (Sorry, I watch a lot of cartoons.)

I've tried a lot of shrimp and grits recipes. Nathalie Dupree has a whole book on the subject. My favorite complicated recipe is the one for 83 East Bay Shrimp and Grits from *The Lee Bros. Southern Cookbook.* Most shrimp and grits recipes have you make a shrimp stock and work it into a gravy, and this gravy plus the grits is the whole point of the dish.

That's fine, but when I'm not up for a full production, I still want shrimp and grits. So I came up with a convenient and admittedly nontraditional version that highlights the flavors of shrimp, bacon, butter, and corn. Serving it at my house is always kind of a crapshoot: I never know if Iris will like shrimp on any given day. And Laurie doesn't like shrimp at all, but she loves grits.

Happiness by the Slice

Straddling the line between kid- and grownup-friendly is easy with pizza, because there's an actual line down the center of the pie. The words "half cheese" have done more for family harmony than any therapist.

Recently, Iris went through a Greek myth phase. Every day, Laurie and I would read to her from *Greek Myths for Young Children,* an incredibly gory cartoon book. When she got bored with reading, she wanted to act out the myths, and when she got bored with that, she wanted us to act out newly made-up myths. The most popular of these involved Persephone (Iris) being kidnapped and taken to the underworld by Hades (me). When Demeter (Laurie) tries to rescue her daughter, Persephone admits that she ate six slices of pomegranate pizza and therefore has to stay in the underworld half the year, helping Hades tend his million-degree pizza oven. This game was really funny the first thirty times we played it.

I'm really not sure how you can feed kids, adults, or demigods without pizza. Until a couple years ago, however, I didn't see any good reason to make pizza at home. We have a good neighborhood pizza place, Pagliacci, where we all go for slices about once a week. They have a 600-degree oven. I don't. They're good at flinging dough. I'm not, although Iris enjoys watching my failed attempts.

Then I read something in Julie Powell's book *Julie and Julia* that made me intensely hungry:

> I reached over Eric, already racked out across the bed from his share of the vodka tonics and the jalapeño-bacon Domino's pizza we'd eaten for dinner.

This was enough to get me on the phone to Domino's in thirty seconds or less. Unfortunately, they'd never heard of jalapeño-bacon. Must have been an old special. If I wanted this pizza (or the pomegranate pie, for that matter), I'd have to make it myself.

Iris doesn't want jalapeños on her pizza at the moment. Or anything else, really, although bacon is acceptable (even if it's not Nueske's). Several times a week we'll walk past Pagliacci and I'll say, "I wonder what slices they have today." I peer inside. "Looks like Grand Salami Primo and Veggie Veggie Combo."

"And cheese?" asks Iris. This is a joke of hers, since she knows they have cheese every day.

Tonight we're doing homemade. I roll out the crust and move the pastry board to the kitchen floor, and Iris helps with the toppings. Pizza is good no matter how haphazardly the toppings are applied, of course, so I can let her do her thing without hovering. She puts the jalapeños on, then licks her spicy finger and complains that it is spicy, as if I didn't warn her about this and as if it didn't happen the last six times.

What I like about pizza, besides the obvious, is that it grows with you. When I was Iris's age, my favorite food was pizza and my favorite topping was pepperoni. "Favorite topping" is a euphemism. I mean that I didn't consider any other topping, including plain cheese, to be food. By the time I was in high school, my favorite food was still pizza, but every year on my birthday I'd request a large pie from Hotlips Pizza, topped with pepperoni, sausage, green peppers, mushrooms, and onions. Now my favorite pizza is Pagliacci's Pear Primo, with sliced pears, walnuts, and blue cheese. In high school, I would have considered this the pizza equivalent of classical music and Jane Austen: weird grownup stuff. Hmm — maybe I should look into classical music and Jane Austen.

When Iris is ready to move on from cheese, pizza will be there for her. Pizza can be vegetarian, cheeseless, or gluten-free without losing its basic essence. It can handle a wider range of ingredients than any other food I can think of except maybe pasta. No wonder Hades used it to lure Persephone.

Here's a pizza tip. At around sixteen months, when Iris grew her first top teeth and got interested in pizza, she could chew it pretty well but her tiny hands couldn't maneuver the slice. She needed little half-inch squares of pizza. The folks at our pizza place are very helpful, but not that helpful. So I would bring along a pair of kitchen shears and cut the pizza into bites at the table. Then I'd wrap the scissors in a napkin and wash them at home. Plus, I was all set whenever I needed to fight off a mugger or attend an impromptu ribbon-cutting.

Now Iris can handle a slice just fine, and she routinely eats half as much pizza as I do, even though I am five times her size.

Mac Daddy

Okay. This is embarrassing.

Long before Iris was born, Laurie and I tried a super-cheesy macaroni recipe from a magazine. It called for nearly a pound of Cheddar, plus evaporated milk and eggs. It was quite tasty. It also made me want to lie down afterward. In a casket. I like rich food, but this was too much.

I've never made that recipe again, but, perhaps embarrassed about the stash of blue and purple boxes in the pantry, I've tried others. I've made custardy, cheesy, stovetop, and oven versions. The result is always the same: Iris is fine with any macaroni as long as the cheese is fully melted and dissolved ("This noodle has too much Parmigiano," she told me recently). But her parents, nursing painful memories of the macaroni of death, prefer the stuff from the box. Look, we're not into canned ravioli or frozen burger patties. I make my own panko-breaded chicken strips, okay? (See page 194.) But boxed macaroni is just the thing.

That's not to say that we eat the contents of the Kraft or Annie's box unadulterated.

Our most common Sunday lunch after a trip to the farmers' market is mac and broc. You can throw broccoli right in with the boiling macaroni.

Cauliflower works well, too. Sautéed corn off the cob nestles nicely into the pasta shells. Fresh or frozen peas would be lovely.

Mac and cheese is also good with salsa or sriracha. I take a couple of tablespoons of homemade or commercial salsa and strain it in a sieve to thicken it while I make the macaroni, then stir it in at the end. I especially like a spicy green tomatillo salsa for this purpose.

In the spring, I sauté morels and stir them into the boxed mac after it's cooked and sauced. Wouldn't it be cool if Kraft made a variety that included a packet of dried morels to throw in with the noodles? They could sell it for ten bucks. I'd buy it.

Finally, I wondered whether I could devise a homemade cheesy vegetable pasta dish, something with sophisticated flavor and no cheese powder packet, but with a monochrome palette so Iris wouldn't complain about flecks of green on her noodles. It took a few tries, but baked pasta with cauliflower and cream is an unqualified hit.

French Fries from Hell

Before Iris was born, I had lunch at a restaurant in downtown Seattle known for its kobe beef burgers. The burger was pretty good. The shoestring fries were fabulous — slender, golden, cognizant of one of the key rules of deep-frying: more surface area equals more crunchy goodness.

The fries seemed easy enough to recreate at home. I gave it a practice run and they came out perfect. So I told Laurie we would be having homemade fries with dinner. Brimming with confidence, I overheated the oil, and when I put the potatoes in, it bubbled over and ignited on the burner. I was sure the whole building was going to burn down. Laurie reminded me we had a fire extinguisher. Fire extinguishers really work! Nothing was destroyed but a saucepan, the fries, and a peaceful evening.

I do not make fries anymore, unless they come frozen in a bag, in which case I pan-fry them in just a few tablespoons of oil. I do make crunchy potatoes, though: see my recipe for duck hash (page 48).

STICKY RICE

⏰ 1 hour, plus soaking time

🍳 Cheesecloth, stockpot with steamer basket

What do you do with sticky rice, other than shovel it in? Use it as a fork: gather a small ball with your fingers, flatten it into a sheet, and use it to pick up salads, curries, grilled chicken, whatever.

Serves 4

> 2 cups Thai white sticky rice, soaked in ample water
> for at least 4 hours

1. Drain the sticky rice and wrap in moist cheesecloth. (Note: Someone gave us a pack of gauze diapers as a baby present, and I don't understand how they could possibly work as diapers, but they're great in the kitchen in lieu of cheesecloth. Do not substitute Huggies for cheesecloth.) Place in the steamer insert.

2. Bring a couple inches of water to boil in the pot and place the steamer insert in the pot. Cover, reduce heat to medium, and steam 45 minutes, flipping the rice packet over once, halfway through

cooking. Unwrap and serve immediately. Sticky rice dries out easily, so keep the serving bowl covered with some damp cheesecloth
during dinner.

BIBIMBAP

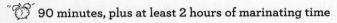 90 minutes, plus at least 2 hours of marinating time

Other popular toppings include carrots, spinach, zucchini, mushrooms, and daikon, but try the simple version below first. And by all
means try a vegetarian version, with tofu or without. The beef will
be easier to slice if you freeze it for 30 to 60 minutes first. If you have
access to a Japanese or Korean grocery, you'll find good-quality
presliced beef labeled for sukiyaki or bulgogi — a real timesaver.
My favorite bowls for serving bibimbap (and many other rice and
noodle dishes) are Crate and Barrel's inexpensive Bistro Bowls.

Serves 4

FOR THE BULGOGI MARINADE

- ¼ cup soy sauce
- 1½ tablespoons sugar
- 2 tablespoons finely grated Asian pear or Granny
  Smith apple
- 1 scallion, thinly sliced
- 1 medium clove garlic, minced
- 2 tablespoons toasted sesame seeds
- 2 tablespoons sesame oil
- ½ tablespoon ground black pepper

- 1 pound beef flank steak, halved lengthwise,
  then cut crosswise into very thin slices
- 8 ounces bean sprouts
- 4 eggs
  peanut oil

10 cups hot cooked medium-grain (Calrose) rice
   (from about 3½ cups uncooked rice)
 8 ounces napa cabbage kimchi (see note)
   gochujang (Korean hot sauce), thinned to pourable
   texture with rice wine vinegar or water (see note)
 4 large bowls

1. Combine the soy sauce, sugar, pear, scallions, garlic, sesame seeds, oil, and pepper in a bowl. Add the meat and refrigerate for at least 2 hours or up to 24 hours. Put the meat and the marinade in a skillet over medium-high heat and cook just until no trace of pink remains in the meat. Set aside.

2. Blanch the bean sprouts in boiling salted water for 2 minutes.

3. Fry the eggs in a bit of peanut oil in a large skillet. (A runny yolk is best here, because the heat of the rice will cook it.)

4. Place 2½ cups of rice in each bowl. Top each bowl with one-quarter of the beef, bean sprouts, and kimchi — arranging them reasonably artfully around the edge of the bowl — and place a fried egg in the middle.

5. Serve immediately. Each diner should add gochujang to taste and stir everything together, including the egg. Eat with a spoon.

NOTES ON INGREDIENTS

Kimchi is sold in jars in the refrigerated section of the supermarket, usually near the produce with the Asian noodles and tofu. The kind I call for is the most common variety and needs no prep before serving other than slicing it and putting it atop the bibimbap.

Gochujang is sold in Korean and other Asian groceries, generally in a red plastic box. If you can't find it, substitute Rooster brand sriracha sauce, sold in a clear plastic squeeze bottle in most supermarkets. If you use sriracha, there's no need to thin it with vinegar or water.

SHRIMP and GRITS

🕐 2 hours, mostly unattended

If using stone-ground grits, it's best to soak the grits for at least a couple of hours ahead of time. If you skip soaking, the texture will be, well, grittier, but still tasty.

Serves 4

- 1½ cups grits, preferably stone-ground
- 1½ cups whole milk
- 4½ cups water
- 2 teaspoons kosher salt
- 2 tablespoons unsalted butter, divided use
- 4 slices bacon, cut crosswise into ½-inch pieces
- 1 pound large (21–25 or 26–30) shrimp, peeled and, if desired, deveined

1. Turn the oven on to 350°F. Combine the grits, milk, water, salt, and 1 tablespoon butter in a large saucepan. Place in the oven (no need to preheat it all the way) and bake 1 hour. Stir. Bake another 15 minutes or until thick and creamy. When you remove the pan from the oven, place a potholder over the handle so you don't burn yourself like I always do. Add the additional 1 tablespoon butter and stir vigorously.

2. Meanwhile, cook the bacon in a large skillet over medium heat until just starting to crisp. Remove the bacon to a paper towel–lined plate, reserving the fat in the pan. Raise the heat to medium-high. Add half the shrimp and cook 3 minutes or until just cooked through, flipping the shrimp halfway through the cooking time. Repeat with the remaining shrimp.

3. Divide the grits between four bowls and top with the shrimp and bacon. Braised kale is a great side dish.

CHEESY VARIATION After the grits come out of the oven, add 1 cup shredded sharp Cheddar along with the additional butter.

GRIT CAKES

! QUICK

"⏰" 20 minutes

When life gives you leftover grits (or polenta), make grit cakes. Pour the leftovers into a mini-loaf pan and refrigerate overnight. In the morning, unmold the now solid grit loaf onto a cutting board and cut it into one-third-inch slices. Using a nonstick skillet, fry the slices in butter over medium-high until well browned on both sides. This will take longer than you expect — ten minutes per side is not unheard of. Serve with scrambled eggs, bacon, or leftover shrimp. Grit cakes work better with noncheesy grits; the cheesy ones are easy to burn.

BACON-JALAPEÑO PIZZA

"⏰" 30 minutes, not counting time to make pizza dough

🍲 Pizza stone, parchment paper

LITTLE FINGERS: Kids can roll out small pizzas and top them. Pizza stones cause third-degree burns.

I don't want to give exact quantities for this recipe, because only youknow how spicy, saucy, or cheesy you like your pizza. I generally use 4 slices of bacon, 1½ cups of cheese, and a whole lot of jalapeños — and I almost always use canned or jarred tomato sauce here.

Serves 3

> 1 recipe Cornmeal Pizza Dough (see below)
> bacon, preferably double-smoked, cut crosswise into ½-inch lengths
> tomato sauce of your choice
> low-moisture whole-milk mozzarella, shredded
> Parmigiano-Reggiano, grated
> pickled jalapeño slices

1. Place a pizza stone on the bottom rack of the oven and pre-heat the oven to 500°F. Let the oven preheat for at least 30 minutes and preferably 1 hour.

2. While the oven is preheating, cook the bacon in a skillet until crisp. Drain and set aside.

3. Place a sheet of parchment paper on a rimless cookie sheet or pizza peel. Place the dough on the parchment and roll it out, flour-ing the top as needed, until very thin (⅛ inch) and about 12 inches in diameter. It's fine for the dough to stick to the parchment.

4. Top with tomato sauce, cheese, bacon, and jalapeños. Trim the parchment so only a small amount protrudes beyond the edge of the pizza.

5. Slide the pizza, parchment and all, onto the pizza stone. Bake 6 to 7 minutes, or until the cheese is bubbly and well browned.

Cornmeal Pizza Dough

! EASY

⏲ 10 minutes, plus 90 minutes rising time

LITTLE FINGERS: Kids can help measure ingredients and punch down dough.

This recipe is adapted from *The Way to Cook,* by Julia Child.

  1   teaspoon instant yeast
  ½   teaspoon sugar
  5   ounces all-purpose flour
  2   ounces cornmeal
  1½ teaspoons salt
  ¼   cup milk
  ¼   cup water
  2   tablespoons olive oil

1. Combine the yeast, sugar, flour, cornmeal, and salt in the bowl of a food processor and pulse briefly to mix. Add the milk,

water, and olive oil, and process until the dough comes together into a ball. It's a fairly wet and sticky dough.

2. Place the ball of dough in an oiled mixing bowl and cover with plastic wrap. Let rise at room temperature for 90 minutes, punching down once, or refrigerate up to two days or freeze up to a month.

MAC and BROC

! QUICK & EASY

🕑 20 minutes

Other vegetable ideas: cauliflower, corn, sautéed mushrooms, and peas. Use about 1 cup of vegetables.

Serves 3

> 1 medium head broccoli
> 1 box (6 to 7.25 ounces) macaroni and cheese
> 2 tablespoons butter
> ¼ cup milk

1. Bring a pot of salted water to a boil. Meanwhile, cut the broccoli into florets. Peel the stem and cut it into half-inch slices. (I think the broccoli stem is the tastiest part, and Iris likes it because it doesn't look so much like a *vegetable.*)

2. If you are using macaroni shells: Add the shells to the boiling water. Boil 4 minutes. Add the broccoli, return to a boil, and boil 6 additional minutes, for a total of ten minutes. Drain. **If you are using elbow macaroni:** Add the elbows and broccoli to the boiling water simultaneously. Boil 6 minutes. Drain. **If you are using SpongeBob or other pasta shapes:** You're on your own there, buddy.

3. Return the pot to medium heat. Melt the butter and add the milk and cheese powder. Return the macaroni to the pot and stir to combine with the sauce. Serve.

BAKED PASTA with CAULIFLOWER

⏲ 45 minutes

🍲 Ovenproof ceramic baking dishes (or substitute a
9 x 13 Pyrex baking pan)

This is based on a technique from *Cucina Simpatica*, by Johanne
Killeen and George Germon. Colorful French ceramic bakeware,
such as Emile Henri or Le Creuset, works great for this recipe, but
you may also use one 9 x 13 baking pan. If you don't want to buy
a whole tub of ricotta to get 2 tablespoons, some cheese counters
sell it in bulk — or you can just leave it out and nothing bad will
happen.

WARNING: Do I have to mention that you should not place a
500-degree dish in front of a toddler?

Serves 4

- 2 cups heavy cream
- 1½ ounces (½ cup) grated pecorino Romano or Parmigiano
- ½ cup shredded low-moisture whole-milk mozzarella
- 2 tablespoons ricotta
- 1½ teaspoons kosher salt
- 12 ounces penne rigate or farfalle
- 1 medium head cauliflower (about 1½ pounds), cut into small florets
- 4 tablespoons unsalted butter

1. Preheat oven to 500°F. Stir together the cream, cheeses, and
salt in a large bowl.

2. Boil the pasta and cauliflower together in salted water for
four minutes and drain.

3. Toss the drained pasta and cauliflower into the bowl with the
cream and cheeses. Divide into four shallow 24-ounce (3 cups or
700 milliliters) baking dishes. Dot the top of each dish with 1 tablespoon butter, cut into bits. Bake 10 to 12 minutes, or until some of
the pasta is well browned and crunchy. Serve immediately.

12

Welcome to *The Jungle*

THE MONKEY AND THE
MEAT GRINDER

ON OUR BOOKSHELF is a charming 1968 volume entitled *What to Do When "There's Nothing to Do."* It's full of wholesome rainy-day activities to keep kids and parents entertained.

"Teach your child how to operate a meat grinder" does not appear in the book.

But Iris's face lights up on Ants on a Tree night when it's time for her to push chunks of pork into the feed tube of the KitchenAid grinder attachment — using a wooden dowel, I should add. (The dowel is technically known, much to Iris's delight, as a *stomper.*) Not with her fingers. That would be dangerous.

We grind our own meat for two reasons.

Fun. We started grinding meat at home because Iris and I were at the supermarket one day buying ground pork to make Ants on a Tree (see chapter 5). "Why does it look like worms?" asked Iris.

"It's because it comes out of the holes in the grinder plate and . . . wait a minute, I think we have a meat grinder at home. You can see for yourself." We bought some pork shoulder instead and I found the meat grinder attachment in the closet. Iris and I assembled the grinder, fed in the pork, and watched the "worms" come out the other end. When people talk about wanting to teach children where their food comes from, I'm not sure this is what they mean. But it should be. Iris has been grinding meat for almost two years now, and she still loves the worms. It's one of the few kitchen tasks, other than measuring (i.e., tasting) sugar, that she always wants to help out with.

Quality. The ground pork they sell at our supermarket is lousy — it's too lean, too finely ground, and too stale. Freshly ground meat is always much tastier than ground meat that's been sitting around for even a few hours. The culprit is oxygen, which causes chemical reactions that make meat taste stale. Unlike a steak, ground meat has tons of surface area and it gets stale fast. (I say "stale" because the meat is still safe to eat; it just doesn't taste as good as fresh.)

I was hoping to be able to report that grinding meat at home also reduces the risk of foodborne illness. Unfortunately, an expert at the American Meat Institute told me it doesn't. This was disappointing, but it did get me thinking: Wouldn't it be awesome to be able to tell people that you work for the American Meat Institute? Especially vegetarians.

If I can't persuade you to grind your own meat, there is a trick you should know about. If your supermarket has a staffed butcher counter, you can bring up a piece of meat and ask them to grind it for you. (I mean, you have to buy it in the same store. Don't bring in some random meat from your fridge.) And some stores have a policy of grinding their own meat daily; here in Seattle, the ground pork from Uwajimaya, the big Asian supermarket, is fresh and fabulous. I've read that you can grind beef for burgers in the food processor, but I've had zero luck with this, personally; the texture always comes out wrong for me. I've had better luck with chicken; see the Chicken and Spinach Meatballs recipe at the end of the chapter.

Sauce on the Side

Iris likes her burgers absolutely plain. My philosophy is, if I'm going to make a plain burger, it has to be the greatest plain burger you can imagine. I am going to make a burger so good, Iris will be humiliated when friends take her to McDonald's, because she will ask why the burger is so lousy. Yes, I'm completely out of touch with reality.

So we've taken care of the meat for a great burger. Now we have a bun problem. Iris and I like a sesame seed bun. For no reason that I can understand, all of the sesame seed buns sold in our neighborhood are gargantuan. They're like truck hubcaps. A patty big enough to fit one of these buns would require at least half a cow.

There is a bakery in Seattle that makes excellent sesame buns of modest size, but it's several miles from our house. So I muddled through with the plain supermarket buns for a while. Then I put my foot down: we were going to have sesame buns with our burgers or else! Or else . . . I was going to write an angry letter to a bakery, I guess. I'd prefer it if you imagine me with a flaming torch, though. Thanks.

First I made homemade buns using a brioche recipe. I'm pretty sure just the word *brioche* cancels out the manliness of grinding your own meat. The brioche buns were good, but even I am not going to make homemade buns every time I want a burger. Besides, the homemade buns weren't as good as the faraway bakery buns. (The bakery buns do freeze well, though.)

Then I tried cutting the XXL sesame buns down to size with a biscuit cutter. This resulted in a silly-looking thing with a frayed edge. I gave up — until one night when I asked Iris, "So, you want burgers for dinner?"

"Sure. And will there be sesame buns?"

Oh, dear. Well, I write for a newspaper, and deadlines are my life. So, stop the presses: I'd just have to figure something out in the remaining two hours before dinner.

And I did! Here's how you convert regular buns into sesame. Preheat the oven to 300°F. Make a loose egg wash by beating 1 egg with 2 tablespoons water. Place the tops of the buns on a foil-lined baking sheet, brush them lightly with egg wash, and let Iris sprinkle them with toasted sesame seeds. If Iris is unavailable, substitute as necessary. Bake 7 minutes or until the egg wash is dry.

Now, with fresh-ground meat and sesamized buns, we can create the ultimate burgers.

What about cheese and other toppings? Up to you, of course. I find that a big, juicy, fresh-ground burger doesn't need cheese. My favorite thing to put on a burger is sautéed onions — not caramelized onions, but yellow onion slices quickly charred in a pan. (Or on a grill, of course, if you're grilling your burgers.) Onions and a little A1 sauce, and I'm thrilled. I'd rather have other vegetables in a salad or side dish.

Hot Dogs for Papaya People

Don't worry! I'm not going to tell you to make your own hot dogs.

Everything I know about hot dogs I learned at Mike's Papaya in New York City. Mike's is one of many knockoffs of Papaya King, the original New York hot dog and papaya drink stand that appeared in an episode of *Seinfeld*. While living in New York, I also visited Gray's Papaya and Frank's Papaya. It hasn't yet reached Ray's Pizza proportions, but there are a lot of papaya places.

Here's what I learned from the papaya people. Buy hot dogs with natural casings. Cook them slowly on a griddle until the skin gets a little browned, shriveled, and crunchy. Don't charge more than a dollar per hot dog. Serve papaya drinks. Okay, I never serve papaya drinks at home, but I hew closely to the rest of the papaya commandments.

Americans are, by and large, opposed to natural casings on their hot dogs. I urge you to join the old-school vanguard. Be a papaya person. I say this even though Iris's preferred method of eating hot dogs is to pull the skin off of each piece with her teeth, eat the interior, then eat the skin. You are so lucky you don't have to see this.

Here's how you recreate the papaya experience at home. Heat a large skillet over medium heat with a bit of vegetable oil. Add the hot dogs. Cook, rolling them around occasionally, for 10 or 15 minutes, until the skin is a bit browned. Place a bun over each dog, cover the pan, and let the buns warm and toast for a minute or two. My favorite toppings are sauerkraut and pickled jalapeños; Iris, you will be shocked to hear, prefers hers plain.

I've tried most of the hot dogs available in my local markets, and the best are Boar's Head all-beef hot dogs with natural casings. They come in a package of seven dogs, presumably just to provide fodder for stand-up comedians. ("You ever notice how they sell hot dogs in packs of seven and buns in packs of eight? Ho ho.")

Spaghetti and Meatballs Are Friends

There's no diplomatic way to say this: our favorite meatballs contain spinach. I'm not trying to sneak spinach into my family, as recommended in books like *The Sneaky Chef* and *Deceptively Delicious*; I use it because, as Iris once put it, "Those meatballs good! Not too spinachy." They became our house meatball after I gave up on trying to find a traditional spaghetti and meatballs recipe that I actually liked.

Don't get me wrong: I love the idea of spaghetti and meatballs. I think I first tried to make it after Iris and I read *Bread and Jam for Frances* and Frances's picky-eating phase comes to an abrupt end after she is confronted with an irresistible plate of the stuff.

To me, though, the spaghetti and the meatball are just too . . . separate. You've got the vulnerable pasta and then this big meaty thing lurking thuggishly nearby. Furthermore, I'm not really a fan of ground beef outside of a burger.

So I've attacked this very serious problem in two ways: one chicken meatball with spinach and a sweet-and-sour sauce, and one miniature pork meatball. I often serve the chicken meatballs without pasta, but I can always make some spaghetti if Iris insists. The little pork meatballs are meant to go with spaghetti; they're small enough that they're somewhere between traditional meatballs and meat sauce.

The thing I realized about meatballs while coming up with the pork recipe is this: fillers are good. My instinct when making a meatball, and perhaps yours, too, is to be generous with the meat. This is admirable but dumb. A great meatball is light and tender, and it gets that way by having enough bread and milk in it that it just barely holds together before cooking. A meatball with insufficient fillers is a puck.

The first time I made the pork meatballs, I started with half a pound of leftover ground pork and browned the meatballs in olive oil, drained them, and finished simmering them in tomato sauce. With spaghetti, it was the perfect amount for the three of us, and Iris ate numerous meatballs. First, though, she looked at her plate, where I had carefully cut a meatball into bites for her, and said, "But where is my meatball?" She sounded exactly like Frances.

What's For Dinner

Steak was a staple of my youth — as I recall, my mom would buy "London broil," which I now understand means basically any cheap, thick cut that goes on sale a lot. Then my dad would cook them up on the gas grill, and every time, my mom would say, "I think this is the best steak we've ever had." I must have overdosed on steak as a kid, though, because I can remember cooking it myself exactly one time before Iris was born. Lobel's, a high-end butcher in New York, was having an impossible-to-ignore fifty-dollars-off mail-order special. That covered one free ten-ounce prime strip steak, which I ate for lunch while Laurie was at work. In my defense, Laurie didn't like steak. Yet.

Then, on a trip to the supermarket when Iris was two, we passed the meat counter and the butcher handed her a free sample of steak. It was the perfect kid-size bite, and she loved it. "We could make steak at home," I found myself saying.

"Tonight," said Iris.

So I bought the steak that was on sale, which was top sirloin with the supermarket's "signature herb rub" — you know, where they shake on five cents' worth of dried herbs and charge an extra dollar. For the grownups, I turned the steak into a salad with arugula, olive oil, and lemon juice. I still don't have much interest in an unadorned hunk of beef the way Iris does, but steak salad is wonderful and the source of infinite variations. I've made it with blue cheese, pecans, and sherry vinegar, and my favorite is Thai-style, with cucumbers, lime juice, fish sauce, and chiles.

We still don't have steak often, and I rarely buy the bargain-basement beef anymore. I wish I could say this is because of my well-developed sense of ethics, but actually it's because I wrote a column about dry-aged steaks and found them so much tastier that they're hard to pass up, even at eighteen dollars a pound or more. That sounds like a hell of a splurge, but a pound of steak is plenty to serve all three of us, and we can easily spend more than eighteen bucks going out for pizza. If there's a butcher, farmer, or supermarket near you selling dry-aged beef, give it a try. Don't blame me if you get hooked.

If I'm not buying dry-aged, my favorite cuts of beef are the midpriced chewy-but-flavorful ones, flank and skirt. (Hanger steak is also in this category, but I almost never see it for sale.) Iris likes flank steak so much that when we pick up the weekly supermarket circular in the lobby, she'll take a look and say, "Oh yeah! Flank steak!" Flank is also the ultimate beef for stir-frying; just freeze it for half an hour, raw, and slice it thin across the grain, as seen in my bulgogi recipe. I'd never buy precut "beef for stir-fry," which is usually cut from the round and guaranteed to cook up tough and flavorless.

If your family loves steak enough that you're getting bored with it, inspiration can be found in Cree LeFavour's book *The New Steak,* which has dozens of great recipes for marinades, rubs, sides, and so on.

CHICKEN and SPINACH MEATBALLS

 90 minutes

You'll need a food processor and a 12-inch nonstick skillet with lid. Well-seasoned cast iron would be okay, but do not try this with a stainless-surface pan or they will stick like hell. An instant-read thermometer is also handy but not required.

This recipe is descended from one in Lynne Rossetto Kasper's *The Italian Country Table,* but I've changed it around quite a bit. It's a rather involved, weekend recipe, but it doubles very well if you have a fourteen-cup food processor, and leftovers reheat perfectly and make great meatball sandwiches or midnight snacks. Cook the meatballs in two batches if you double. And feel free to skip the sweet-and-sour sauce and just use regular spaghetti sauce.

Makes about 12 meatballs, serving 4

FOR THE MEATBALLS

  1 slice rustic bread, crusts removed
  2 large cloves garlic, peeled
  2 ounces pepperoni slices
 12 ounces boneless, skinless chicken thighs
  5 ounces frozen spinach, defrosted and squeezed dry
  1 small onion, coarsely chopped
 ¼ teaspoon cinnamon
 ½ teaspoon kosher salt
    few grinds black pepper

1 tablespoon red wine vinegar
1 ounce grated Parmesan cheese
zest of 1 lemon
1 large egg

FOR THE SAUCE
1 tablespoon extra-virgin olive oil
½ cup dry white wine
2 teaspoons sugar
2 tablespoons red wine vinegar
1 cup canned low-sodium chicken broth (or homemade)

1. Place the bread in a food processor and grind into crumbs. You should have about ½ cup. Remove to a separate large bowl.

2. Place the garlic and pepperoni in the food processor and process until very finely chopped.

3. Add the chicken, spinach, onion, cinnamon, salt, and pepper, and process until well mixed. Poke through with a fork or spoon looking for unincorporated chicken chunks, and process further until you don't find any. You're not looking for a mousse texture, but pretty close. Remove to the bowl with the bread crumbs.

4. Stir in the 1 tablespoon vinegar, cheese, lemon zest, and egg. With your hands, form the meat mixture into two-inch meatballs, placing them in a single layer on a large plate. You may cover the meatballs with plastic wrap at this point and place them in the fridge for several hours.

5. Pour the olive oil into a 12-inch nonstick skillet and heat over medium-high. Add the meatballs to the pan and cook until well browned on all sides, turning carefully with tongs. Turn the heat down if they're browning too fast. This will take about 10 minutes. Pour off or blot any excess fat.

6. Return the heat to medium-high (if necessary) and add the wine. Cook until nearly completely reduced, about 2 minutes. Add the sugar, vinegar, and broth, bring to a simmer, reduce heat to low, and cover. Simmer 12 to 15 minutes, turning the meatballs once, until the meatballs are firm and register between 165°F and 170°F in the center.

7. Remove the meatballs to a bowl, raise the heat to medium-high, and boil the sauce down until it's sour, sweet, and salty enough to your taste. Pour over the meatballs and serve immediately with rice or noodles.

SPAGHETTI with
PORK MINI-MEATBALLS

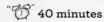 40 minutes

Meat grinder, if you'd like to grind your own pork

Serves 4

FOR THE MEATBALLS

  2 slices white sandwich bread, crusts removed, torn into pieces
  ½ cup milk
  1 large egg, beaten
  2 ounces grated Parmigiano-Reggiano
  2 tablespoons minced fresh oregano
  2 cloves garlic, minced
  1 teaspoon kosher salt
     pepper to taste
  1 pound ground pork

FOR THE SAUCE

  2 tablespoons olive oil
  2 cloves garlic, minced
  1 28-ounce can diced tomatoes with juice
  1 tablespoon tomato paste

¼ teaspoon sugar

salt and pepper

1 pound spaghetti

1. In a bowl, combine the bread and milk and mash with a fork until it forms a paste. Stir in the egg, Parmigiano, oregano, garlic, salt, and pepper. Add the pork and mix (hands work well) until well combined.

2. Heat the olive oil in a large nonstick skillet over medium-high. Drop 1-tablespoon dollops of meat mixture into the skillet. (The meat mixture will be too soft to form the meatballs ahead of time, and they'll come out a bit like thick sausage patties. Yes, they're supposed to be like that.) Working in two batches, brown the meatballs on two sides, about 2 minutes per side, and transfer to a plate.

3. Add the remaining garlic and cook until fragrant, about 15 seconds. Add the tomatoes, tomato paste, and sugar and bring to a boil. Cook over medium-high 10 minutes, until thickened, reducing heat if the sauce spatters too much. Return the meatballs to the pan, reduce heat to medium-low, and cover. Cook 10 minutes or until meatballs are cooked through, stirring occasionally. Season sauce with salt and pepper to taste.

4. Meanwhile, bring a large pot of salted water to a boil. Add the spaghetti and cook until al dente. Drain. Combine the pasta, sauce, and meatballs and serve.

BURGERS

" ⏰ " 40 minutes

🍶 Meat grinder

LITTLE FINGERS: Kids can help grind and season the meat, form patties, and butter buns. If your kids are ready to use an electric frying pan with supervision, a burger patty is a great item to practice with.

This is enough to make two 6-ounce burgers and one 4-ounce burger, which is just right for us. Feel free to increase as needed. I call for grinding the meat twice through the coarse plate, because I think you get the best texture this way, but you can also grind once through the fine plate; it's not a huge difference.

Serves 2 adults and 1 child

- 1 pound chuck roast, cut into 1-inch cubes (or a little more, because some will get stuck in the grinder)
  kosher salt
- 3 sesame seed buns
- 2 tablespoons butter, melted

1. The first rule of meat grinding is this: keep everything cold. While you're cutting up the meat, put the grinder attachment and a bowl in the freezer. It wouldn't hurt to freeze the meat chunks for a few minutes before grinding, either.

2. Assemble the grinder with the coarse plate (this is butcher-speak for "the one with the big holes") and attach to your stand mixer. Put it on low speed and grind the meat into a cold bowl. When it's done, feed the ground meat through the grinder a second time.

3. Form the meat into two 6-ounce patties and one 4-ounce patty. It takes a little practice to pack them tightly enough so they hang together but not so tight that they're dense and dry. Make a slightly thicker ridge around the edge of the patty, like you would with a pizza crust, and the patty will end up evenly thick when it's done cooking. Season the patties generously on both sides with salt.

4. Heat a cast-iron or nonstick skillet over medium-high heat for 3 to 5 minutes or until hot. Place the patties in the pan. There are many factors that determine how fast a burger cooks: the size and thickness of the patty, the heat of your stove, the type of pan, how tightly you packed them, and so on. You can use a meat thermometer to judge doneness, but there's really no substitute for making burgers several times and falling into a routine. I cook my 6-ounce patties for 3 minutes per side and the 4-ounce patties for 3 minutes on the first side and 1 minute on the second side.

5. While the patties are cooking, brush the buns with melted butter and toast them in a hot skillet or under a broiler. Assemble the burgers and serve immediately.

13

Monkey Goes to Market

SHOPPING OUR WAY
THROUGH SEATTLE

GROCERY SHOPPING IS one of my favorite forms of entertainment. It's not just the produce, either — I can get lost in the baking aisle geekily comparing different brands of flour. According to the Food Marketing Institute, the average American shops 1.9 times per week. Daily shoppers like me account for about 1 percent of Americans. "Let me just say that we love you," a guy from FMI told me. The industry loves me because the more often I set foot in the store, the more impulse buys I'm likely to make. I'm not even going to try to deny it.

My daily shopping habit is equal parts necessity and mania. We have three supermarkets within easy walking distance, so there's no need to load the kid into the car for a quick shopping trip. (In fact, we don't have a car.) And I like a quick trip. Unfurling a book-length shopping list and ticking it off as I plow down every aisle does not appeal to me. We don't have a garage or a basement, so we're not going to be loading up a chest freezer anytime soon. Some people find a full fridge reassuring; to me it looks like clutter.

On the positive side, shopping makes me feel useful. Sure, Laurie brings home the bacon, metaphorically speaking, but I *literally bring home bacon.* I like watching the neighborhood supermarket try to keep up with Whole Foods and other specialty stores; the cheese department has gone from Velveeta to Vacherin in the decade we've lived here. They now carry good-quality Thai curry paste (Mae Ploy is my favorite brand) and coconut milk (Chaokoh). And there are certain vegetables, such as fennel, that I like better at the supermarket than at the farmers' market. The supermarket still can't sell a decent tomato, though.

Iris doesn't share my enthusiasm for grocery shopping, so I don't take her to the supermarket very often. Maybe once a week, when just the two of us are home in the afternoon and I realize I'm missing an ingredient for dinner. Then I can say, "If you want Ants on a Tree tonight, we have to go get some noodles," which usually wins her over. But shopping at the supermarket with Iris brings up the kind of stereotypical parent-child issues that I like to pretend I can opt out of. As in: Iris tries to convince me to buy some stupid product. I say no. She whines. I relent. When we get home we eat 10 percent of the product and the rest goes stale. This happened most recently with frozen pretzels, which I agreed to buy even though we make homemade pretzels and Iris loves to sprinkle salt on them. She had one pretzel for snack and the rest are still taking up space in the freezer, wondering why no one has inquired after them.

Embarrassingly, I'm perfectly capable of making the same mistake on my own. I will always buy the latest limited-edition candy bar, for example, no matter how ill conceived. (Mass-market coffee-flavored candy bars are never, ever good.)

When people suggest leaving the kids at home when you go shopping, my knee-jerk reaction is to say, hey, there are fun experiences and learning opportunities at the supermarket. This is true, but on the whole I have to agree: I'd rather do it myself. Unlike cooking and eating, grocery shopping just doesn't seem to be a point of agreement for me and Iris. She's never once asked to go to the store, and I don't see a good reason to convince her to come along more often. I shop at urban supermarkets with small aisles, and I don't want to be the guy with the kid getting in your way and upsetting the apple display.

Recently QFC added this new kind of cart that is, like the Grim Reaper, simultaneously great and terrifying. It's a small cart with two baskets stacked vertically. Each basket is the size of one of those hand-carried plastic shopping baskets. I have my top basket and Iris takes the bottom one. It's terrifying because now it's that much harder to say no to Crunch Berries, but my ability to convince Iris to come along to the supermarket took a big hit when she outgrew the seat in the regular-size cart. "You can put your stuff in the bottom basket" has been a semi-successful replacement.

The two-basket cart gave me a flashback to when Iris was nine months old and outgrowing the Baby Bjorn carrier. She loved the Bjorn because she could ride facing out and greet people at eye level. Suddenly she was relegated to the stroller, and it felt like we had taken her out of her social milieu and socked her away in a rolling drawer to be sniffed by dogs. (Okay, actually she loved being sniffed by dogs.) The little cart makes her a first-class citizen of the supermarket republic. Maybe she'll grow up to be a daily shopper like her dad. I'll be proud, especially if she pays for her own Crunch Berries.

As for the fact that Iris isn't into comparing unit pricing, however, that's just unacceptable.

So instead of any further griping about how Iris is missing out on the joys of comparing bulk and packaged nut prices, let me tell you about a few places where she *does* love to shop.

Bavarian Meats

"Would you like a wiener?" asked the old German lady at Bavarian Meats. She was talking to Iris.

Bavarian Meats is a German sausage emporium in Pike Place Market. We shop there for slab bacon and Westphalian ham, Iris's favorite. I am working up the courage to try their *bundnerfleisch,* a hard beef sausage that is literally black. They give kids free wieners, wrapped in a napkin for immediate consumption. "And could I have a hot dog?" Iris asked the last time we went in.

"We don't have hot dogs! Only wieners!" replied the counterwoman, who was not intentionally doing a John Belushi impression.

They also sell the European confection known as Kinder eggs. You split open a chocolate egg and find a colored plastic egg inside. Open that, and there's the toy. Some assembly required. A lot of assembly, if you're lucky. The best Kinder toys are the ones that come in twelve tiny plastic pieces and have to be assembled with a magnifying glass and tweezers. Sometimes you get a little action figure with no moving parts, and this is a big disappointment. It feels like if your spouse gave you cash for your birthday. Iris keeps her favorite Kinder toys in a small box, and you can fit a *lot* of Kinder toys in a small box; at the bottom of the box you can find random plastic parts that snapped off, like unpopped popcorn kernels at the bottom of a bowl.

It would be nice to report that the Kinder corporation takes their chocolate as seriously as their toys, but the Kinder egg chocolate may be the worst chocolate in the world. It tastes like highly sweetened margarine. If you hold an unwrapped Kinder egg in your hand for a few minutes, it will coat your hand with chocolate so sticky, it could be substituted for Krazy Glue.

On one of our visits to Bavarian Meats, they were giving out free samples of *landjager,* a hard German salami stick. I tried it and warned Iris that it might be too chewy. By the time we got halfway down the block she had finished it, and we had to go back and buy some. Iris will try absolutely anything offered as a free sample. Once I tried to kiss her good night and she said, "No free samples!"

Uwajimaya

If you're shopping at Uwajimaya in downtown Seattle and you notice a thirty-something guy and his daughter loitering near the chiles and scallions and looking shifty, I can explain. We're not terrorists, but we *are* waiting for something to explode. Several times an hour, the sound of thunder rings out over the produce department, followed by an anticlimactic sprinkle of water over the greens.

Iris thinks this is the best thing ever. Now we have to go to the produce department first thing, which is fine with me, because I also think the produce department at Uwajimaya is the best thing ever. They always have fresh turmeric, shiso leaves, and lime leaves. There are a dozen varieties of Chinese greens, two dozen fresh chiles, and green mangoes and papayas for making crunchy salads.

Uwajimaya is to ordinary Asian supermarkets as the giant Mekong catfish is to a pet goldfish. The store is huge and they stock everything for cooking East Asian food, with a particular emphasis on Japanese and Hawaiian products. When I say "Hawaiian products," I mean Spam sushi. This is not a joke. They also carry Vermont Curry, my favorite brand of Japanese curry-in-a-box.

As much as Iris enjoys the produce thunderstorms, she may like the Pocky aisle even better. Made in Japan, Pocky Sticks are chocolate-dipped pretzels, but they come in about three dozen varieties, and Iris is determined to try them all. Last time she selected Pocky Mousse Tiramisu. Many Pocky flavors are, in a very Japanese touch, made with hydrogenated fish oil. Is it good for you because it's fish oil or bad for you because it's hydrogenated? With flavors like these, who cares! My favorite Pocky is Chocolate Crush, which has chocolate cookie crumbs in it.

There's a big paper dragon hanging from the ceiling of Uwajimaya, and it is Iris's friend. Once we had left the store and had to go back in because, as a despondent Iris sobbed, "We forgot to feed the dragon some Pockys."

Pocky (pronounced "pokey") is apparently most popular among young girls in Japan, so in an effort to expand its market, the manufacturer introduced Men's Pocky, which is made with bittersweet chocolate and comes in a manly green box. (It's great.) On another visit to Uwajimaya, Iris picked out a cookie called, I kid you not, Couque d'Asses. Also made in Japan.

She also likes to shop for mackerel, her favorite fish. It's a bit heretical to be an American mackerel lover; this is not a popular fish, even by American standards. It has a powerfully smoky flavor, loads of fat (the good fish-oil kind, if you care), and lots of little bones to watch out for. I used to go to this Japanese luncheonette called Takohachi, where the signature dishes were broiled mackerel (*saba shioyaki*) and bacon fried rice (*bacon fried rice!*). The mackerel was sprinkled with lots of sea salt before broiling, and the result was a sensual salt- and fish-oil-seasoned experience. But Takohachi went out of business and I went into mackerel withdrawal.

Then one day in the freezer section of Uwajimaya I noticed frozen fillets of Norwegian mackerel. It looked perfect, and it was six dollars for two fillets. With its shiny striped (and completely edible) skin, mackerel is among the flashiest of fish, which is probably why *maquereau* is French for "pimp." (The word *morue* is French for "cod" and "hooker." I assume there is another French word that means both "John Dory" and "john.")

I was really nervous about whether I would cook the mackerel properly and whether Iris would like it. I broiled it with a little soy sauce, and it turns out mackerel is almost impossible to screw up (the oil content keeps it moist), and the quality doesn't suffer at all for being frozen.

"I just knew I'd love that mackerel," said Iris after devouring about half a fillet. Now I keep mackerel in my freezer at all times (did I mention Norwegian mackerel is sustainably fished?), and I recommend you do the same. It's great broiled with salt, miso, or homemade teriyaki sauce. Sometimes I buy the whole fish and roast it with slices of lemon. Basically, think of mackerel as aquatic beef: it can take any strong flavors you throw at it.

Broadway Farmers Market

Remember the episode of *Sex and the City* with the guy who never left Manhattan? I used to live in Manhattan, and I was that guy. Now I'm even worse. I rarely leave my Seattle neighborhood, Capitol Hill. I walk Iris to school. My parents live a few blocks away. Sometimes Iris and I take the bus downtown or to University Seafood and Poultry, but fundamentally, we're walkers. If you told me I could never leave the Hill again, that would be totally fine.

Iris was a late walker. She finally got the hang of it at twenty months. Now, however, she will race me the nine blocks home from preschool, and this is after chasing other children around for half an hour. (Okay, more often she'll chase other children around for half an hour and then claim she is too tired to walk home.)

So when our farmers' market opened three years ago, it was the last piece of the neighborhood puzzle for me. We have the library, the supermarkets, schools, parks, and now the farmers' market. In the ecosystem of gourmet shopping, big markets such as Pike Place or the Ferry Plaza market in San Francisco are the charismatic species — the mountain gorilla, the Bengal tiger. Little neighborhood markets like mine are the unknown insect species that you've never even heard of, but if it goes extinct, you're hosed. Besides, our market may be small, but it would be great even if the only vendor was Alvarez Farm.

Alvarez Farm is a large organic farm in eastern Washington. They concentrate on New World produce: corn, eggplant, potatoes, tomatillos, and dozens of varieties of peppers. When Iris was infatuated with dried chiles, we bought a colorful fresh ristra from Alvarez and hung it from her ceiling so she could watch it dry, which is about ten percent more exciting than watching paint dry. Alvarez grows peanuts and sells them roasted or raw. (Raw peanuts taste exactly like beans, which they are.) They also sell fresh chickpeas, which come in a bouquet and are labor-intensive but have an amazingly green flavor.

I'd like to tell you that the guys at the Alvarez stand recognize Iris and ply her with peppers and corn. Actually, it's the bakery guy who recognizes her and plies her with pretzels. Iris does enjoy husking corn, though. Once when she was two, she picked up an ear of corn, handed it to me, and said very clearly, "Dada, suck it."

"What?" I boggled.

"Dada, shuck it!"

When you shop at the farmers' market, you start to get a sense of which items are really better at the market and which offer only a karmic benefit. I refuse to buy corn from anyone other than Alvarez, because doing so is always disappointing. Oh, and local, organic food, the stuff that has a reputation for being expensive and elitist, is a bargain. They have the gall to sell celery root for five dollars a pound at my local supermarket. One day we brought home a gargantuan two-and-a-half-pound celery root from the farmers' market. A brain surgeon could have operated on it for practice. It was two dollars. This is not just an anecdote: a Seattle University professor did a study comparing supermarket and Broadway Farmers Market prices on fifteen items, and the farmers' market won.

Aside from saving money and being a good citizen and stuff, I like scaring Iris with warty fingerling potatoes and weird gourds, both of which are sold in abundance on Broadway in the fall. After the market closes for the year, in November, I get a little depressed and eat few vegetables until spring.

A Date with Death

During October, I have no trouble persuading Iris to come along to the supermarket. And it's not because of candy.

One Halloween, before Iris turned two, I took her to QFC and she fell in love . . . with a giant inflatable Grim Reaper candy display. It's about eight feet tall, with glowing red eyes, and you can walk inside his cloak to grab a bag of candy. Perhaps this is a commentary on modern times. In the olden days Death rode a pale horse. Now it's the 3 Musketeers of the apocalypse.

When you enter the Reaper, lights flash and the Reaper cackles. Iris was a little scared of it at first but wanted to go back and visit again and again. This had better not portend a bad-boy penchant.

Iris tried to tell my mom about her new friend. "Tell Grandma what you saw at QFC," I prompted.

"The Greemreaper," said Iris.

"The what?" asked my mom. "The Green Reaper?"

"Its name is Beth."

"You mean Death?" I asked.

"Yes. Beth."

Happily, the Reaper has come back every year. This year, I found Iris stroking its skeletal hand and whispering, "I'm so glad you're back." I waved my hand in front of the sensor to make the Reaper cackle. "You got reaped!" howled Iris. No one has ever been happier to see the Grim Reaper approaching.

BROILED TERIYAKI MACKEREL

! QUICK & EASY

 15 minutes

Mackerel fillets are bony, I'm afraid. Serve kids from the tail section, which is the least likely to have bones. If you're not sure you like mackerel and are planning to skip this recipe, I'll make you a deal. If you eat some of this mackerel, you can have two cupcakes.

Serves 2 adults and 1 child

- 2 mackerel fillets, 6 to 8 ounces each
- 1 tablespoon soy sauce
- 1 teaspoon mirin
  lemon wedges, for serving

Preheat the broiler. Stir the soy sauce and mirin together and brush onto both sides of the fillets. Place on a foil-lined baking sheet and broil, skin-side down, five minutes. Carefully flip the fillets (use two spatulas) and broil on the other side 3 to 5 minutes until skin is a bit charred and the fish is cooked through. Serve immediately with rice or roasted potatoes.

PRETZELS

⏰ 2 hours, including rising time

🍲 Stand mixer

LITTLE FINGERS: After I let Iris help shape pretzels, she invented this game where she curls a rubber band or piece of string into a squiggle and asks, "Would you eat a pretzel shaped like THIS? Yes or no?" Repeat a hundred times. Other than that and the obvious warnings about the electric mixer and the oven, I have no caveats about letting your children help make pretzels.

Makes 6 pretzels

> 8 ounces all-purpose flour
> 1 teaspoon instant yeast
> 1 teaspoon kosher salt
> 1 tablespoon honey
> ½ cup lukewarm water
>   cooking spray
> 2 tablespoons baking soda
>   kosher or pretzel salt for sprinkling

1. In the bowl of a stand mixer fitted with the paddle attachment, stir together the flour, yeast, and salt. Stir the honey into the water until it begins to dissolve, then add the honey-water mixture to the dry ingredients. Mix with the paddle on low speed until the dough starts to come together, then switch to the dough hook and knead on medium speed (4 on the KitchenAid) for 4 minutes. If the dough is very dry (bits are refusing to incorporate) add an additional tablespoon of water. Spray a bowl with cooking spray and place the dough in it. Spray a bit more cooking spray on top of the dough, cover the bowl with plastic wrap, and let rise 75 minutes, punching down the dough after 45 minutes.

2. Line a large baking sheet with parchment and spray with cooking spray. Divide the dough into 6 pieces (about 2 ounces each). (It will be easier to form the pretzels if you cut the dough into strips with a bench knife rather than pulling off balls of dough by hand.) Roll each piece into a long (18-inch) snake and form into a pretzel. Place the formed pretzels on the baking sheet.

3. Preheat oven to 450°F. Bring 2 quarts of water and the baking soda to a boil in a saucepan. Add 3 pretzels to the boiling water and boil 30 seconds. Flip the pretzels, boil an additional 30 seconds, and return them to the baking sheet. Repeat with remaining pretzels. Sprinkle the pretzels with kosher salt or with pretzel salt (available from kingarthurflour.com) if you have it.

4. Bake 9 to 10 minutes or until deep golden brown. Cool pretzels on a rack and serve warm.

14

Can a Monkey Make Dinner?

Let's just say we cut ourselves a lot in the
kitchen and leave it at that.
— Anthony Bourdain, *Kitchen Confidential*

ACTUALLY, MORE OFTEN I burn myself. Sometimes it's an accident: the potholder slips as I reach
into the oven. Sometimes it's the kind of macho stuff I'm prone to
after reading too much *Kitchen Confidential*. Like, the heating ele-
ments on our stove are kind of loose, and they don't always heat
up when I turn the knob. I've been known to put a pot of water on
to boil and then realize two minutes later that I'm not sure if the
burner is on. So I poke the coil with my finger. If you hear a howl of
pain, it's working! It's the worst kind of pain, too: the kind that de-
serves no sympathy.

The other day I closed the dishwasher on my finger and took off
several layers of skin. Sometimes I bang my head into the corner
of the cabinet door. I've reached into the dishwasher to grab some
silverware and impaled myself on the kitchen scissors, which some
idiot (hi!) has put in there with the points up.

Yes, the kitchen can be a dangerous place, and I'm not eager to put my only child in harm's way. (Those of you with multiple children: Good move! Always keep a backup.)

Normally when I let Iris help in the kitchen it's because we're making cookies. I let her measure the flour and sugar, maybe crack an egg, and put on the sprinkles. In fact, we don't even do these things *in* the kitchen — we use the dining room table.

For Iris's second birthday, we got her a little wooden toy kitchen. She took to it immediately, inventing a game called "Ding! It's Ready!" the rules of which you can surely divine. She used her Melissa & Doug cutting food toy and her wooden knives to prepare me hundreds of meals — all some combination of fake cucumber, carrot, fried eggs, pizza, tomato, and watermelon. In other words, she's well equipped to open a pizza place in Japan.

Laurie and I nursed an absurd fantasy about the toy kitchen: when one of us was in the real kitchen, Iris would station herself at the toy kitchen and keep herself busy mimicking dinner prep. Nice try. To Iris, it's not really play unless someone is playing *with* her. Did I mention she's an only child?

Then one fall day we invited ourselves over to Lara Ferroni's house. Lara is a great food photographer whose work can be found at cookandeat.com. I wanted some pictures of Iris and me cooking together. I asked Iris what she'd like to make for lunch at Lara's house, and she said Ants on a Tree (see recipe, chapter 5), which sounded perfect, because there would be photos of Iris operating the meat grinder.

After the meat grinding, I thought maybe Iris would be bored of posing and want to play with Laurie while I finished making lunch. But no, she wanted to be the chef. We sat on stools at the kitchen table, and Lara handed me the coolest thing: a Kuhn Rikon paring knife, red from point to handle. Iris commandeered it and semi-deftly sliced some peppers and scallions. No blood was drawn.

I pulled her stool over to the stove and handed her a spatula.

"These noodles are going to be Iris-made," she declared. We fried up the noodles. "Do you want to try some noodles?" Iris asked Lara's husband, Cam. "They're homemade."

Iris asked if the paring knife came in other colors, like, say, pink. It did. Clearly it was time to bring Iris into the kitchen . . .

. . . which is about thirty square feet. I'm a nice guy, but when people come into the kitchen while I'm cooking, I get stabby. Even if they're coming to help. Even if they've just come from Whole Foods and are bringing me a present. I wanted Iris to learn to cook, but did it have to be in *my* kitchen?

It's amazing, the ability of small children to independently invent things that seem like learned behavior. Iris, for example, had never seen anyone cover their ears and spout gibberish to avoid hearing unwanted advice. She recreated this practice on her own. She also invents nice things, like describing her stuffed animals as an extended family. ("And these are their babies. And this is Ducky's cousin. And Blue Sweetie is . . . their butler.")

I wanted to teach Iris a few things about cooking without actually *teaching* anything in the sense of pontificating, which would definitely be greeted with covered ears and gibberish. Plus, I've always wanted a sous-chef.

I started by letting Iris make her own pizza. There was no question about whether she'd eat the result, and if she turned out to be any good at it, it would make a great summer job in a few years. I gave her a small ball of cornmeal pizza dough, some mozzarella, pepperoni, and sauce. When her rolling pin stuck to the dough, I offered to help, but she gave the dough a light dusting of flour and shooed me away. I went to check the oven temperature, and when I got back, there was a perfect pizza — well, fairly misshapen, but rolled out flat and topped with even layers of sauce, cheese, and pepperoni.

"I guess you didn't need help," I said. *I have a pizza prodigy!*

"Why didn't we throw it?" asked Iris.

"Huh?"

"Like at Pag." At Pagliacci, our local pizzeria, the crust is confidently hand-thrown.

"Oh. Well, you can't throw the cornmeal dough or it would just break. I'll make some regular dough and we can practice throwing it." I slid Iris's pizza into the oven, where it baked on the hot pizza stone for about six minutes. It was not only good, but it was better than the pizza I made, because I didn't have the patience to roll it as thin as Iris's. Hers had a nice char around the edge.

Pizza is uncontroversial. Wouldn't it be nice, though, if I could convince Iris to eat more vegetables simply by getting her involved in their preparation? It worked with the homegrown cilantro, after all.

Iris eagerly agreed to help me tear Brussels sprouts into individual leaves for a simple sauté with butter and lemon juice. In no time, thanks to her determination and tiny fingers, she had mastered it. Then I made the mistake of asking, "So, do you want to eat some of these leaves tonight?"

"Sure," replied Iris, sounding anything but sure. Of course, she didn't eat any. Ellyn Satter predicted my failure:

> Some parents cook or grow gardens with their children in hopes that doing so will make them eat better. It won't work. If that is your motive, your child will be onto you in a flash and will be less, not more, likely to eat even the food he grew with his own hands.

Don't you hate it when people know more about your kids than you do?

> Ideally you will be working at a child-size table, using a table-top electric skillet for any child-centered cooking. That way, you can sit with your children and work side-by-side, rather than dealing with kids on high stools in front of a stove.
>
> — Mollie Katzen, *Salad People*

I'm pretty sure "Child-Centered Cooking" is the title of a canni-
bal cookbook, and I am prejudiced against cannibals and electric
frying pans. I already have a working stove. Why would I need a
smaller stove that takes up shelf space? I try to keep my kitchen free
of extraneous devices, and I thought *I* took a hard line about this
until I saw the episode of *Good Eats* in which Alton Brown throws a
rice cooker out the window.

Then Iris came along and the answer was obvious. Katzen was
right. The electric skillet could be *Iris's* stove. That way I wouldn't
have to bring her up to stove level in the kitchen, which would make
her susceptible to toppling over (or getting in my way) while flipping pancakes.

It turns out they sell electric skillets at my local supermarket
for twenty-five dollars. I bought a small one and decided to teach
Iris to make pancakes. We set up the skillet on the kitchen floor
and got to work mixing. (Iris requested blueberry-buckwheat and
ate numerous frozen blueberries while cooking.) I showed Iris how
to brush the pan with oil and ladle out a small amount of batter.
She worked her spatula under a pancake and flipped it perfectly.
She was, I would have to say, more proficient than many actual
diner cooks. Then, while flipping the next pancake, she burned
her wrist.

I *told* her to watch out for the hot top edge of the skillet. I don't
know why they can't build them with a ring of heatproof material
shielding the edge. Iris cried for about a minute, then started laughing when she saw the ragged excuse for a pancake that had resulted
from her mishap.

After I ate the defective pancake and cooked the next batch,
we had breakfast on the floor. Bacon was also served. Iris was delighted with this farmhouse breakfast from her own little stove, and
the burn didn't even leave a mark. While eating, I decided I was
glad she'd burned herself right away. It would teach her a healthy
degree of caution: it hurt, so she'll be more careful, but it didn't
hurt so much that she'll never cook again. Then I felt guilty for be-

ing glad that she'd burned herself. Then I ate more bacon. It was a full morning.

And Iris did cook again. She made grilled cheese sandwiches for lunch the same day. I grated the cheese and melted the butter. She did everything else — sprinkled cheese between slices of bread, brushed them with butter, and cooked them. She even mastered peeking underneath the bread to see if the sandwich was browning. "Are we going to flip these?" Iris asked.

"Go for it," I said. She flipped.

"Anybody would like this sandwich," mused Iris while eating her creation.

"Definitely," I said. I had put pickled jalapeños on mine.

"I mean, even somebody who didn't like grilled cheese would like this sandwich."

Next: scrambled eggs. Iris whisked up the eggs, salt, and milk, and promptly dumped them onto the rug. This was my punishment for insisting we cook outside the kitchen. I cleaned up the mess and we started over, this time on the kitchen floor. As the eggs finished cooking, Iris said, "They're done? I made them?" Now she wants to learn macaroni and cheese. "You boil the noodles and I'll make the cheese sauce," she told me. "I might taste the cheese sauce with a little spoon to make sure it's good."

I get the feeling she's going to open one of those restaurants where the chef is bigger than Jesus. "Chef Amster-Burton's grilled cheese is legendary," the waiter will say. "Even somebody who didn't like grilled cheese would like this sandwich."

Shortly after this string of successes, Iris and I were out buying a balloon. "It's for my mom's birthday," Iris told the balloon guy.

"Are you going to make her breakfast in bed?" he asked.

"Yes," said Iris, "because I'm a great cook." A couple of days later we were talking about cooking classes for kids, and Iris asked, "Can you take a cooking class even if you already know how to cook?"

Okay, I'm glad she was confident in her skills. But I had to show this kid that there was more to cooking than topping a pizza or making grilled cheese. I had another project in mind: lasagna bolognese. Even if Iris didn't participate, I wanted to show her what real cooking was all about. And I did, although not exactly in the way I intended.

Lasagna bolognese is the ultimate lasagna. The noodles are homemade. It has alternating layers of meaty bolognese ragu and smooth béchamel, each layer lightly sprinkled with Parmigiano-Reggiano. You top it off with lots of Parmigiano and bake it until crusty on top and perfectly tender beneath. There is no ricotta or cottage cheese in this lasagna.

It's such a production that I hadn't made it since Iris was born. Just walking through the steps on paper makes me want to take a nap. (If you want the complete recipe, it's in Marcella Hazan's *Essentials of Classic Italian Cooking*.)

1. Make the ragu. (This takes at least four hours.)
2. Make the béchamel. I hate doing this. Every time I make béchamel, I stand there stirring for ages, inching the heat up and wondering if it's ever going to thicken.
3. Make the fresh pasta sheets.
4. Boil the pasta sheets, a couple at a time. Yes, you have to do this even though they're already soft. If you make the lasagna with unboiled pasta sheets, they'll soak up too much sauce and Marcella Hazan will cry.
5. Grate the cheese.
6. Assemble the lasagna, with alternating layers of béchamel and ragu, Parmigiano on every layer, and lots of extra Parmigiano on top to become brown and crispy.
7. Bake.

Perhaps you're already thinking of shortcuts: no-boil noodles, pre-grated cheese, sauce from a jar. Perhaps you want to get yourself *banned from Italy*. Don't get me wrong — I use all of those things, but not here, where it would be like designing the Taj Mahal and then deciding to save money by using plywood.

Lasagna bolognese takes basically all day, and I would never do it except that it's one of the most delicious things in the world and restaurants tend to charge thirty dollars for it. If I could get Iris to do some of these steps — preferably all of them — we would all eat this lasagna more often (like, once a year instead of never) and be that much happier.

Iris already knows how to use the pasta machine. I know this because I bought this absurd pasta drying rack from the King Arthur Flour catalog. It's about eighteen inches tall, with rods that fan out like an angry porcupine when you turn a wheel. You can hang a lot of noodles on it. As soon as Iris saw it, she demanded we make pasta immediately, so I dusted off my underused pasta machine and made her operate the crank.

My pasta machine is one of those heavy metal manual models, and it's a real tease. Every pasta machine works the same way. There's a pair of metal rollers, and the distance between them is adjustable. You roll the dough through several times on the thickest setting to knead it, then steadily narrow the setting until the pasta is see-through. For noodles, you can stop on the next-to-last setting. But for lasagna, you have to go all the way. And the difference between those last two clicks is a doozy. The dough tends to stick, buckle, and tear. You know how it's easier for a camel to pass through the eye of a needle than for a rich man to enter the kingdom of heaven? Well, passing pasta dough through the last setting on the Imperia pasta machine is harder than either of those things.

(Some people roll their pasta dough out by hand. I don't even want to think about this.)

If Iris could transfer her mad pizza skills to the pasta arena, we'd be able to enter the kingdom of heavenly lasagna on a whim. Just to keep the pressure on, I invited our friends Molly and Brandon over for Iris's lasagna debut. Molly is author of the cookbook-memoir *A Homemade Life*. Brandon is a vegetarian and a restaurant cook. My theory was that Iris would make the meat lasagna and I would make the vegetarian lasagna. And it couldn't be one of those per-functory veggie lasagnas with canned mushrooms. Cookbook author in attendance!

"What can we bring?" asked Molly.

"Plenty of beer," I replied.

Then Iris came down with one of those mysterious "my tummy hurts" childhood ailments. She perked up enough to work the pasta machine, however, and she was a champ, cranking that thing like she was starting a 1920s jalopy. No pasta dough stuck to the rollers. We hung the pasta sheets on the drying rack and Iris went back to lying on the couch and looking sickly while I ruined the vegetarian lasagna filling.

It was a classic kitchen blunder. I had a one-ounce bag of beautiful dried morel mushrooms, hand gathered by local foragers and sold at the farmers' market. An ounce is quite a lot of dried morels. It cost ten bucks. I soaked the morels in hot water, chopped them, and added them to my sauce-in-progress, which consisted of leeks, fresh cremini mushrooms, and cream. I tasted it and crunched down on a mouthful of sand. I'd forgotten to wash the very dirty reconstituted mushrooms in several changes of water. Morels have a characteristic honeycomb texture that picks up dirt like a three-year-old at the playground.

So I had to chuck the fantastically tasty but sandy sauce and send Laurie out for some dried porcini. I'd like to pretend I handled this in a manly fashion, but the truth is, I literally cried. I've already mentioned how Iris takes big disappointments stoically and breaks down over absurd small stuff. I guess she learned it from watching me.

The leek-porcini filling turned out blessedly grit-free. Then I started making the béchamel. I told you there were a lot of steps.

"Are you going to try both of these delicious lasagnas?" I asked Iris while I was boiling the noodles.

"The only thing that can make my tummy feel better is a chocolate malt sandwich cookie," she moaned. The previous day, Laurie and Iris had made a big batch of them, my favorite cookies in the world.

"Will you help me put the lasagnas together?"

"I'm too busy lying on the couch."

I assembled the lasagnas myself, topping each with a blizzard of grated Parmigiano-Reggiano. When Molly and Brandon arrived with a six-pack of New Belgium's powerful 2 Below winter brew, Iris dragged herself to the table and, true to her word, ate no lasagna but finished an entire chocolate malt sandwich cookie, which you will be amazed to hear did not make her tummy feel better. The lasagnas were excellent — thanks for asking. Next time I would put more cream and a little white wine or lemon juice in the mushroom lasagna, but nobody complained. The adults ate two and a half chocolate malt sandwich cookies each.

A couple days later, Iris's tummy took a turn for the worse, and she threw up. After I cleaned her up, we had this actual conversation:

IRIS: Are you going to throw up too?

ME: I don't think so. I don't throw up very often.

IRIS: Why not?

ME: I don't know. I think I've only thrown up once in the last twenty years.

IRIS: You mean in the eighties?

"So, what would you like for dinner this week?" I asked Iris.

"How about pork on a stick?"

"You mean like pork satay?"

"Sure!"

Satay is wonderful. There's the aroma of slightly charred meat, the spicy peanut sauce, the fun of eating with only a skewer for a utensil. Everything tastes better on a stick, right? The only thing standing between us and the ultimate home satay experience was that we have no grill. I've made satay under the broiler a couple of times, and it's good, but it's not quite the full experience.

"You know," said Laurie, "they have a little gas grill on sale for twenty bucks at the store." I was out the door and back with a grill and a can of propane in minutes. It was Memorial Day, so the clerks were used to dealing with barbecue-crazed customers.

There are hardly any grilling recipes in this book, you'll notice. That's because I don't know how to do it. The only grilling I've ever done in my life is frozen hamburgers when I was a hungry teenager.

Laurie, with some help from Iris, got to work assembling the grill while I sliced pork tenderloin and marinated it in dark soy sauce, ginger, garlic, lemon juice, and honey. A reassuring level of grumbling told me that progress was being made in the living room. "Can I help?" I asked.

"Yeah," said Laurie, her hands full of parts. "You can play Uno with Iris."

A few Wild Draw Fours later, the grill was assembled and I took it out on the balcony. Because I am opposed to Iris catching fire, I made her watch through the glass door while I lit up the grill. It worked! Fire! I called Laurie's dad to ask whether the sputtering sound coming from the propane can meant it was about to explode. "Um, that's normal," he said. "And before you call again, if the canister gets covered in condensation, that's also normal."

Iris and I got to work threading the meat onto skewers. "How you like THAT?" she asked, nearly poking me with a skewer full of pork. Without much of a demonstration, she'd figured out how to sew the meat onto the skewer so it doesn't fall off. When we ran out of meat, Iris was still holding one skewer. "I wanted to do one more," she said, her lip quivering.

Iris pressed her face up against the door and watched me put meat (and some asparagus spears) on the grill. It went pretty well. A twenty-dollar grill, you'll be surprised to hear, does not heat very evenly or very hot, but it's hard to ruin marinated pork, and some pieces even had grill marks. Iris especially liked the crispy edges. Clearly she understands grilling.

The only downside to the whole experience was being banished to the balcony tending meat while the rest of the family ate in the dining room. What I really wanted, I realized, was a grill built into my stove, like you see on TV cooking shows. Failing that, since nothing exploded, next time I'll invite Laurie and Iris to pull up folding chairs and join me on the balcony. The whole family can gather around the fire and enjoy charred meat, spicy sauce, and, with a little luck, no more than first-degree burns.

Iris gets to choose dinner one night a week, and Laurie and I are not allowed to veto her choice. Laurie also gets a pick. I like this system, because discussing dinner with the family is exactly like getting a group of friends to decide on a restaurant. It's nice to have the responsibilities clearly delineated. When Iris was a baby I interviewed the Australian cookbook author Donna Hay, who surprised me by admitting that she also hates deciding what to make for dinner. "Even if they just give you a category, like, 'I feel like beef tonight, or I feel like chicken, or I feel like noodles,' I'm fine with that," she said, "but I'm not fine with the whole open book." This from a woman who's written a dozen hit cookbooks.

Iris's most common picks are Ants on a Tree and "crispy duck leg." I interpret "crispy duck leg" as I like: sometimes it's duck confit, sometimes regular duck leg, with various sauces and accompaniments. As long as it has crispy skin, there are no complaints. The other night, and after gnawing her duck leg scrupulously clean of meat, Iris clutched the bone between her teeth and said, "GRRRRR."

"You look like a savage," said Laurie.

"Yes! I am!" said Iris. "What's a savage?"

Given how much of a pain it is to plan dinners, we've been trying to put even more responsibility for meal planning onto Iris's plate. Sometimes her suggestions are less than imaginative. Brandon is opening a pizza place, and he told Iris that he would name a pizza after her and put it on the menu if she came up with the toppings.

"Okay, how about tomato sauce and cheese?" said Iris.

"I don't think that's quite what he had in mind," I said.

"Cheese and pepperoni?"

I told her she'd have to come up with a pizza with two toppings in addition to sauce and cheese. Several weeks later, she's still working on that.

But sometimes Iris's simple tastes produce a result worthy of Alice Waters. "If you were going to make a sauce to go on farfalle, what would it have in it?" Laurie asked her one night. Farfalle, the little bow ties, are Iris's favorite pasta shape. I'm so glad I already liked short pasta before having a kid, because watching a child smear herself with spaghetti is something I can only handle once in a while, especially if the spaghetti is topped with . . .

"Tomato sauce," said Iris.

"Anything else?"

"And ham." I was standing about two feet from where this conversation took place. Nevertheless, Iris turned to me and said, "If I was a cook I'd make farfalle with tomato sauce and ham."

"You *are* a cook," I said, putting it on the schedule. "We can even make that in your frying pan. What would you serve for dessert?"

"Ice cream sundaes," she replied. "A scoop of vanilla ice cream, chocolate sauce, and a cherry."

"Some people put other things on a sundae, like crumbled Oreos," said Laurie.

"AND THAT."

The tomato and ham sauce was a real winner: simple, delicious, and not something I would have thought to make. Iris smashed some garlic with a tin can and extreme prejudice. We cooked a little prosciutto in her frying pan, then set it aside and browned the garlic in the rendered prosciutto fat and some olive oil. We added canned tomatoes and cooked them down for about ten minutes. Then we passed the sauce through the food mill to puree it. (Yes, in addition to the meat grinder attachment, I do actually have a hand-cranked food mill; it wasn't a rhetorical device.)

. Iris was in charge of tearing basil leaves, and as with cilantro, she kept sneaking them into her mouth. I've always said I should cook more with fresh herbs, and now I have an herb sous-chef. Awesome.

After we ate much farfalle with Iris's tomato-ham-basil sauce, it was sundae time. Laurie put the Oreos in a Ziploc bag and let Iris loose on them with the chicken pounder. There should be a children's cookbook in which every recipe has an ingredient that must be brutally pounded or mashed. The sundaes were, well, they were ice cream sundaes. There's no such thing as a bad one.

"What toppings would you like to put on your sundae next time?" asked Laurie.

"I'VE GOT IT!" said Iris, then turned to me and whispered, "Dada, do you know any sweet toppings?" By the time I stopped laughing, however, she had thought of some. "I want to make a three-scoop sundae. One scoop with apples around it, one scoop with pears around it, and one scoop with grapes around it." This doesn't sound like my dream sundae, but hey, I hear she's a great cook.

BLUEBERRY-BUCKWHEAT PANCAKES

! QUICK & EASY

20 minutes

LITTLE FINGERS: Children can measure and whisk batter, place blueberries (careful of the hot pan), and learn to flip pancakes.

If buckwheat isn't your favorite thing but you'd like to get some whole grain into your pancakes, try substituting Kamut flour, an organic whole-wheat flour that adds a bit of fine cornmeal texture but tastes basically like white flour. Find Kamut flour at natural foods stores or order online from bobsredmill.com.

Makes 8 four-inch pancakes

- 2 tablespoons butter, melted and cooled slightly, plus more for greasing the pan
- ½ cup (2½ ounces) all-purpose flour
- ½ cup (2½ ounces) buckwheat flour
- 1 tablespoon sugar
- 1 teaspoon baking powder
- ¼ teaspoon baking soda
- ½ teaspoon kosher salt
- ¾ cup buttermilk
- ¼ cup milk
- 1 large egg
- ¼ cup frozen wild blueberries (or regular blueberries, fresh or frozen)

1. Stir together the flours, sugar, baking powder, baking soda, and salt in a large liquid measuring cup. Combine the buttermilk and milk in a bowl. Stir the egg into the melted butter, then stir the egg-butter mixture into the buttermilk mixture.

2. Dump the liquid ingredients all at once onto the dry ingredients. Whisk until just barely combined. Heat a large skillet or griddle over medium-high and grease with butter. Pour as many four-inch pancakes as will comfortably fit. When they begin to set up, top each pancake with a generous teaspoon of blueberries. (It's tempting to use more, but if you do, the center of the pancake won't cook, and raw pancake batter is really gross.) Flip and finish cooking. Cook remaining pancakes, greasing pan and reducing heat as necessary. Serve with maple syrup or fake syrup.

FARFALLE with TOMATO SAUCE and HAM

! QUICK & EASY

"⏰" 30 minutes

🍲 Food mill, blender, or food processor

LITTLE FINGERS: This is a perfect recipe to make in a child's electric frying pan, with the usual caveats about oil splatters and hot surfaces. Place the pan on a large towel and send the kid away to tear basil leaves after the tomatoes go in. Otherwise, flying tomato droplets will turn your child into a measles-pocked disaster area.

Serves 4

- 12 ounces farfalle
- 3 tablespoons olive oil
- ¼ pound thinly sliced prosciutto ham, diced
- 3 cloves garlic, smashed and peeled
- 1 28-ounce can diced tomatoes
- ½ teaspoon sugar
- fresh basil to taste, torn
- salt and pepper
- Parmesan cheese

1. Heat 1 tablespoon olive oil in a skillet over medium heat. Add the ham and cook, stirring frequently, until ham begins to brown, 3 to 5 minutes. Remove ham to a bowl.

2. Heat the remaining 2 tablespoons olive oil. Add the garlic and cook until beginning to brown, about 2 minutes. Add tomatoes and sugar. Raise heat to medium-high and cook, stirring occasionally, 10 minutes or until juice no longer looks watery.

3. Meanwhile, boil a large pot of salted water and cook the farfalle until al dente.

4. Pass the contents of the pan through a food mill (coarse plate) or blend in a blender or food processor and return to the pan. Add the reserved ham, basil leaves, and salt and pepper to taste. If the sauce is too loose, simmer another 2 minutes or so. Drain the pasta and add to the sauce, stirring to combine. Serve with freshly grated Parmesan cheese.

15

Magic Cooking Robots

FUN WITH THE SLOW COOKER AND PRESSURE COOKER

A LOT OF COOKBOOKS offer tips for saving time in the kitchen. I like helpful hints, but spending less time in the kitchen isn't a priority for me, because it's my favorite room in the house. As the productivity expert Merlin Mann put it, "It's like wanting less steak or less *The Wire* or less French kissing. Just lost on me why you'd want to truncate one of life's most sublime pleasures." (Actually, he was talking about sleep, but the point stands.)

But I'm not going to be a jerk and wag my finger and say that you, for the sake of yourself and your children, must make more time for cooking. Neither am I going to say something like "Grinding your own flour doesn't take nearly as long as you think!" That strikes me as a pretty jerky thing to say, and maybe you already think I'm a jerk, since you figured this book might give you some ideas for your own life and your own kids and then it turns out that the author has two hours each day to make dinner. Man of the people, my ass!

Sometimes, though, work catches up with me and when Laurie

gets home I head out to the tea shop to grab an hour to type on the baby computer. I return at five-thirty p.m. and have to serve dinner at six p.m., because if we don't start eating at that time, certain family members (Laurie, Iris, and Matthew) start to get cranky.

I don't have an eight-to-five job and a commute, and I don't want to sound like the kid who comes back from a weeklong school band trip and now *totally gets* France. But I do spend some days each month cooking ahead and cooking fast, and I even enlist Iris's help at times, so I want to share what I've learned.

Because I'm a guy, I don't feel like I'm really solving a problem until I've acquired a new piece of equipment. There are three popular gadgets designed for convenience cooking, and I already own two of them, the pressure cooker and the microwave.

The pressure cooker will be covered later in this chapter. As for the microwave, I've owned one all my adult life and have never actually cooked anything in it. I use it for reheating leftovers, melting butter, defrosting frozen vegetables, and heating the occasional Stouffer's frozen panini.

So I had my eye on the third convenience device: the slow cooker.

My mom offered me her Crock-Pot years ago and I declined. I was haughty about it and said something like "I'm not a Crock-Pot kind of guy." She gave it to my sister-in-law Daysha instead. When I decided to try slow cooking, I called up Daysha and sheepishly asked to borrow her Crock-Pot. She agreed. Probably if I'd waited a few days, a free slow cooker would have appeared in my building lobby. Like exercise bikes, the supply of used slow cookers greatly exceeds the demand.

I've resisted the slow cooker, pressure cooker, and microwave in part because you don't get to play with the food while it's cooking. Watch any TV cooking show and you'll see the same thing over and over: sauté. It's the most prestigious station in a restaurant kitchen, and for most cooks, it defines what cooking is all about. With this trio of devices, you put the food inside, set a timer, and see if the food is done when it goes off. Is that cooking?

"I asked Daysha if we could borrow her Crock-Pot," I told Iris. "Want to help me try it out?"

"What is it?"

"Well, it's like a pot where you put in the ingredients in the morning and turn it on, and it cooks all day and the food is ready at dinnertime."

Here's why I love kids. If you told an adult you wanted help with your Crock-Pot, they'd call security. Whereas . . .

"That sounds FUN!" replied Iris. Then she started singing, "Crock-Pot, Crock-Pot, what are you doing? / Crock-Pot, Crock-Pot, what are you cooking?"

Good question! The answer, in short, is meat. Or beans. Or soup, which Iris would like to remind you she hates. What she loves is pork, so for our Crock-Pot debut we decided on Chinese-style spareribs. I sliced the rack of ribs into individual pieces. If we were in culinary school this would fall under the heading of *meat fabrication,* which is fun to say. Sometimes Iris asks what I'm doing in the kitchen and I say, "Oh, just a little meat fabrication."

Iris used her pink knife to cut the scallions into two-inch lengths. She was also in charge of loading the ingredients into the slow cooker. "What is THAT?" she asked, holding out a star anise.

"It's star anise," I said. "It smells kind of like licorice." We have this same conversation every time I use star anise. I don't let Iris play with it because it's expensive, which is silly of me because it's much less expensive than actual toys and smells better.

Iris threw in a few lumps of rock sugar, which is basically just big crystals of semi-refined sugar, sold in Asian groceries. I doubt you could tell the difference between rock sugar and granulated sugar in the finished recipe, but it's traditional for Chinese braising, and the box has a satisfying rattle. Also, it can be used as a toy. "Can we play Rock Sugar Toss?" asked Iris, explaining that this involves seeing who can throw rock sugar farther down the hall. Because every piece of rock sugar looks like just every other piece of rock sugar, however, Iris decided after each throw that whichever one went farther, that was hers. When she grows up, Iris is going to be a cruise ship shuffleboard hustler. After about two hundred rounds of Rock Sugar Toss, I asked her if she'd help me remember what we put in the Crock-Pot so I could write the recipe. "Let's see, there was pork, poison sauce —"

"Did you just say 'poison sauce'?"

"I said *hoisin* sauce. And what was that star-shaped stuff?"

After a few hours, the ribs started smelling really good. Slow cooker tip: if you're a confirmed kitchen fiddler like me, use the slow cooker on a day when you're actually going to be out of the house. I couldn't resist removing the lid and stirring the ribs, even though I knew this wasn't necessary and would release heat from the pot and risk knocking the meat off the bones.

I was worried that the ribs might not be done in time for dinner, but they were ready by five p.m. It was Sunday (I was too nervous to inaugurate the slow cooker on an actual weekday), so I had extra time and was tempted to cheat by crisping up the ribs in the oven, or reducing the sauce, or making a vegetable garnish. Instead, I made some rice in the rice cooker and threw together a quick salad with greens from the farmers' market.

Existential question: Why do good slow cookers cost like twenty dollars and good rice cookers cost a hundred dollars and up? And why do fancy rice cookers always come with "fuzzy logic"? Does anybody know what fuzzy logic is? Is fuzzy logic something that costs eighty dollars?

Iris thought ribs and rice was a great dinner. "Could I please hold one star anise?" she asked after dinner. I found a whole one with a stem on it, and she spun it around in her little fingers and breathed deep. "It's so fragrant," she said.

After dinner I strained the braising liquid and put the leftover ribs and broth into the fridge. The next night, at five-thirty p.m. sharp, I skimmed off the fat and preheated the oven to 450°F. I poured the braising liquid into a saucepan and boiled it down to about a quarter cup, forming a glaze. Laurie and Iris put some jasmine rice in the (non-fuzzy) rice cooker.

I put the ribs on a baking sheet and asked Iris to brush on the glaze, but by then she was too busy winning a game of Uno. I applied the glaze and put the ribs in the oven. While they heated up, I made another salad, with leftover salad greens and homemade peanut dressing.

For extra credit, I put a little asparagus in the oven to roast with the ribs and threw the roasted asparagus into the salad. The leftover rib glaze went on the table for dipping and drizzling on rice. Dinner was on the table on time, and it was great — even better as leftovers than in its original incarnation. Maybe there is something to this Crock-Pot thing.

The next day, Iris agreed to load up the slow cooker with dried black beans, onions, garlic, olive oil, and water. "Check the beans and make sure there are no rocks," I said.

Iris took this to mean that she should examine each individual bean before putting it into the pot. "I think I found a rock!" she said, handing me a gray object that turned out to be a stunted bean. Over the next ten minutes, I was asked, like a Civil War triage nurse, to decide the fate of a dozen additional beans. Then I turned on the pot and we headed out to a playdate with one of Iris's preschool friends.

Now, a normal person would have left it at that: a pot of beans with warm corn tortillas is dinner for several million people on any given night. But I eyed our container of masa harina and recalled a Rick Bayless recipe for black beans with masa "gnocchi," from his book *Mexico One Plate at a Time*. Because when you think of quick cooking, you think homemade gnocchi, right? (Seriously, for those of you who are not insane like me, those packaged gnocchi sold in the supermarket pasta aisle are really good, easy for young kids to eat, and a great alternative to pasta yet again.)

It never got that far, though, because I checked the beans at five-thirty and they weren't done. So we had homemade potstickers from the freezer. This, I have to admit, was the best dinner yet.

So, the Crock-Pot is great if you're a gambler: dinner might be ready . . . or it might not! Do you feel hungry, punk?

The beans finished cooking at about ten p.m. At five-thirty p.m. the next day, I started warming them up and put Iris and Laurie to work making gnocchi. I rolled a little marble of dough, pressed my thumb into it, and placed it on the plate. "This is the sample," I announced.

Iris promptly rolled and thumbed her own *gnocco*, which was a little smaller but perfectly formed. (I guess that describes Iris, too.) "I think this should be the new sample," she intoned. This was the first kitchen task I can think of that Iris completely and totally nailed: She was actually helping rather than learning or, well, getting in the way.

I threw some baby spinach in with the simmering beans and put the gnocchi on top. It's an oddball rustic soup, and I really enjoyed it, especially the way the fresh spinach soaked up the broth and got juicy. Iris ate a bunch of plain gnocchi, or, as they are called in Spanish, *chochoyotitos.*

And, hell yeah, everything was done in half an hour, including prep. I swear on my chochoyotitos. It happened thanks to a combination of good planning and luck. The beans were already cooked. Iris made the gnocchi. The spinach came out of a plastic tub. A squeeze of lime, and dinner was served.

Contrary to the scenario promoted by Rival, you can't always spend five minutes dumping ingredients into the Crock-Pot before work and come home to a perfectly satisfying dinner. That worked for the ribs, but with other dishes I ran into roadblocks, some of which could be averted with practice:

- It's dinnertime but the food isn't done. As long as you allow for this possibility, it's not a big deal, because you can do as we did with the beans and make today's Crock-Pot contents into tomorrow night's dinner. This is obviously more likely to be a problem with beans (which have inconsistent cooking times) than anything else.
- You start the food in the morning but it only takes five hours to cook, and by dinnertime it's overcooked. (As Beth Hensperger and Julie Kaufmann put it in *Not Your Mother's Slow Cooker Cookbook,* "Some foods cannot cook all day and still be recognizable.") This happened to us when we made a stew with chicken thighs, tomatoes, smoked paprika, and red wine (Iris was in charge of adding the paprika and wine). Luckily, we happened to get home in time to save the chicken. Many slow cooker models have a timer to avoid this problem, and it's a feature I'd recommend. Also, be sure to buy one with fuzzy logic. Just kidding.
- Some ingredients have to be pre-cooked before going into the pot if you want them to be any good when they come out. This is more than I can handle in the morning. My two all-time favorite ingredients, bacon and onions, are in this category.
- Not a lot of liquid evaporates from the slow cooker, which is fine for soup, but if you're making a stew, you have to fully submerge the meat if you want it to come out tender. Therefore, you'll need to reduce the liquid before dinner, which can take quite a while.

I have to admit, the slow cooker makes possible some amazing feats: when making the chicken thighs, I managed to reduce the sauce and make caramelized fennel and mashed potatoes, all between 5:25 and 6:00 p.m.

If I were less interested in active, standing-at-the-stove cooking, I'd probably be in love with the slow cooker, but after a couple of weeks, I gave it back to Daysha. I guess I'm really not a Crock-Pot kind of guy. I turned my sights to a louder and scarier cooking tool.

If the pressure cooker and the slow cooker played siblings in a wacky comedy, the pressure cooker would be the high-powered stockbroker and the slow cooker would be the stoner. They both get the job done, but one does it in eight minutes and the other takes all day. Both of them excel at the same task, braising, but they exemplify two solutions to the problem of not enough time to cook. You can either cook at top speed just before dinner, or throw some ingredients in the slow cooker before work and assume it'll turn into dinner by the time you get home. (Or make stew on Sunday.)

I got the pressure cooker for my birthday when Iris was one and a half. She woke up, crawled out into the living room, and said, "New pot!" Three years later, we still call the pressure cooker the New Pot, in the same way we call our neighborhood park New Park, even though that's not its name and it opened in 2004. ("It's called Cal Anderson Park, not New Park," Iris patiently explains to us.)

The first time I released the pressure on the New Pot and sent a geyser of steam into the living room, Iris, who is not scared of anything, screamed and hid her face. It's hilarious when something like this scares her. Once when she was a baby she was shaking a plastic container of unpopped popcorn, and it came open and scattered popcorn, and she gave me the look of ultimate terror before bursting into tears. Probably I am a jerk for thinking this is funny. I figure, hey, there are a lot of genuinely scary things in the world I can't save her from, but flying popcorn is not a major threat.

If you're also scared of pressure cookers, know that today's models have multiple safety features and never explode. Some of you will, I know, find this a little disappointing.

So the pressure cooker is clearly entertaining, but could it save dinner? I consulted Lorna Sass's book *Pressure Perfect,* which is one of only a few pressure cooker cookbooks in English. (The pressure cooker is popular in Europe and ubiquitous in India.)

My goal: taco night. Laurie and I prefer shredded beef tacos rather than ground beef, so I put some cubes of beef chuck in the pressure cooker and Iris helped me add ancho chile powder, cider vinegar, oregano, cumin seed, salt and pepper, and water. Her measuring (and reading) skills are steadily improving, almost to the point where I can hand her instructions and trust that she'll measure correctly. I still have to mop up afterward, but that's true when I measure spices, too.

There was a detour on the way to dinner because I made a discovery while looking for the cumin. "Hey, Iris, I found some whole vanilla beans!" I shouted. "Want to see?"

"Coming!" She sniffed a bean. "That's strong. Hey, I got some tiny vanilla seeds on my finger. Can I lick them?" These vanilla beans had been hanging out in the back of the cupboard for years and didn't actually taste like much, but the seeds sure look cool.

Dried chiles are a magical vegetable-spice hybrid. This recipe had one-fourth cup of ancho chile powder. What other spice can you measure with cups rather than spoons and have it come out great?

The beef cooked at high pressure for about twenty minutes. Learning the pressure cooker takes practice, but not any more so than the slow cooker. You have to look up cooking times and remember which foods require natural pressure release (that is, no shower of steam). Some seasonings tend to behave in strange ways at high temperature: curry powder, for example, tends to get washed out, and citrus juices become dominant.

I was pretty proud of the rich, chile-laden meat. I sent Laurie and Iris out to the balcony to gather cilantro while I put together some other condiments: red onion, grated cheese, fire-roasted canned tomatoes. I also fried up some taco shells; I don't make homemade shells every time, but they really are better than store-bought. And I put out some warm soft corn tortillas so we could have our choice of hard or soft tacos, just like at Taco Bell. (The Taco Bell down the street from us recently closed. I bought lunch there for me and Iris exactly once, and Iris didn't like it at all. Nevertheless, she asked, "Why did it have to close? The tacos were so good.")

"Let's see," said Iris, taking a taco shell and a soft tortilla. "I want one of these crispies on the side, and one of those for making my taco." Completely ignoring my succulent pressure-cooked beef, she put a handful of Monterey jack on her taco. "I want a little cheese . . . hmm, a lot of cheese. And some fire-roasted." I helped her fold her taco and watched her eat it, torn between disappointment that she rejected the beef and elation that she was eating cheese.

Iris took a bite of the taco shell. "I give this sideways thumbs," she said. "It's a little too corny." (She feels the same way about my jokes.)

At its best, the pressure cooker is capable of magic. I made a great taco filling in thirty-five minutes that would have taken at least two hours in the oven. It works wonders on cabbage and other greens. But it's also the kind of cooking least suited to assistance from a child, since it mostly involves fiddling with knobs on the stove. Plus — you never know — it might explode.

STICKY CHINESE-STYLE SPARERIBS

 8 hours, mostly unattended

 Slow cooker

 LITTLE FINGERS: Kids can measure rock sugar and sniff star anise, and if they're ready for liquid measures, let them measure the liquid ingredients. Scallions are hard to cut all the way through and are therefore not ideal for learning knife skills.

I prefer to eat spareribs that have been scrupulously trimmed, with the breastbone and the floppy section (the skirt) removed. Sometimes this is called St. Louis–style trim. If your butcher won't do this for you, find an instructional video on YouTube. There's a lot of meat in the skirt, which can be braised with a can of tomatoes — in the slow cooker, if you like — to make pasta sauce. For information on rock sugar, see below.

Serves 4

- 1 rack spareribs (about 3½ pounds), trimmed and cut into individual ribs
- 1-inch piece of ginger, sliced thin
- 1 bunch scallions, cut into 2-inch lengths
- 4 cloves garlic, smashed and peeled
- 2 star anise
- ¼ cup rock sugar or 2 tablespoons granulated sugar
- ½ cup soy sauce
- 1½ cups low-sodium chicken broth
- 2 tablespoons hoisin sauce
- 2 tablespoons rice vinegar

Place all ingredients in a slow cooker and cook on low heat 7 to 8 hours or until the meat is very tender.

NOTE Rock sugar is crystallized sugar similar to rock candy, sold in Asian groceries. It comes in irregular light-brown pieces or in gem-shaped clear rocks, and it may come in an opaque box so you can't tell which you're getting. Luckily, either is fine.

CHICKEN STEW with SMOKED PAPRIKA

"⏰" About 6 hours, mostly unattended

🍲 Slow cooker

Serves 4

1 medium onion, sliced
1 carrot, peeled and diced
1 rib celery, diced
8 bone-in chicken thighs, skin removed
1 15-ounce can diced tomatoes, drained
3 tablespoons smoked Spanish paprika
¾ cup red wine
  salt and pepper

1. Place the onion, carrot, and celery in a slow cooker. Add the chicken thighs, stacking them in two layers, bone-side up. Add tomatoes, paprika, wine, and salt to taste. Cover and cook on low heat 5 hours or until the meat is very tender.

2. Remove chicken and most of the tomatoes to a platter. Strain liquid into a saucepan. Discard onion, carrot, and celery. Bring the liquid to a boil and reduce to less than one cup. Add pepper to taste. Serve chicken with mashed potatoes and reduced braising liquid for drizzling.

SHREDDED BEEF TACOS

! EASY

"⏰" 45 minutes

🍲 Pressure cooker

LITTLE FINGERS: Kids can measure spices and toss beef cubes into the cooker. I'd let an adult handle the vinegar, though.

Spice Islands brand ancho chile powder is sold in supermarkets, but it's cheaper when purchased at a Latin grocery or from Penzeys .com.

Serves 4

2   pounds beef chuck, trimmed of excess fat and cut
    into 1-inch cubes
¼   cup ancho chile powder
2   tablespoons cider vinegar
1   teaspoon Mexican oregano
1   teaspoon cumin seeds
    salt
½   cup water

In a pressure cooker, combine all ingredients and cover. Bring to
high pressure and cook 20 minutes. Remove from heat and let pressure release naturally, about 10 minutes. Shred meat lightly with
two forks and serve with soft corn tortillas or taco shells, or in a
burrito.

16

Fast but Not Furious

QUICK AND EASY MEALS

As much as i enjoyed playing with the Crock-Pot and pressure cooker with Iris, I'd rather spend thirty minutes in the kitchen cooking something hot and fast.

You can do a lot with the slow cooker and pressure cooker, but you can't make food that is crunchy on the outside with a chewy center, like the old Far Side cartoon. Chefs will tell you that the best way to sell a dish on the menu is to call it "crispy" (hey, no wonder we always order Crispy Duck Leg). To get crispy, you have to fry, roast, or sauté.

The best shortcut to crispy is the Japanese bread crumbs called *panko*. Panko is now widely available in supermarkets (Kikkoman makes it, for example), and for breading, it's not only better than other supermarket bread crumbs but better than homemade bread crumbs.

Panko was born to be the last step of a three-part breading. You can't just dip your poultry in panko and start frying, or the panko will fall off, so you have to sort of glue the panko to the protein. This is the kind of thing you can just barely get done in half an hour, but it's totally worth it, and you can enlist kids to help as long as they don't mind getting messy. (That's a joke.)

This works with meat, firm-fleshed fish, or chicken (this is how you make homemade chicken nuggets or strips). Line up three cake or pie pans. Put flour in the first. Crack a couple of eggs in the second and whisk them with a tablespoon of vegetable oil. Put panko in the third. At this point, Iris says, "Can I taste a little panko?" Uncooked panko tastes like really stale bread, but if it makes her happy, whatever.

Then dip your protein in each pan: flour, eggs, panko. Place the breaded protein on a rack to dry for a couple of minutes before shallow-frying in oil. I've heard assorted tips for keeping clean while doing a three-part breading, but I always end up breading my hand, and this always makes Iris laugh.

Making great food fast requires practice — ever seen a professional chef chop an onion? But more than that, it requires getting friendly with flavorful ingredients.

Have you ever made a Thai salad dressing? It's a combination of five common ingredients: fish sauce, lime juice, chiles (preferably Thai, but the ubiquitous green serranos are fine), garlic, and sugar. You can put the ingredients into a mini-chopper and have the dressing ready in less than two minutes. Grill or pan-fry a steak, slice it, open a bag of salad greens or slice a cucumber, and toss the meat and greens with the dressing. If you have any toasted rice powder (see page 54), sprinkle some on top. Serve rice (regular or sticky) on the side.

If your child is old enough to chew steak, this is an absolutely perfect dinner. Kids who don't like salad can eat steak and rice. If they don't like spicy food, leave the chiles out of the dressing and put a dish of sliced chiles in fish sauce (*nam pla prik*) on the table.

You hardly ever see quick and full-flavored ethnic foods like this in a quick cookbook, despite the fact that, in this case, the ingredients are available in regular supermarkets and it's a snap to make.

When a quick cookbook uses the word "Thai," it usually means something drenched in peanut sauce (Rachael Ray's "Thai Salad with Peanut Dressing," for example), even though peanut sauce is not particularly popular in Thailand. Salad with peanut sauce, *gado-gado,* is an Indonesian thing.

The book *Desperation Dinners* offers "Thai Beef Salad with Red-Hot Dressing," which is closer to the real thing, but the dressing contains Dijon mustard, peanut oil, and Worcestershire sauce, all of which are unnecessary and make the recipe take longer. It also calls for deli roast beef, which certainly saves time, but yeesh. If there isn't time to cook and slice a steak, a better choice is leftover cooked steak from a previous day; there's no need to reheat it.

Nancie McDermott's book *Quick and Easy Thai* has a great beef salad recipe and a bunch of other great Thai recipes that do not make me go off on a rant.

But the best quick-cooking source isn't a book. It's a magazine: Martha Stewart's *Everyday Food.* The cover story is always something like "Five Easy Pastas!" or "Weeknight Wonders!" (It's like how *Cosmo* has a groundbreaking all-new sex survey every month. Not that I ever read *Cosmo* while waiting in line at the supermarket.)

Iris is a huge fan of *Everyday Food.* When she was a baby she would stack and restack the issues, which are conveniently the size of a skinny paperback novel. Once she learned to talk, she'd welcome Laurie home with, "Mama! We got a new *Everyday Food!*" (Between this and the cookie magazine, I realize I'm making it sound like Iris spent her entire infancy reading Martha Stewart publications, which is not true. She also read other food magazines.)

And now she can flip through and actually choose something for dinner, since there's a photo accompanying every recipe. Recently Iris picked a cover recipe for chicken milanese with arugula salad. She even requested some leaves of arugula with her chicken. "That looks good," said Iris, taking a bite of arugula. "Too bad I don't like salad!" She hastily ushered the rest of her salad onto her mother's plate.

The editors of *Everyday Food* have struck a great balance between convenience and quality. The chicken took half an hour and the recipe didn't call for anything weird like instant mashed potatoes. If you're a beginning cook, *Everyday Food* will ask you to stretch, but not very far. There's a monthly feature called "Have you tried . . . ?" introducing a special ingredient, such as canned chipotles in adobo, pecorino Romano, or radicchio. (If I were the editor, for the April issue I would feature something like "Have you tried . . . chicken?" or "Have you tried . . . beer?")

The other reason I like *Everyday Food* is that you keep getting it month after month. Maybe it's just me, but after I've had a cookbook sitting on the shelf for a while, it's hard to get excited about the recipes in it. The most delicious food, for me, is ripped from today's headlines. I always have a special sense of accomplishment when I read about something in the Wednesday *New York Times* or the new issue of *Everyday Food* and have it on the table that night.

I've already admitted to a string of lucky breaks that make me somewhat unlike the average weekday cook. So I called my sister-in-law Kathleen, a working mom with three adorable girls, and asked her about her dinner schedule. She said she starts cooking at five-thirty p.m. and has dinner ready between six and six-thirty p.m. Fresh ingredients are important to her, and the only time she really gets stressed out about cooking is when she hasn't planned dinners ahead or runs out of something during the week — because she tends to shop once a week. Until she said that, we were pretty much on the same page.

As I've mentioned, Laurie and I hit the supermarket about eight times a week, plus our weekly farmers' market outing, even when I'm under brutal deadline pressure. I know most people don't shop this way. Kathleen is a lot more typical.

One reason we shop often is that we don't have much pantry

space, and our freezer is more subcompact than Sub-Zero. Another reason is that we live three blocks from the grocery store. But frequent shopping obviously isn't the only way to make good quick meals happen.

Convenience cookbooks tend to assume you don't care about fresh produce. I do like frozen potatoes and Brussels sprouts, but canned green beans? Forget it. The worst feeling I ever have as a cook is when it's five o'clock, I have no idea what I'm making for dinner, and I'm sticking my head repeatedly into the refrigerator, hoping some appealing produce will magically appear. Here are four strategies I use to avoid that plight:

1. Shop at the farmers' market. Yeah, you hear this all the time, but I'm not going to talk about your carbon footprint here. Most farmers' market produce is days, sometimes weeks, fresher than imported supermarket stuff. This means better flavor and texture, sure, but it also means that, in many cases, you can let it sit around in your fridge for a week and it'll still be good. Those supermarket bags of salad are fine, but they're not nearly as tasty as farmers' market salad blends, which last at least four days in the crisper drawer.

2. Alternatively, look into joining a CSA (community-supported agriculture) program, in which you buy a seasonal share of a local farm and receive a weekly produce delivery. CSAs are becoming more sophisticated: more pickup locations, more choice of produce, and a wider variety of items, since some are run by a consortium of farms. For the busy cook, the key is that you don't even need to think about what produce to buy; it just keeps coming in. The disadvantages are also obvious (do you know a plant called chard? you will), but CSAs are relatively inexpensive.

3. **Wrap.** The main enemy of fresh produce is water loss. Water keeps leaves crisp. Place fresh herbs in a Ziploc bag with a wet paper towel, and they'll last at least a week — even the wimpiest ones, like cilantro. For root vegetables with attached greens, such as carrots and turnips, twist off the greens, cook them if you like, and store the roots in a Ziploc.

4. **Cook and store.** Some vegetables are better cooked right away, then refrigerated and enjoyed for several days. Braising greens like chard, kale, and collards are in this category.

Even if it weren't a requirement of my job, I'd try new things in the kitchen on a regular basis. And sometimes they don't work. When I say, "This is an experimental dinner," Iris and Laurie have learned to brace for the worst: scrambled eggs, toast, grumpy dad. Not that Iris has any problem with scrambled eggs. She probably prefers them to whatever it is I was trying to make.

The best situation would be to always have easily reheated leftovers on call when I'm making a new recipe — working with a net, you might call it. The proper rate of leftover generation is an advanced skill, though. Have you noticed this, that whenever you have the time and money to make something new, you also have leftovers saying "eat me"? I find leftovers come calling just when I'm least happy to see them, unless we're talking about leftover enchiladas, which always make me happy.

Some cooks, I know, are very skilled at using the freezer. I'm not. Really, I'm physically inept at putting things into the freezer. About once a week I will have to call Laurie over for help getting the freezer door to close. I know I shouldn't treat the freezer the way a kid cleaning her room treats the closet, but it's a hard habit to break. I do freeze homemade potstickers (see chapter 21) and try to have those on hand at all times, and I like frozen ravioli. Sometimes

I make homemade sausage and freeze that. Chili, most stews, and most pasta sauces freeze well. Mostly, though, defrosting feels like a cop-out to me. I imagine how customers in a restaurant would feel if they knew the chef was merely defrosting some food he cooked last month. This is completely insane, I know, since Laurie and Iris don't care how hard I worked on dinner, but every cook has his own personal neuroses, right?

My favorite thing to find in the fridge is semi-leftovers, the kind that can quickly turn into a rerun of a favorite dinner with just a bit of actual cooking. The stacked enchiladas of chapter 5 are exactly the sort of thing I have in mind. I always make them two days in a row. After the first night, there's leftover chicken, green chile sauce, and cowboy beans. On day two, all I have to do is fry the tortillas, layer, and broil. Every time I do this, Iris says, "More crunchy cheese?" like she can't believe her good luck. And I'm happy because it felt like real cooking, not reheating. (I'm also happy because of crunchy cheese.)

But neither enchiladas (too slow) nor salad (not Iris-oriented, unless there are homemade croutons) works as a backup dinner. Invariably, I turn to frozen potstickers, pancakes, or waffles, any of which can be ready in ten minutes. I try to have frozen blueberries on hand for pancake emergencies, so at least there's some fruit involved.

I've been cooking for more than ten years, and sometimes — generally around five-thirty p.m. — I still feel like grabbing the stove by the lapels and saying, "Why? Why do you treat me this way?" So, I hope Iris will learn enough about cooking to step into the kitchen and say, "We can fix this." She could point out, for example, that overcooked steak can turn into a nice stir-fry; undercooked beans can go into the pressure cooker; and scrambled eggs for dinner isn't so bad.

But if she wants to just stick with her technique of patting me on the shoulder and saying, "It's okay, Dada," that's fine, too.

CHICKEN STRIPS

! QUICK & EASY

⏰ 30 minutes

LITTLE FINGERS: Iris loves breading things. It's like a science experiment.

Substitute cubes of pork loin for the chicken, serve them on toothpicks, and you'll have another of Iris's favorite dinners.

Makes about 12 strips, serving 3

- 2 boneless, skinless chicken breast halves, about 1 pound
  salt and pepper
- ½ cup flour
- 2 eggs
- 1 tablespoon vegetable oil
- 1 cup panko
- ½ cup lard or vegetable shortening

1. Slice the chicken breasts lengthwise into strips approximately a half-inch thick and one inch wide. This is easier if you freeze the chicken for 20 to 30 minutes before slicing, but if you don't have time, don't worry about it.

2. Place the flour into a cake or pie pan. Beat the eggs and vegetable oil together in a second cake or pie pan. Place the panko in a third cake or pie pan.

3. Salt and pepper the chicken strips generously. Flour one chicken strip on both sides and shake off the excess. Dip the chicken strip into the egg, then the panko, shaking off excess. Place on a large plate and repeat with remaining chicken.

4. Heat the lard or vegetable shortening over medium-high in a large skillet until shimmering. Add as many breaded chicken strips as will fit loosely; don't crowd the pan. Cook 2 minutes per side or until panko is golden brown and chicken is cooked through. Drain on paper towels and serve with your favorite dipping sauce.

THAI SALAD DRESSING

! QUICK & EASY

⏰ 5 minutes

You can quickly mince the chiles and garlic in a spice grinder or mini-chopper.

Makes ½ cup

- 3 tablespoons fish sauce
- 3 tablespoons fresh lime juice
- 2 teaspoons sugar
- 3 Thai or 2 serrano chiles, or to taste
- 2 medium cloves garlic, minced to a paste

Stir together all ingredients until sugar is dissolved. Serve over steak, grilled chicken, cucumbers, salmon . . . seriously, this stuff is good on everything short of ice cream.

17

Tradition Without Turkey

THANKSGIVING
IN THE MONKEY HOUSE

WHEN LAURIE AND I were twenty and first living in Seattle, I had blue hair and was in a punk rock band. Celebrating Thanksgiving definitely would not have fit with my self-image at the time. Thanksgiving is the least punk rock of all holidays. Nothing gets blown up, and you can't give ironic presents or black heart valentines. The most punk rock thing that ever happens on Thanksgiving is a turkey fryer injury. That first year, Laurie and I bought pirozhkis on Thanksgiving. One year we went out for Indian food — I mean, not Native American food, which would have been appropriate, but curry.

Once we had a baby, though, I had to concede that some kind of family tradition would not be out of place. Like many children, Iris thrives on routine. She loves preschool's arbitrary rules. (I hope she doesn't join the army.) We have dinner at six p.m. every day. Every night we have a tightly prescribed hourlong bedtime ritual which does nothing to prevent Iris from popping out of her room and saying, "I just need a sip of water and one extra hug." Pirozhkis for Thanksgiving weren't going to cut it, not when she was learning turkey songs at school.

Fine, I could handle that I was no longer a twenty-year-old punk rocker. My hair was no longer blue. (The old me would totally spit on the current version.) I could do Thanksgiving. What I wasn't ready to embrace was the traditional turkey dinner. The food is too bland, too sweet, and too lacking in acid. Turkey is boring. I don't even like pumpkin pie, but I realize this doesn't make me rebellious, just weird. Laurie loves pumpkin pie.

I thought about reinventing the traditional dishes in a more modern style — a "have your tradition and overthrow it, too" approach. Maybe cook the turkey in the style of Thai grilled chicken, *gai yang,* marinating it with lemongrass and coconut milk and serving it with a trio of spicy dipping sauces. But this was a little too *Gourmet* magazine — *reinvent your Thanksgiving with international flair!*

We did end up tricking out our Thanksgiving with international flair, but not the kind that you'd see on a magazine cover: we found the centerpiece of our Thanksgiving table in England.

Laurie has family in Cornwall, and when you say "traditional food" in Cornwall, you can only be talking about Cornish pasties. Having visited Laurie's various cousins in Cornwall and pronounced them charming, I'm ready to fight for the honor of England's most southwestern province and its favorite meal. And let me tell you, the Cornish pasty is an argument disguised as a meat pie. Take the case of Nigella Lawson's pasty recipe.

I'm a fan of Lawson. What's not to like about a pretty woman with an accent who likes to make cookies? (Hmm, if Laurie could pick up an accent, that would make her three for three. I'll drop her an email.) But I am not a fan of Nigella's Cornish pasty recipe. You see, she *pre-cooks the filling.* This is apparently a very bad thing to do, and if I mention it, Laurie gets mad.

A pasty is a football-shaped pastry crust pleated together on top and filled with beef, potatoes, onions, and sometimes rutabagas, which are known as "swedes" in Cornwall. The first time I had a pasty was at Laurie's grandparents' house in Lompoc, California, where grandmother Betty Burton makes the family recipe, the one she passed down to her daughter-in-law, Laurie's mother, Susan. On one trip to Portland, I asked Susan to show me how to make pasties. This struck me as delightfully contemporary, since traditionally, my mother is supposed to teach Laurie how to cook the ethnic foods of my youth. Since the ethnic foods of my youth were enjoyed at dim sum parlors, I'll stick with pasty lessons.

We have a notebook prepared years ago and given by Betty Burton to Susan Burton, and it's about the best introduction to pasty making a person could have. "The dough for pasty," Granny Burton writes, "shouldn't be rich like for a fruit pie — but a little stretchier like pizza dough . . . so that it is crisp and hard when cooked, not rich and flaky like regular pie pastry."

If you don't have access to the Burton family's pasty notebook, Hettie Merrick's *Pasty Book* is the next best thing. (It's easily available from Amazon.co.uk.) Merrick founded a quintessential pasty shop in the Lizard, which is the real name of a peninsula and town in Cornwall; her daughter, Ann Muller, runs the shop today and defends the pasty against people like Lawson.

When we needed something seasonally and culturally appropriate to serve on Thanksgiving, the pasty became the obvious place to alight. Just look at this unbiased scientific comparison of two favorite Thanksgiving entrees:

	PASTY	TURKEY
Comforting and filling	X	X
Nap-inducing	X	X
Makes great leftovers	X	X
Easy to make	X	
Actually tasty	X	

Furthermore, while the standard pasty is large enough to over-hang a dinner plate, it's easy to make in any size you like, which means Iris can have her own little pasty. Shops in Cornwall sell mini-pasties like this, advertised as "for the cheel," which either means "children" or "time around three p.m. when you want a little snack."

For this year's Thanksgiving, I invited Laurie's parents to come up from Portland for dinner so I could show off my pasty tech-nique — well, that, and see if Susan could teach me how to crimp the top without mauling it.

To be journalistically accurate, we didn't actually have my in-laws over on Thanksgiving proper. It was the Sunday before Thanksgiv-ing. I thought this was a clever and original move — have people over on a different day so no one can complain about the lack of tur-key. Then on Saturday I was listening to the radio and there was the L.A.-based food critic Jonathan Gold talking about how he always invites people over the Sunday before Thanksgiving to try out his nontraditional recipes. These Hollywood types are always stealing my ideas.

I made the dough in the morning. "I am not going to put too much water in the dough like I did last time," I announced. I proceeded to put too much water in the dough, but only a little too much. Bruce and Susan came over while I was cutting the meat into cubes and ar-ranging all the fillings in bowls on the dining room table.

Iris made the first pasty. She rolled out a little ball of dough with her rolling pin. "This is going to be a GOOD pasty," she said.

"What are you going to put in it?" I asked.

"Beef." And sure enough, she put in beef. And salt. You can't ar-gue with people about their pasty fillings. It's a religious practice. I piled mine high with potatoes, beef, rutabaga, onions, and pars-ley. My crimping skills were pretty good. We piled the pasties onto parchment-lined baking sheets and wrote the owner's name on the parchment (Bruce does *not* like rutabaga).

I put a little beef suet, left over from trimming the meat, into one of them as an experiment, because I've seen Susan do so in the past. To make the suet, I just whizzed up the beef trimmings in the food processor. As I said while putting this on the table, you can think of it as suet, or you can think of it as 10-percent-lean ground beef.

While the pasties baked, I cooked Brussels sprouts and asked Bruce about the pasties of his childhood. "We had them about once a week," he said. Susan gave me a look, like, *He always says that, but it's not actually true, and I know more about his family than he does.* If you doubt that all this can be communicated in a look, you haven't been married as long as I have.

Bruce admitted that it was probably more like once every two weeks. He grew up in the small Southern California town of Lompoc, a town best known for its prison. Lompoc has become TV shorthand for a really hard-core joint, and the TV thugs usually mispronounce the name. (It's "LOM-poke," not "LOM-pock.")

Susan told me about learning to make pasties. "Bruce sat me down on this stool next to his mother. I was under the impression we weren't getting married unless I sat and learned," she said.

My introduction to the world of pasties was altogether less fraught. I don't want to make too much of it — Susan was obviously being facetious — but there are issues associated with being a female cook that I will never have to worry about. Men hardly ever feel like they're trapped in the kitchen turning out dinner for an ungrateful family, and they never worry about whether they will be considered bad feminists if they love to cook. I'm simultaneously grateful that I don't have to worry about these things and depressed that anyone has to.

During this grownup talk, Iris went around untying people's shoes. Then the pasties were ready. I put them on the cooling rack and immediately lost track of which pasty was whose. Which one had no rutabaga? Which one had the suet? Only Iris's little one was obvious. We examined the crimp on each pasty and eventually divvied them up correctly.

"Thumbs-up or thumbs-down?" Iris asked everyone around the table. (This is one of her current things.) We all gave the thumbs-up. Laurie lucked out with the suet-augmented filling. A little beef fat goes a long way; her pasty was incomparably juicy. The crust was crisp and just a little flaky.

I sent a small leftover all-beef pasty to school in Iris's lunch. She's my little Cornish tin miner. Actually, I put in a little onion and parsley. Don't tell her. When I picked her up, she said, "That pasty tasted like real beef." I peeked inside her lunch box. She'd only eaten the crust. "I didn't quite eat the whole thing," she backpedaled, "but the crust had real beef flavor."

Now that I've mastered the Cornish pasty, I'm ready to move on to another Cornish delicacy, stargazy pie. It's a pie made with whole fish, with the fish heads poking through the top crust with their dead eyes gazing at the stars. (Do not Google "stargazy pie" at work. Or, like, ever.) When we were in Cornwall, I asked around. "Nobody actually eats that," I was told. But isn't that just what you would tell nosy foreigners if you were a stargazy pie fan and wanted to keep all the fish heads for yourself? Maybe I could get Iris to eat another fish eyeball.

CORNISH PASTIES

2½ hours

LITTLE FINGERS: Children can easily fill and (with a bit of help) fold a small pasty.

Rib-eye steak makes the ultimate pasty, but it's not cheap. For more economical alternatives, try top blade steak, flatiron steak, or sirloin tip steak. Leftover cooked pasties can be frozen, thawed in the refrigerator, and reheated in a low oven; do not attempt to freeze raw pasties.

Makes 5 large pasties

    5 cups (25 ounces) all-purpose flour

1½ teaspoons table salt

2½ ounces cold lard, cut into chunks

    1 stick (4 ounces) cold unsalted butter, cut into chunks
       cold water to moisten

FOR THE FILLING

    2 pounds rib-eye steak, cut into ½-inch cubes

    2 pounds russet potatoes, peeled, quartered lengthwise,
       and thinly sliced

    1 small rutabaga, peeled and minced

    1 medium onion, diced
       flour
       salt and pepper

    2 tablespoons minced fresh parsley

TO FINISH

    1 egg

    1 tablespoon milk

1. Preheat oven to 400°F. In a large bowl, combine the flour, salt, lard, and butter, mixing with your hands until the fat is in pea-size chunks. Add water slowly, taking care not to make the dough too wet — check by pressing it into a ball; if it doesn't fall apart into dry chunks, it's ready. Err on the side of too dry. About 1½ cups of water is a good place to start.

2. Divide the dough into five balls (about 9 ounces each) and roll the first piece out to a 9-inch circle. Pile the center of the dough with generous layers of rutabaga, potatoes, meat, onion, parsley, and 1 teaspoon flour. Sprinkle each layer generously with salt and pepper. Moisten edge with water and lift the two sides of the pastry to seal on top. Crimp edge with your fingers. Place on a sturdy, parchment-lined cookie sheet. Repeat with remaining balls of dough.

3. Beat the egg and milk together in a small bowl. Brush each pasty with egg mixture and cut two slits with a sharp knife. Bake 30 minutes, then reduce oven to 350°F and continue baking 30 more minutes. Cool on a rack 10 minutes before serving.

18

Life in the Sushi Belt

I HAVE A FOOD FANTASY.

When Iris is six, I'm going to take her to Tokyo. Just the two of us, dad and daughter, in the big city, kickin' it Japanese-style.

Laurie will stay home, because — this is her only fault — she doesn't like Japanese food. Sometimes she comes along for sushi, but she says it makes her feel like a philistine, because she only eats the easy bits, like tempura.

So, while Laurie eats whatever it is she eats when we're not around, Iris and I will eat at a skeezy yakitori joint and enjoy char-grilled chicken parts on a stick. We'll go to an eel restaurant and eat several courses of eel, my favorite fish. Iris's favorite is mackerel, so we'll also eat plenty of salt-broiled mackerel, *saba shioyaki,* tearing off fatty bits with our chopsticks. We will eat our weight in rice.

We'll ride the Tokyo subway, perhaps take the bullet train to a *ryokan* in the country. We may, possibly, purchase some Hello Kitty merchandise. We'll have breakfast at Tsukiji, the world's largest fish market. And we'll eat plenty of sushi from a conveyor belt.

Conveyor belt sushi (in Japanese, *kaiten-zushi*) was invented in

Japan in the 1950s. You sit at a counter and watch the sushi pieces roll by on the belt, taking whatever you like. At the end of the meal, they total up your plates, which are color-coded. So tamago, the omelet on rice, might cost one hundred yen, and sea urchin, six hundred yen. A radio-frequency ID tag system makes sure no plate stays on the belt too long: plates pass an antenna that alerts a robotic arm (or a human) to remove that forty-five-minute-old shrimp roll.

In preparation for our Tokyo trip, we practice at a kaiten-zushi place in Seattle, Blue C Sushi. The creators of Blue C have figured out how to make a sushi place supremely kid-friendly. They have three locations and an average customer age of about thirteen. Iris has been eating at Blue C since before she was two.

The worst part of taking a kid to a restaurant is the period between the time you sit down and when the food finally arrives. This is hard enough for me as an adult. With a toddler, you can watch the stomach take over the rest of the body. One moment: laughing and coloring with crayons. Next moment: ready to eat other customers.

These are our basic dining-with-Iris rules:

- We don't go to restaurants where you have to wait for a table.
- No kid restaurants, unless we're just going to play. If there's a play area, Iris won't bother to eat. Crayons are fine.
- Lunch is better than dinner. If lunch takes longer than expected, no big deal (at least, now that Iris no longer takes a nap). If dinner runs long, well, I don't want to see the resulting tantrum any more than you do.

No type of restaurant fills this finicky bill better than a kaiten-zushi place. You walk in, sit down, and start eating immediately. It's faster than a salad bar or Mongolian barbecue. It's faster than *Mc-*

Donald's. If you need assistance, you press a button and a blue light over your head illuminates, just like on a plane.

It's also entertaining for me to see which items Iris will enjoy on a particular day. There have been trips to Blue C when she would eat literally nothing other than rice. Then there was one day when we'd been playing hard all morning and Iris had had only a few sips of smoothie for snack. I asked her what she'd like for lunch and she said sushi. So we caught the bus to Fremont and took our seats at the conveyor belt.

I watched in astonishment as Iris put away mackerel, tuna, tempura roll, salmon, and pickled ginger (usually dismissed as too spicy). She didn't go for the eel or the watercress that came with the fruit salad. When we got home I measured Iris on her growth chart and she had grown three-fourths of an inch in a week. We are constructing a human out of recycled sushi.

The belt at Blue C holds more than just sushi. They have sesame noodles, shrimp tempura, potato croquettes, and juice. The thing that keeps Iris coming back to Blue C is the cream puff, available with chocolate or vanilla filling. Iris and I have a deal: she can only have one cream puff, but she can get it anytime. In practice, it's never our first or last item. Sometimes she sees the puff going by but isn't ready for it because she has a shrimp in her hand. This causes significant inner turmoil. "But someone else might take it," she whispers to me.

Sushi is the only food I can think of that has gone from the punch line of a joke ("Those crazy Japanese eat *raw fish*!") to total mainstream acceptance in my lifetime — at least in my cloistered, urban part of the country. There's a book by Rosemary Wells called *Yoko* about a girl (actually a cat) who brings sushi to school for lunch and is mocked by her peers. It was published in 1998. Today, a kid in Seattle who *didn't* like sushi would be mocked. I suspect sushi will be a major part of Iris's diet when she's a teenager.

Is it safe for a baby to eat raw fish? Sure. Iris's first encounter with sushi was when she was about eleven months old and willing to eat anything, and her favorite item was the mashed tuna from the spicy tuna roll. People always say they're looking for freshness when they go out for sushi, but all of the fish you eat at a typical sushi joint has been defrosted after spending time in a deep-freeze to kill parasites and retard bacterial growth. Some high-end places buy fresh tuna (and take scrupulous care of it), but nobody serves fresh salmon. It's too risky. You could get sick from eating sushi, maybe from a cook who didn't wash his hands before touching your fish, but it's no more likely than getting sick from salad.

As I write this, however, there's a huge controversy over high mercury levels in bluefin tuna and whether it is safe for anyone to eat, let alone young children. Furthermore, conservation groups say that bluefin is critically endangered and nobody should eat it anyway. I'm going to duck these issues completely, because with a young child in the house, we can no longer afford bluefin tuna.

When we get home from eating sushi, we play Conveyor Belt, a game Iris invented. There's a wheelchair ramp in front of our building and Iris can slide under the railing, inch along, and pretend it's a conveyor belt and she is the sushi.

IRIS: What kind would you like?
MATTHEW: What kind are you?
IRIS: You have to say.
MATTHEW: But you're on the conveyor belt. Isn't that your job?
IRIS: But I'm just a sushi. And sushis can't think.

There's also a wooden sushi toy set, made by Melissa & Doug. Their other food-related toys are a vegetable slicing kit, a pizza set, and a sandwich set. I can hear the frazzled parent telling the pediatrician, "She won't eat *anything* except sandwiches, pizza, and sushi."

Iris gave me the sushi toy for my birthday. She is like Susan in Carol Ryrie Brink's classic book *Family Grandstand:*

> Susan thrust her package into George's hand. "Here, George."
>
> George shook it. "It rattles," he said, "but I guess it isn't alive. Thank you, Susy!" He unwrapped the paper, and the rich warm smell reached his nose. "Oh boy!" he cried. "It's Susan's favorite candy!"

The toy sushi set is very clever. It comes with pickled ginger made of felt, sushi rolls you can cut with a knife (included), and velcro chopsticks that adhere to the sushi. We pulled out Iris's little table and she dubbed herself the sushi chef. "When I come in, you say *'Irasshaimase,'*" I explained. "It's 'welcome' in Japanese."

"Uh, I think I'll just say, 'What would you like to order?'"

Iris likes to ride down the elevator to the basement to take out the recycling, because on the way up she turns into a robot. She puts the wastebasket — one of those IKEA models that looks like the trash can on a Mac — over her head and does her best robot voice. As robots go, she's like Adam on season four of *Buffy the Vampire Slayer:* not very scary, but funny.

Hmm. Iris loves robots. She loves sushi. She needed to see a sushi robot in action. This would be a pure act of fatherly love and would have nothing to do with her father's love of expensive gadgets.

I first learned about sushi robots from a sign in the window (WATCH OUR ROBOTS MAKE SUSHI) at a restaurant outside the Vancouver, British Columbia, public library. The robots are the behind-the-scenes heroes of modern sushi. They're about the size of a small frozen yogurt machine and are able to produce up to 2,400 nigiri sushi per hour. Obviously, someday they will become sentient and decide to make humans into sushi, but it is *so* worth it.

Unfortunately, sushi robots cost $20,000, and no Seattle restaurant I called would admit to having one. So we decided instead to try making sushi at home, by hand, while talking in robot voices. Some company needs to make a ninety-nine-dollar home version of the sushi robot. If it only made a hundred sushi pieces per hour, that would be plenty. If people will buy a three-hundred-dollar fuzzy logic rice cooker, they (meaning "I") would totally buy the sushi robot.

We invited Tara Austen Weaver over for a sushi party. Tara, who used to live in Japan and has sushi in her blood, is the author of the forthcoming book *The Butcher and the Vegetarian.*

Tara brought rolling mats and seaweed and pickled ginger. I imagine she has these in a bag by her door, ready to go in case someone calls with a sushi emergency. Before the sushi party, she asked if Iris liked anything special in her sushi. "Just rice," answered Iris.

"Isn't there anything else you'd like with the rice?" asked Laurie.

Iris thought. "Um. Ham?"

Tara asked me to make rice. I used too much water and made mushy rice, so she took over. I sliced the yellow pickled daikon and shiso leaf. And yes, I julienned the ham. Iris and I fanned the rice with manila file folders to dry it off to the proper level of stickiness, while Tara stirred in sweetened vinegar.

"You should spread your rice a little thinner," Tara told me as I spread a thick layer of sushi rice over my seaweed. In that respect, sushi rolls are like dumplings: the beginner tends to overfill. She showed us how to spread the rice over most of the nori, leaving a bare strip at the top to seal the roll shut.

My best roll featured shiitake mushrooms, cucumber, blanched carrots, and pickled ginger. (Tara doesn't cut fish. She leaves that to trained professionals.) "I invented this roll, so I get to name it," I explained. "I'm calling it the Iris roll. What do you call your roll, Iris?"

"The ham covered in rice and wrapped in seaweed roll," she said, nibbling at the nori. "I don't like this kind of sushi. How can I invent it if I don't like it?" She ate a bunch of ham strips off the platter and ran off to play.

A few minutes later, while I was rolling my next sushi, a shriek came from the living room: "I LOOOOOVE HAM."

I did try the ham roll. Iris was right. It wasn't that great. It needed more ham.

HAM-and-EGG SUSHI ROLL

 45 minutes

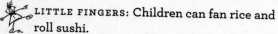 LITTLE FINGERS: Children can fan rice and roll sushi.

After all the talk about our Tokyo adventure, this will probably get me banned from Japan. But it's great for breakfast. Scallions would also be good in this roll, if your kids let you get away with something green.

Makes 3 rolls, serving about 3 (or more as part of a meal)

FOR THE SUSHI RICE

- 1½ cups Japanese-style short-grain (Calrose) rice
- 1½ cups water
- 2 tablespoons rice vinegar
- 4 teaspoons sugar
- ¼ teaspoon salt

FOR THE OMELET

- 2 large eggs
- ½ teaspoon soy sauce
- 2 teaspoons sugar
- 1 teaspoon vegetable oil

FOR THE SUSHI ROLL

- 1½ ounces smoked ham, thin-sliced and cut into strips
- 3 sheets yakinori (toasted seaweed, available at health food stores and Asian groceries)

1. Make the rice. Wash the rice in several changes of cold water and drain. Cook the rice with 1½ cups water in a rice cooker or saucepan. If using a saucepan, bring to a boil, reduce heat to low, cover, and cook about 20 minutes. In either case, allow the rice to rest 20 to 30 minutes before proceeding.

2. Make the omelet. Meanwhile, beat the eggs, soy sauce, and 2 teaspoons sugar together with a fork. Heat the oil in a nonstick skillet over medium heat and add the eggs. When the top is nearly set, roll up the omelet into a coil and transfer to a plate. If you're not very good at making rolled omelets, join the club and don't worry about it. Let cool to room temperature. Cut the omelet into long half-inch-wide strips.

3. Season the rice. In a small saucepan, combine the vinegar, 4 teaspoons sugar, and salt. Warm over medium heat, stirring frequently, until the sugar dissolves. (Alternatively, combine the ingredients in a bowl, heat 30 seconds on high power in the microwave, and stir.) Turn the rice out onto a cutting board or into a large bowl. Add 1 tablespoon of the vinegar mixture and "cut" it into the rice using a large spoon or spatula, using a motion similar to how you'd fold egg whites into batter. Add the remaining vinegar mixture and continue folding it into the rice. If you have a helper available, have her fan the rice to cool it during this process. (A child with a manila envelope works well.) Continue mixing until the rice is no longer steaming. Allow the rice to cool to room temperature.

4. Assemble the sushi roll. Spread a thin layer of rice (about 6 ounces) over the dull side of a sheet of nori, leaving a half-inch strip clear at the top to seal the roll. Make a line of ham and omelet about one inch from the bottom. Roll up — you don't need one of those bamboo mats; hands work fine. Slice the roll into three-quarter-inch pieces and serve.

19

The Lobster Chronicles

"**I**S IT OKAY IF the lobster pinches your finger?" Iris asked me. We were making lobster chowder, and she had a few questions.

Lobster and corn chowder is the signature recipe of Boston chef Jasper White, and it appears in his books *Lobster at Home* and *50 Chowders*. The latter is one of my favorite books. Every recipe is basically the same: boil up pork, potatoes, and onions with some kind of main ingredient and enrich with cream. But there's no sense that Jasper (who seems like such an easygoing sort that it's impossible not to call him Jasper) is just padding out the cookbook.

I've made a bunch of chowders from *50 Chowders:* classic New England fish, chanterelle, corn, chicken, and so on. Iris's favorite part of any chowder dinner is the common crackers, which are little silver dollar–size crackers that you split in half, brush with butter, and toast in the oven. We order them online from VermontCountryStore.com.

"Is it okay if the lobster pinches your hand?" asked Iris. "Does that not hurt?"

Once I read Jasper's lobster chowder recipe, I had to make it. It sounded delicious, and it also sounded like an adventure. Not only had I never made lobster at home, but I'd barely ever eaten lobster. Blame it on the Northwest. We've got brilliant clams, mussels, oysters, crabs, and fish, but no lobster, and we're a bit xenophobic. Lobsters in Seattle are tolerated up to a point, but you don't want to invite them over for dinner — same as with Californians. Probably the majority of lobsters in town are served at Red Lobster, and I can't think of any restaurant more disdained by foodies than Red Lobster, except perhaps the Olive Garden, which is part of the same company but offers breadsticks in place of crab legs.

With the lobster chowder recipe in hand, therefore, I felt like a guy in Iceland longing to enter a chili cookoff.

"Do lobsters have crabby hands?" asked Iris, clicking her fingertips together like castanets.

Jasper's recipe calls for three lobsters. When we got to the fish market, University Seafood and Poultry, there was only one lobster left. "You should have called ahead to reserve them," said the fishmonger. I hadn't realized lobsters were like new DVD releases. Actually, it was a relief — I'd showed up expecting to battle all three musketeers, but instead I'd just be going mano a claw with, uh, Porthos. Porthos the lobster. Also, this way I only risked ruining twenty-five dollars' worth of lobster instead of seventy-five dollars' worth.

Because now I only had enough lobster for a cup of chowder per person, I also made Southwestern Corn Chowder.

Cooking the lobster was easier than I expected, both physically and mentally. Having read David Foster Wallace's essay "Consider the Lobster," in which he tries to decide whether a lobster festival constitutes a holocaust, I expected to feel a twinge of guilt as I slipped the live crustacean into the boiling pot. But it was actually a relief to snuff out its flame of existence, because I'd already been feeling guilty about keeping a live animal in my refrigerator.

Extracting the lobster meat from the shell was no big deal, either, although a hammer probably isn't a traditional tool for the job. I chopped up the lobster meat and made the chowder.

After you've made chowder a few times, it becomes a meditative activity. Every chowder is the same and different: you build a sturdy but bland scaffold for a flavorful main ingredient, and then vary the main ingredient. Jasper writes that he planned to include a potato chowder in his book — that is, a chowder without a signature ingredient — but "as it turned out it was too humble, and novelty was not a reason to include it," so he added Cheddar cheese. The main ingredient doesn't have to be something luxurious like lobster or strong-flavored like clams: chicken chowder is one of our favorites, but even in this case, the chowder teaches us that chicken wasn't as boring a flavor as we thought.

Okay, I said chowdering was meditative, but you don't actually get to have meditative activities with a preschooler in the house. While I cooked, I had to prevent Iris from eating all the lobster meat. I couldn't blame her, because I was having trouble restraining myself. In fact, I was simultaneously batting her hand away from the lobster bowl and swelling with pride (my kid likes *lobster*!), which is a lot better than swelling from a shellfish allergy.

"Can we have the chowder right now?" Iris asked.

Iris is always eager to help me prepare a new dish, even if it's something she has no intention of trying. I figured this would probably be one of those. But lobster, it turned out, is as child-friendly as a marshmallow. It's mostly white and the flavor is mild.

"Why did the lobster not pinch Dada?" I heard Iris ask Laurie. Iris's ideal lobster experience, apparently, would have been one hour of the lobster savaging me with its claws followed by two hours of cooking it in a pot.

Both chowders were brilliant, of course — all praise be to Jasper. Iris ate a bunch of common crackers and all the lobster chunks out of her chowder and pushed the rest around with her spoon. Later I found her rolling the rubber band from one of the lobster claws between her fingers and muttering, "Who was wearing that rubber band?"

. . .

A few weeks later, Laurie went out of town. In the morning, I told Iris she could choose anything she wanted for dinner. "Lobster!" Iris shouted.

"Okay," I said. "We'll go to QFC and see if there are any lobsters in the tank."

Iris thought about this. "But the best lobsters are from University Seafood and Poultry."

I had to concede this. University Seafood and Poultry was once described by the local paper as "the fish market that time forgot." Prices are not posted. When you ask how much for the salmon, the counterman, who looks like he just stepped off a boat, names a figure that is lower than you expected but not low enough to make you nervous.

Later that morning, Iris eagerly told her babysitter Sarah about our lobster plans. Sarah is used to my weird habits by now. I am always dropping Iris off and saying things like, "I have to go to a chocolate tasting today." She probably thinks I'm actually not a food writer but a drug kingpin with a weird set of euphemisms.

In the afternoon, we went to University Seafood and Poultry. Iris chose a lobster, and we rode home on the bus with the lobster in a box on our laps. We were like Amy in *Little Women:*

> In stumbling to the door, she upset the basket, and — oh horror! — the lobster, in all its vulgar size and brilliancy, was revealed . . .

Except that, as literary characters go, Iris and I are superior, because our lobster was alive and Amy's was precooked. And we didn't let ours escape.

"Could I eat the claw meat?" asked Iris.

"Sure. How about you eat one and I eat one?"

"I should eat both of them," she replied. Oh, *fine.*

I boiled up the lobster, melted some butter, and cut a lemon into wedges. Iris did eat a claw, but what she really wanted, it turned out, was the microscopic slivers of meat inside the lobster legs. This required toothpick-aided surgical extraction. I ate the whole lobster tail. Boo-ya!

That night I interviewed Iris about the lobster and posted it on my blog, explaining to her that this is called a podcast. In the podcast (www.rootsandgrubs.com/2007/02/21/iris-out-loud-2-the-claw-game/), Iris expounds on her favorite parts of the lobster in anatomical detail worthy of a veterinary textbook.

The next day, Sarah asked Iris, "So, how was your lobster?"

"Didn't you listen to my podcast?" asked Iris.

When some friends of mine rented a house in Maine and invited me along, I shouldn't have agreed. It meant a big expense and a week away from Laurie and Iris. And I would have said no, if not for two words rattling inside my head: *lobster roll*.

The lobster roll is the ultimate way to serve lobster. You make a salad with big chunks of lobster and a little mayo, maybe a fresh herb or celery. Serve a healthy scoop of this on a toasted hot dog bun. Lettuce is optional. They have regional hot dog buns in New England that look like a folded slice of white bread. The bun is split on the top and the sides are buttered and toasted. It's required for a lobster roll. If you don't live in New England, you can bake the buns yourself with a pan available from the King Arthur Flour catalog, and if you bake your own hot dog buns, you are a better foodie than I.

This was all theory to me, because I'd never had a lobster roll. So I went to Maine. I drove up from Boston with my friends Dan and Liza. We planned to stop for lunch in Portland. First we had to escape from Massachusetts, which took hours. Then there was a stop for liquor in New Hampshire, where the tax-free liquor sales are trumpeted on highway signs. By the time we got to Portland it was after three p.m. and we were about ready to stop at Taco Bell and pray for a lobster chalupa.

We got off the freeway and rolled up almost immediately at a roadside shack called Benny's, which advertised the best lobster rolls in Maine. Also the best fried clams, clam burger, and other local specialties. We sat in the shady, wooded seating area, and the waiter brought us our lobster rolls. I don't know if they were the best lobster rolls in Maine, but they were definitely the best lobster rolls I'd ever had: a quarter-pound of lobster nestled in a leaf of butter lettuce on a toasted bun.

That night I called Iris and told her about the lobster roll. "Oh, barnacles!" she said, quoting SpongeBob. I had to promise to make her one as soon as I got back.

But when I got back, Iris was sick. She had a cold and an earache and refused to take any Tylenol. "I can't eat the medicine," she wailed. Eventually we had to take her to the emergency room, where we got two prescriptions: amoxicillin and Tylenol suppositories. Then the cold headed over to Laurie and gave her three days of total laryngitis. This was one mean virus.

Luckily, Laurie and I hardly ever get each other's colds. This makes some scientific sense. A few years back there was a study that suggested that one of the roots of sexual attraction is divergent immune systems — you're likely to get turned on by the scent of someone whose immune system is primed to fight off a different array of diseases than yours. That way, your kids will be immune to more diseases than you or your mate.

As soon as the family had recovered, I headed over to University Seafood and Poultry and came back with two lobsters. It hurt to fork over the fifty-seven dollars, since I'd just seen lobsters in Maine going for twelve bucks or less. I yearned for the old days, when lobsters, oysters, and bluefin tuna were working-class staples.

Iris was excited when I showed her the box of lobsters, but by the time I finished steaming them and pulled off a leg, she declared, "I don't like lobster anymore." Then, while extracting the meat, I cut my thumb and bled all over, which Iris thought was cool because she had to get me a Band-Aid. Why do kids love Band-Aids so much? I guess they're stickers imbued with purpose. Left to her own devices, Iris would completely encrust herself with cartoon character Band-Aids until she looked like a mummy sponsored by Hello Kitty. Iris kept checking the Band-Aid on my thumb and saying, "Why weren't you careful?"

I did pull off a coup with the buns. It turns out they sell unsliced hot dog buns at Trader Joe's. They were much larger than the New England buns, so I top-sliced the buns and cut the edges off, revealing a large, toastable surface which I spread liberally with butter. I toasted the buns in a skillet, covering the pan so the buns would steam a bit and warm throughout. The contrast between a hot bun and cold lobster is key to a great lobster roll. Okay, so I've only eaten two lobster rolls. But I'll be having another for lunch tomorrow, so I'm practically an expert.

At dinner, all Iris ate was French fries, a bit of toasted bun, and a bite of corn on the cob. I was all set to get depressed about this until I realized that *someone* would have to eat Iris's lobster roll.

Maybe Iris is just an ethnocentric Seattleite. She'll wolf down three salmon cakes — preferably made from wild Alaskan sockeye — but no lobster. Though her standard bedtime song is still "A Real Nice Clambake" from *Carousel,* which has a line about cracking into lobster claws with your teeth. Teeth! Why didn't I think of that? It would have either saved me a lot of blood loss or ripped out several of my incisors.

After dinner, I noticed an odd prickly sensation in my throat. Then it started to swell. I'd eaten lobster before with no ill effects, but I concocted a nightmare scenario in which the lobster roll I ate in Maine awakened evil dormant antibodies which, when confronted with even more lobster a week later, went crazy and were sending me into anaphylactic shock.

I woke up with a sore throat, an earache, and a stuffy nose. It was the evil virus. What a relief!

So I can't blame the lobster for anything but a hole in my wallet and my thumb, but all the same, I think my lobster obsession is over for now. Luckily, there's a place at Pike Place Market that makes

Dungeness crab rolls, and we have some gummy lobster candies that I picked up at the airport in Boston. A whole pound for eight dollars!

LOBSTER ROLLS

3 hours, including 2 hours of chilling time

Serves 4

- 2 live lobsters, 1¼ to 1½ pounds each
- 2 tablespoons mayonnaise, or more to taste
- 4 hot dog buns, preferably New England–style
- 2 tablespoons butter, melted
- Boston or butter lettuce
- lemon wedges

1. Boil a big pot of water, large enough to hold two lobsters. Salt the water heavily until it tastes like seawater. Add the lobsters, cover, and return to a boil. Reduce heat to a simmer and simmer 10 minutes. Remove the lobsters to a plate and let cool to room temperature.

2. Remove the tail, knuckle, and claw meat from the lobster and cut into half-inch dice. Gently stir the mayonnaise into the lobster meat and refrigerate at least two hours and up to three days.

3. Brush the hot dog buns with butter and toast in a skillet. Line each bun with a lettuce leaf and top with one-quarter of the lobster. Serve immediately with a squeeze of lemon.

20

Monkey on Vacation

KEEPING FOOD REAL ON THE ROAD

EVERYTHING I'VE SAID in this book about Seattle is true. It's laid-back, pretty, and loaded with more great things to eat every year. Laurie and Iris and I love it here, and we intend to stay.

Like Jimmy Carter, however, I have committed adultery in my heart.

You see, Seattle has a cute neighbor I've been eyeing for a long time. She's got a cunning foreign accent and a trim, efficient midsection. Her name is Vancouver, and she lives less than two hundred miles away. If you can lure Vancouver into a long-term relationship, you can even partake of her bitchin' health insurance. (Though this is also true of Laurie.)

We've not only looked at Vancouver lustfully but consummated the relationship on several occasions.

We first took Iris to Vancouver just before she turned two. We stayed at a hotel that provided a tiny crib in which we managed to wedge Iris at night. She called it "the funny crib." In the morning we'd go out for croissants and these astonishing cookies called Sparkle Cookies, made by the chocolatier Thomas Haas and available at various shops around town, including Haas's own in North Vancouver. Sparkles are very chocolaty little cookies made with almond flour, and the light dusting of powdered sugar against the dark chocolate cookie really does make them sparkle. It got progressively harder to fit Iris into the funny crib over the course of the vacation.

One day we had dim sum with friends at Kirin, a fancy Chinese restaurant downtown. The potstickers were excellent (though Iris never met a potsticker she didn't like), and there was a large tapestry of a lion on the wall for Iris to growl at. We'd been vacationing pretty hard, though, and she started to get fussy, so I took her back to the hotel while Laurie stayed to chat with her friends. It was raining, and Iris started sobbing.

Luckily, nearly every block in downtown Vancouver features a place dispensing a product that can cheer up any kid and most adults: Tim Horton's, the doughnut chain. I've been to Tim Horton's dozens of times and have almost never ordered a whole doughnut, because I can't get past the doughnut holes, known as Timbits.

Here's how seriously Tim Horton's takes doughnut holes: there's a jelly Timbit. It has maybe a teaspoon of jelly inside. This is Iris's favorite. Mine is the rich and tangy sour cream cake Timbit. Eventually it occurred to me that if I like the sour cream so much, I could buy *an entire sour cream doughnut.* Mostly we've stuck to our Timbits, though. They're filed in separate bins, and you can request your favorites when you order. This is what I do, even though it makes me feel like a picky eater ordering sauce on the side. In addition to the jelly and sour cream, we like the Dutchie (apple-cinnamon), chocolate, and honey cruller. The rest of the Timbits all seem to be some incarnation of plain.

After we got back, our Canadian friend Johan asked Iris, "So what was your favorite thing about Canada?"

"Tim Horton's," she replied.

This was our first family vacation, and we enjoyed it so much that we came back the following winter for a whole week and rented an apartment. We also brought along Laurie's sister Wendy and her partner, Nicole, both of whom were smitten with Iris.

I don't think we'll ever vacation without bringing friends or family along again. It's like bringing your nanny along on vacation, but (a) you don't have to pay them, and (b) you don't feel like a rich jackass. Yes, it was a lot of people to cram into a small two-bedroom apartment, but we had a *kitchen*.

The fundamental difference between renting an apartment and staying at a hotel isn't the kitchen. It's that when you lie around in a hotel room, you feel like you're wasting time. When you lie around in an apartment, you feel like you're at home with nothing you have to do. And since living in Vancouver is my fantasy, how could it get better than that? True, when we got there, Iris looked around the living room and asked, "Do they have books in Canada?" I went off to the bookstore and bought her a Mercer Mayer treasury, six books in one, that provided enough reading for the whole week. For the two-year-old, at least. The book has about 187 pages and at one point I think we read it straight through twice in a row. If Mercer Mayer turns up dead, I can think of four suspects.

With Iris in the family, I've pretty much lost the urge to go out for dinner. Lunch, absolutely. But dinner starts to run into bedtime, and you postpone Iris's bedtime at your own peril. With a kitchen in our apartment, we could have Vancouver and eat it, too. We could shop for ingredients at Oyama Sausage, for example.

Oyama is the most fully stocked sausage maker in North America. If you are a sausage lover, go to Oyama's website (oyamasausage.ca) and prepare to drool over their list of, oh, about two hundred different house-made sausages. You never know which Oyama products will make it through customs, although they've been known to "accidentally" mislabel them for a smoother ride across the border. Once I attempted to bring home goose prosciutto and spicy wild boar salami, and the customs agent confiscated the salami but waved the prosciutto through, saying, "That's just ham." I was pleased to learn that there is a "just ham" provision in the USDA standards.

The last time I stopped at Oyama, it was Christmas Eve. I might as well have gone to FAO Schwarz. The line stretched out into neighboring produce stands. People were picking up their foie gras special orders. I wanted some duck confit for making hash, and some Italian sausage, and three or four spur-of-the-moment dried sausages with names I can no longer recall but with flavors that are permanent residents of my psyche.

Oyama is located on Granville Island, which is Vancouver's equivalent of Pike Place Market. It's not as old as Pike Place, and largely for this reason feels a little contrived, but you can arrive by boat. A tiny little ferry called the Aquabus runs every few minutes to and from downtown. It is the cutest thing you've ever seen.

Granville is also the home of Kids Market, an entire building devoted to kid-related activities, including three toy stores. It's complete overkill, but they *do* have Skee-Ball. Iris is appallingly bad at Skee-Ball but keeps popping in quarters and flinging the balls, undeterred by the fact that she never wins a single ticket. I was all set to show her how it is done, but Aunt Nicole turned out to be a Skee-Ball hustler, and we both stood there slack-jawed watching her play. Iris, I could tell, was thinking, *I thought Dada was good at this game, but I was so wrong.*

I managed to lure Iris into Adventure Zone, a play area she was, at age two and a half, much too young for, but they let her in as long as we went together. Adventure Zone has a corkscrew-shaped tube slide three stories high. Iris cried throughout most of Adventure Zone, but she loved the slide as much as I did. When we emerged, she told Laurie, "I was clinging to Dada like a monkey."

Before our next visit to Vancouver, Iris started talking about how she was ready to go back into the Adventure Zone. I was skeptical, but she ended up flinging herself through every section of it for an hour, and only cried when it was time to go. This is pretty much exactly what happened with me and sushi: I mentally retasted it.

I had mixed feelings about taking Iris to my most favorite restaurant in the world. It was like recommending your favorite book to someone you really like: What if they hate it? How could you not think less of them? But she had to try the scallion pancakes.

My family went up to Vancouver in the summer of 1988, and on my birthday my mom handed me *Northwest Best Places* and told me to pick something for dinner. To her relief, I flipped past famous spots like Le Crocodile and Tojo's and settled on Szechuan Chongqing Restaurant, which had a three-star rating:

> The best Szechuan food in the city comes out of this tacky little shoebox of a building. Mr. Wong rules the kitchen and the 170-item menu. It features the northern version of his homeland's cuisine: rich brown sauces, heavy on the garlic; lots of explosive red peppers; and wheat (not rice) as the principal starch. Our favorite dish on a rainy Saturday afternoon is a big bowl of the #148 Deluxe Tan Tan Noodles (Szechuan penicillin), a noodle soup in a rich peanutty broth accented with red chiles, green onions, and crushed peanuts.

If there is any single meal that sealed my fate as a food writer, this was it. Since our first visit, the restaurant has moved and changed ownership. Its star rating slipped to one and then it disappeared from *Best Places* altogether, which is inexplicable, since the food hasn't changed at all. The Tan Tan Noodles still arrive in a large bowl and are portioned out into individual cups at the table by a waiter who never spills a drop. I still spill many drops of broth on my shirt when the noodles whip around on the way to my mouth.

I wish we could have gotten Iris to Szechuan Chongqing before her aversion to spicy food kicked in, because she stuck her tongue out at the noodles. She loved the scallion pancakes, though.

Even though we were already hopped up on Timbits, we stopped at La Casa Gelato after lunch at Szechuan. La Casa Gelato offers 218 flavors of ice cream at any given time. Really. By the time you read this, however, the number will be out of date, because every time I go, there are more flavors. The first time I went, it wasn't even 100 flavors. In fact, by the time you read this, every other place I've mentioned in Vancouver will have been replaced by an expansionist gelato empire.

La Casa Gelato has chocolate-chili, pear-Gorgonzola, and durian ice cream. Durian is a large, spiky fruit from Southeast Asia. Every year, several people are killed when durians fall from the tree onto their heads. If you laugh at this, you are a bad person. Thousands more are figuratively killed by the smell, which is famously pungent. Durians are banned from hotel lobbies and airplanes across Asia. At La Casa Gelato, they have to keep a lid over the durian ice cream so the odor doesn't infect other flavors. I've tasted it, and it's pretty good. I think I may be immune to the smell, though. "You've got your onion in my mango" would be a fair assessment of durian.

I can wholeheartedly recommend the black sesame and pandanus leaf flavors. Pandanus leaf is another Southeast Asian ingredient, a long, thin leaf used to wrap foods for steaming or as an aromatic in soups and curries. It has a vanilla-like flavor and imparts an inviting green tinge to the ice cream, not unlike the color of Baskin-Robbins' Daiquiri Ice.

Iris's pick from the 218 ice cream flavors: strawberry.

Vancouver has a beach. Several, actually, including a clothing-optional one. But English Bay beach is right downtown, one block from a cupcake shop. You might not think going to the beach in

Canada in December would be fun, but Vancouver has a lot of sunny days, and Iris takes to the beach like a starfish.

I grew up going to the ultimate beach, on the Oregon coast. I didn't realize it was one of the world's greatest beaches at the time; it was just the beach we'd go to on family vacations — Seaside or Cannon Beach, Lincoln City or Manzanita.

The Oregon coast is like California minus the crowds and 40 degrees of water temperature, which could, admittedly, explain the lack of crowds. The entire Oregon coast is open to the public. Literally, all of it. You could walk south from Astoria and end up a few days later at the California border, dehydrated and barnacle-encrusted but without having trespassed on anyone's property.

The summer of Iris's third year, we rented a house with a bunch of friends in Lincoln City. This is where Iris invented the game Stewpot.

Stewpot is pretty simple. You dig a big hole in the sand and fill it with water. This is the stew pot. "Now we put in the ingredients," explained Iris. She did not restrict herself to traditional stew ingredients. I believe there were blueberries. I sculpted a lobster out of sand and Iris tossed it in. Later I made another sand lobster and Iris stepped on it.

"Hey!" I said. "Somebody stepped on my sand lobster. Who was it?"

"It wasn't me," said Iris.

"Then who made this little footprint?"

"Okay, it was me. I was just making jokes."

Inspired by Stewpot, I plotted a Thai green curry with assorted seafood for dinner (hold the blueberries). We'd stopped at the Portland farmers' market on the way to the beach, and there was a stand run by a woman who made her own curry pastes. On trips to Thailand, I've admired the mounds of freshly ground curry pastes at market stands, and now here was such a purveyor in Oregon. Admittedly, the pastes were in jars rather than mounds, and they cost a wee bit more than in Thailand, but I was delighted.

I went to the Safeway in Lincoln City with visions of clams, mussels, shrimp, and maybe a few dozen oysters to start us off. I put in a request with the guy at the fish counter, who, unaccountably, had a cockney accent. "We don't have any mussels," he said.

"How about those clams?" I asked. "What's the tag date on those?"

He looked at the tag. "Good lord, you don't want these," he replied, tossing them in the garbage. The only edible shellfish on the premises was frozen shrimp. At the beach. I come from America and intend to stay, but I don't always understand it. The shrimp curry was great, though. Iris loved it because there was rice, and she even consented to some sauce.

Frozen shrimp isn't a bad thing. Nearly all shrimp sold in the United States is frozen at sea, so if you see "fresh" shrimp at a fish counter, it's almost always defrosted — and who knows how long it's been sitting there? Individually quick frozen (IQF) shrimp in a bag is a better choice, especially since you can thaw them under running water in ten minutes.

The best-tasting shrimp, I find, are white or pink shrimp from the Gulf of Mexico, with shells on, without preservatives. (Look for "Ingredients: shrimp, salt" on the bag.) Every once in a while I see fresh shrimp in Seattle, flown in from the Gulf, and I always buy them immediately. Like I said, frozen aren't bad, but fresh shrimp are something really special: Laurie doesn't like shrimp, but she makes an exception for fresh shrimp. When you cook shrimp, please do me a favor and peel the whole thing — don't leave the flared tail piece of shell on. I know it looks nice, but how are you supposed to eat it?

To those of you who live in shrimp country: I am envious. Meanwhile, back in frozen shrimp country: it turns out there is a fish market in Lincoln City — I just couldn't find it. So I'm not knocking the town. Just my shopping skills. And Safeway.

THAI SHRIMP CURRY

! QUICK & EASY

"🔔" 20 minutes

LITTLE FINGERS: Iris isn't into peeling shrimp, but I could see some kids really going for it.

The American brands of curry paste, such as Thai Kitchen, are less spicy but also less flavorful than the Thai brands such as Mae Ploy. If you'd like to add vegetables to this curry, peas, onions, red bell peppers, and green beans are all good choices. Frozen vegetables work very well in curry; add them and heat them through before adding the shrimp. My favorite brands of coconut milk are Chaokoh and Mae Ploy.

See the chapter for shrimp-buying tips. I never bother deveining shrimp; it's extra work and I can't tell the difference.

Serves 4 with rice

- 1 14-ounce can coconut milk
- 2 tablespoons green curry paste
- 1 tablespoon palm sugar (or brown sugar)
- 1 tablespoon fish sauce
- 1 pound large shrimp (21–25 or 26–30), peeled
   fresh basil leaves to taste
- 1 tablespoon fresh lime juice

1. If you think of it, refrigerate the can of coconut milk overnight. This helps it separate into thin and thick milk. Open the can and pour off the watery thin coconut milk into a bowl. Add the thick, chunky milk to a saucepan and bring to a boil over medium-high heat. (If your coconut milk doesn't want to separate, don't worry about it; just pour half into the saucepan and reserve half.)

2. Add the curry paste and stir to dissolve. Cook until the coconut milk is thick and fragrant and hisses when you stir, about 3 minutes. (The coconut milk may begin to separate into oil and solids; this is not a problem.) Add the palm sugar, fish sauce, and reserved thin coconut milk and bring to a boil, stirring frequently until sugar is dissolved.

3. Add the shrimp and cook, stirring frequently, until the shrimp is just opaque throughout, 1½ to 3 minutes. (Test by removing a shrimp and cutting it in half.) Off heat, stir in basil leaves and lime juice and serve with rice.

21

The Only Snack Dad in Preschool

FOR A BABY SHOWER present, we got three-year subscriptions to *Parenting, Child, Parents,* and *Working Mother.* All of these magazines are aimed purely at women, but I read them anyway — even *Working Mother,* which has the best recipes, presumably because the affluent businesswomen who read it are not going to come home from a power lunch at Le Cirque to make Velveeta casseroles. (Also, *Working Mother* has photos of hot working moms. Maybe I should renew.) I got plenty of makeup tips and learned how to handle it when my husband takes care of the baby and does everything wrong because he is an idiot. Plus, how to rekindle the fires of romance after baby comes along!

Stories aimed at stay-at-home dads are even worse. "Don't worry — you can be a full-time caregiver AND a heterosexual!" seems to be the message, and they always have to mention *Mr. Mom,* a movie that is now, by my calculation, 103 years old.

I confess that I don't spend much time worrying, or even thinking, about these things, especially now that our magazine subscriptions have blissfully lapsed. Then Iris started preschool, and parents had to sign up to bring three weeks of snack. I looked over the signup sheet and I couldn't help noticing that I was the only man on the roster.

It was at this point that Laurie taught me the term "snack mom," which generally refers to the mom who brings snacks for sports practice, but can apply to preschool as well. (It does not mean "mom I would like to snack on," not that this was the first thing that came to mind or anything.)

I was now Snack Dad, Purveyor of Nourishment. I wanted to hit this one out of the park and steal home. (Misuse of baseball metaphors may be a sign of threatened manhood.) I would be responsible for nine snacks in a row — Monday, Wednesday, and Friday for three weeks.

Monday, October 1. My debut is inauspicious. I was planning banana muffins, but the bananas aren't ripe enough yet, so I get some Cox's Orange Pippin apples from the farmers' market. These are, apparently, the most popular apple in England, and when I get to the apple stand there is a lineup of English people waiting to buy them. I have no idea where they've come from; it's not like my neighborhood has a charming English quarter.

Iris explains to us that there's an empty napkin in the middle of the table at snacktime where kids can put anything they don't want. "Do you ever put things on the napkin?" asks Laurie.

"*Many* things," Iris replies. "Like apples with skin."

Point taken. I spend the morning peeling apples, slicing them, and dipping them in acidulated water so they won't brown. I slice Tillamook sharp Cheddar cheese and send a box each of Triscuits and Wheat Thins. Nothing flashy, but it's a hit. Iris says the other kids ate all the cheese and one even — get this — made a sandwich with cheese and crackers.

Wednesday, October 3. I make the banana muffins. It's usually Iris's job to brutalize the bananas with a potato masher, but I do it before she wakes up. To make it up to her, I let her eat a muffin for breakfast. She puts on an analytical face. "I think these will be good," she says.

After school, I ask Iris how the kids liked the muffins. "They loved them!" she says. "*Nobody* put them on the Empty Napkin."

All of my ideas now revolve around muffins. Gingerbread! Corn! Blueberry! Laurie says I can't bring muffins twice in a row. I do not want to be typecast as Muffin Guy. "Try this," said Laurie, handing me *Martha Stewart's Hors d'Oeuvres Handbook.* Of course! *Hors d'oeuvre* is just a snooty word for snack. I am set. I will make little empanadas on Friday. First I have to email the school to ask if the snack is allowed to contain meat.

Thursday, October 4. The admissions director replies so quickly it's like she's waiting for my question. "Can I join snack when you're on duty?" she writes. "Empanadas sound terrific, and no, they do not need to be vegetarian."

I whiz up flour, butter, and lard in the food processor to make the empanada dough. I make one beef filling from Martha and one improvised mushroom filling with diced button mushrooms, cumin, onion, parsley, and sherry vinegar. While the empanadas bake, I scour the book for more snack ideas.

Despite its five hundred pages, the hors d'oeuvre book is not the ultimate snack savior. There are not a lot of small foods that are sturdy enough to survive the trip to school and hardy enough to go the two hours before snack without getting yucky. This is especially true if you disqualify things wrapped in phyllo. I hate working with phyllo.

The empanadas are great. How many mini-empanadas can one kid eat? I decide to make thirty. I'll have to wake up at five-thirty tomorrow. It's a good thing I don't have a job.

Friday, October 5. I awake before dawn to spend some quality time, just me and my empanadas. I forget that Laurie gets up every

day at five-thirty to get ready for school; she's not interested in com-
miserating with a part-time baker, so I try to stay out of her way.
It takes me until seven-thirty to make thirty-two mini-empanadas.
When Iris wakes up, I tell her about my morning activities. "I want
three beef," she says.

Only three empanadas are left after snacktime. I am Lord of the
Snack. There's plenty of beef filling and empanada dough left in the
fridge, so I ask Iris after school if she'd mind having more empanadas for dinner. "I want three beef," she says.

I wonder if the future snack moms are hearing about me from
their kids. Are they seething with an explosive combination of re-
sentment and sexual arousal? I assume so.

I ask Iris what she thinks I should make for snack next week. She
suggests pumpkin muffins and dumplings. I can handle that.

Sunday, October 7. Over breakfast, Laurie suggests that I could go
to Iris's school and make dumplings.

"You should stay away," says Iris. She doesn't want me horning
in on her territory — worlds colliding and all that. Every day I ask
her what she did at school and she says, "I forget." She is a thirteen-
year-old in a three-year-old's body. But later she changes her mind
and asks me to come to school, probably because I make such good
dumplings.

The dumplings we're talking about are Chinese potstickers. We
eat frozen ones from Safeway for lunch at least once a week, but obviously I'm not going to bring frozen dumplings to school. I'll be
mixing up pork and bok choy, ginger and scallions, and stuffing it
into dozens of round dumpling skins.

I email the school director to ask about making dumplings at
school. I think about proposing it as a hands-on activity, but the
health department probably would have a few things to say about
a dozen preschoolers handling raw pork. I do promise to talk a little bit about potstickers. If I were evil, I would put together a forty-
five-minute PowerPoint presentation about the history of the pan-

fried dumpling and tell the kids they have to sit through it quietly if they want snack. This would prepare them for college.

How many dumplings can these kids eat, anyway? I can eat a lot of dumplings. I'm sort of hoping the director will tell me to stay away.

Monday, October 8. Muffins are so easy, it feels like cheating. Today it's pumpkin. Muffins are even easier than cupcakes, because you don't have to frost them. Assuming muffins are the next big thing, I could open an organic muffin shop, charge three bucks for fifteen cents' worth of ingredients, and get rich. This is, I assume, exactly how people feel a few months before they declare bankruptcy.

Tuesday, October 9. Still no reply on the dumpling front. Perhaps they are holding an emergency board meeting.

Wednesday, October 10. I make corn pancakes (see page 77) and leave out the pumpkin butter, because a dozen kids spreading pumpkin butter would presumably result in a sticky mass of children having to be pried apart with the jaws of life. I also send a bag of baby carrots. Iris reports that the kids ate all the pancakes, which makes me happy but also makes me wonder whether I made enough food. Poor little waifs.

Thursday, October 11. It's time to settle this dumpling issue. I call the school director. She never got my email. Maybe the word *dumpling* makes spam filters all tingly. We are set for Operation Dumpling on Monday at 1100 hours.

Friday, October 12. In celebration, I slack off and send sharp Cheddar, applesauce, and crackers.

Iris and I discuss the final week of snacks. She leafs through *Martha Stewart's Hors d'Oeuvres Handbook* and suddenly her face lights up. "I want to make those!" she says, indicating pretzel bites sprinkled with various toppings. "We should put on lots and lots of salt." I look at the recipe and start calculating how many tiny pretzel bites the kids would eat.

"Could we make big pretzels instead?" I ask. "You could still sprinkle the salt."

"Sure."

"Should we make some with fennel seeds, too, like in the picture?"

"Hmm . . . no." We also decide on gingerbread muffins. My muffin shop is in full effect.

Sunday, October 14. In the morning, we go out to dim sum with my parents to celebrate my dad's retirement. It's also a dumpling reconnaissance mission. I'm delighted to get some of those pan-fried shrimp buns with sesame seeds and chives. I'm also delighted not to see any potstickers go by, because that way Iris can't compare them favorably to mine. Iris's favorite item is a sesame ball with the red bean paste scraped out of the center. I'd scoff at this, but I don't like red bean paste, either.

We stop at Uwajimaya afterward for dumpling ingredients and a box of Chocolate Crush Pocky. I mix up my usual pork and bok choy filling, from Eileen Yin-Fei Lo's *Dim Sum Dumpling Book,* and an improvised vegetarian filling consisting of mushroom, carrot, lotus root, ginger, scallions, sesame oil, and soy sauce. After dinner, I fry some test dumplings. (I cautioned Laurie and Iris to save room for a dumpling, then realized this was stupid — who doesn't have room for a dumpling?)

The dumplings are perfect. Lotus root is a great secret ingredient. It's available in every Asian grocery, cheap, and has a crunchy texture that stays crunchy even when cooked. I got the idea to put it in a dumpling after reading about it in, um, the ingredient list on the back of the Safeway frozen dumpling bag.

Monday, October 15. Waking up early to fold, wrap, or fry something is becoming routine. Folding potstickers is pretty easy. As you get the hang of it, you can fit more and more filling into each dumpling without leakage.

I arrive at school to find my electric frying pan set up on a table with a circle of tiny chairs around it. I was not expecting Kitchen Stadium. I put on my apron and warm the pan up while the children file in. Iris looks very grown up. "You brought the new spatula!" she says excitedly. Yes, I brought the new plastic spatula.

I sort of had the idea that because I think of myself as an overgrown kid, the class would immediately pick up on this and welcome me as one of their own. Not really. "Sometimes I help my mommy make breakfast," says one boy while the dumplings sizzle.

"That smells good!" says Georgia, a girl who chases Iris around after school. I mention that there are pork dumplings and vegetable dumplings. Why do I keep thinking four-year-olds will want a vegetarian option? Nobody wants the vegetable dumplings, lotus root or no lotus root. Most of them eat the pork dumplings, but I confused the issue by putting bok choy in the pork dumplings. I see a few dumplings go onto the Empty Napkin. One kid eats all around the crunchy edge of the dumpling and leaves the middle.

Would the school think I was crazy if I asked for a do-over? If you happen to be making dumplings for a bunch of kids, use napa cabbage rather than bok choy (it's paler, so you can't see it through the wrapper), and do not make vegetable dumplings unless it's some kind of hippie-oriented facility. Dumplings with just pork and no vegetables are too dense and not as tasty. I tell Iris about my clever plan to fool the hypothetical kids with pale cabbage instead of bok choy. "But I love bok choy," she says. "You should make some with cabbage and some with bok choy for me." Yeah, that's going to happen.

Wednesday, October 17. Gingerbread muffins and apple slices. I'd better get this muffin shop open soon.

Thursday, October 18. Time for the homemade pretzels. I mix the dough and Iris and I make a test pretzel. She sprinkles the salt; I boil and bake the pretzel. Jesus Christ, these are good. When Laurie gets home from work, I present her with a hot soft pretzel. Does your spouse do this?

Friday, October 19. I wake up at six-fifteen to roll out pretzels. It is relaxing, but not as relaxing as being asleep. While the pretzels bake, I stir some of our homemade raspberry freezer jam from last summer into a tub of organic whole-milk plain yogurt. This is a thousand times better than pre-made fruit-flavored yogurt. Low-fat yogurt and I are through.

The pretzels are a huge success, although Iris's teacher tells me that some of the kids think they are cinnamon doughnuts.

Monday, October 22. It's not my turn to make snack anymore. What am I supposed to do all morning?

After school, I pepper Iris with snack questions. "We had crackers. And soft cheese with a red stick, and bananas," she says. "I didn't put anything on the Empty Napkin. That was some good cheese." So, Iris won't eat Cheddar, Parmigiano-Reggiano, or Cashel Blue, but she's all over Handi-Snacks-Kraft Crackers 'n Cheez. Is there such a thing as culinary preschool?

Want to take a peek inside Iris's Hello Kitty lunch box? I think that can be arranged, but don't get too excited.

Breakfast, they say, is the most conservative meal of the day, when people eat the same thing daily for years. They're wrong: it's school lunch. I vary the contents of Iris's lunch box a bit, but I do so more for my own self-image than for her nutrition or satisfaction. And in my experience, school lunch — not breakfast — is the meal most likely to be skipped.

Before Iris started school, when she was going to the babysitter, she carried the same sack lunch that every other kid in America did until recently: peanut butter and jelly. Iris's preschool, however, is nut-free. Occasionally I've made her a butter and jelly sandwich, which is exactly what it sounds like but tastes better than it sounds, especially if you use whole-grain bread and Iris's favorite jelly.

There's a jam seller at our farmers' market, and last summer we let Iris go crazy with the free samples and told her to pick a jar to take home. The result was the opposite of our experience at La Casa Gelato: this time, after tasting approximately twenty-three jams, Iris selected lavender jelly. Let me tell you, we ate through that jar like we were looking for the prize at the bottom. The jelly was a beautiful pale pink and hit the tongue like rosemary but gave way to a more floral finish. We ate it on English muffins and waffles, on French toast and in sandwiches.

Now that we've finished off the lavender, I'm back to sending boring lunches that at least stand a fifty-fifty chance of being eaten: strips of ham, frozen spinach-ricotta ravioli, potstickers, Triscuits, grapes, apple slices, cookies. Leftovers, no matter how eagerly Iris devoured them the night before, are usually a bad bet, even though her teachers are happy to microwave.

Recently I found a magical ingredient that makes lunch so much easier: sunflower seed butter. For some reason, sunflower seeds don't provoke deadly allergies the way peanuts do, so they're legal at Iris's school. Sunflower seed butter is as smooth and calorie-dense as peanut butter and, most important, tastes great. As Iris put it, "Sunflower butter is suh-weet!" Trader Joe's sells it, or you can order it from sunbutter.com. I'm not a shill: I would personally slather this stuff on celery or sneak a midnight mouthful off the knife. It's suh-weet.

The temptation, of course, is to forget the quest for peanut analogues and just pack Iris's lunch with her classmates' parents in mind. *Mommy, guess what Iris brought today? A delicious vegetable dish! You should ask her dad for the recipe.* I need to contrive a way to visit Iris's school around lunchtime — maybe to pick her up early for an unspecified appointment — and see what the other kids are bringing, both to cadge ideas and to gloat unjustifiably over their Go-Gurt.

So far I've resisted those urges, but I did make one rookie mistake. One day, while Iris was helping me make grilled cheese sandwiches, I caught her sneaking bits of grated Cheddar. That's right, *Iris was eating nonmelted cheese.* "I could put some cheese in your lunch . . ." I said. "Only cheese strips," said Iris.

Laurie suggested I could slice the cheese and cut it into flower shapes with a fluted biscuit cutter. Iris agreed. So I sent a bunch of cheese flowers in her lunch and of course they all came back uneaten.

"It was too cheesy," Iris reported.

POTSTICKERS

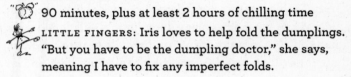 90 minutes, plus at least 2 hours of chilling time

LITTLE FINGERS: Iris loves to help fold the dumplings. "But you have to be the dumpling doctor," she says, meaning I have to fix any imperfect folds.

If your supermarket only carries lean ground pork, try an Asian grocery or bring a boneless pork shoulder roast up to the butcher counter and ask them to grind it. I like to serve these with a simple dipping sauce of soy sauce combined with Frank's RedHot sauce. They freeze very well and can be cooked directly from frozen.

Makes about 44 dumplings

- 10 ounces napa cabbage, shredded
- 12 ounces ground pork (not too lean)
- 3 scallions, white parts only, thinly sliced
- 2 teaspoons minced ginger
- 1 tablespoon oyster sauce
- 2 teaspoons sesame oil
- 1 teaspoon soy sauce

1 teaspoon salt
¼ cup minced lotus root (optional)
1 egg
1 package gyoza wrappers, preferably Twin Dragon brand
   peanut or canola oil

1. Bring a pot of salted water to a boil and add the cabbage. Return to a boil and boil one minute. Strain in a colander and run under cold water until cool. Squeeze the cabbage out in a towel and place in a mixing bowl.

2. To the bowl with the cabbage, add the pork, scallions, ginger, oyster sauce, sesame oil, soy sauce, salt, lotus root, and egg. Stir well to combine. (Hands are good here.) Refrigerate at least 2 hours and up to 24 hours.

3. Place 1 tablespoon of filling in each gyoza skin, wet the edge with water, and fold over, pressing firmly to seal.

4. Heat 2 tablespoons oil in a large nonstick skillet over medium-high. When hot, add as many dumplings as will fit and cook 1 minute. Add ½ cup water, cover, and reduce heat to medium. Steam 6 minutes. Remove cover, raise heat to medium-high, and let any remaining water evaporate. Continue cooking until the dumplings are dark brown on the bottom. Remove to a paper towel–lined plate and repeat with remaining dumplings.

epilogue

End of the Monkey Tale

IRIS IS FOUR YEARS old now. Please don't ask us when we're having another. We're not.

Because of global warming.

Just kidding. Actually it's because having another child might affect our lifestyle. (Saying something this self-absorbed is, I realize, just *asking* for a reproductive mishap.)

Having a kid changed my life, of course, but it's not like we bought a house and started ranting about how the world was so much better when we were kids. The world is a lot better now (Thai eggplants at the supermarket? excellent), and we still live in a seven-hundred-square-foot apartment. Laurie and I enjoy living in a small space — it's very easy to clean — and Iris doesn't mind. She did once tell me we should move to a big house so she can have her own gigantic inflatable Grim Reaper. But the reaper is always grimmer on the other side: the other day Iris had a friend over, and the friend emerged from our elevator saying, "I wish we could live in a building. We only have a house."

It bothers me when people say, "Children need a yard," because what they're really saying is that their own child enjoys having a yard and therefore this must be the best thing for all children. This overgeneralizing of personal experience is so easy to fall into, and I've tried to avoid it in this book. (If you're going to accuse me of bad parenting, please stick to an easy target like letting Iris eat too many doughnuts.)

Every child is a roll of the dice, and if we had another, I'd be worried about rolling one who *did* need a yard. I'd worry about making Iris share her room — not because I think there's anything unfair about making a child share a room (Laurie grew up sharing a room with two sisters) but because the fallout might drive *me* nuts. And most important, I'd worry about having a child who didn't like to eat *any* of the same things I do.

My sister-in-law sent me a photocopied chapter from the book *The Tightwad Gazette II* by Amy Dacyczyn. Food waste drives Dacyczyn crazy, so she has instituted a classic "clean plate club" rule: her kids will eat everything on their plate without complaining, or they will be punished. To me this sounded grim, cruel, and likely to produce a spate of *Mommy Dearest*–style memoirs down the road.

After the foam around my mouth subsided, I reconsidered, recalling that when Iris was about nine months old and still not sleeping through the night, we instituted a version of the Ferber method for sleep training. Instead of Laurie going in to nurse Iris every time she cried, I would go in with a bottle. That was bad enough, since Iris didn't want a bottle, but to make matters worse, I would reduce the amount of formula in the bottle each night, until it was empty. After feeding Iris, I would plunk her back in the crib and immediately walk out. It was a harsh regime, and it worked. I can't say Iris has never had a bad night's sleep since then, but she sleeps very well, and that was the turning point.

In hindsight, I can see that there is not much difference between Dacyczyn's clean plate club and my skulking into Iris's room with an empty bottle. You could argue that we were even worse, because you can't explain the rules of the game to a nine-month-old the way Dacyczyn lays down the law to her older kids. I can scoff at her tough-mom act now, but that's because I lucked out: Iris happens to respond well to the methods that I feel comfortable with. That could just as easily have been me, saying, "You are going to eat that lobster, young lady, and you are going to like it." (Not that the author of the The Tightwad Gazette would ever serve lobster.)

If you've read this far, you're probably thinking that this book was supposed to be about the challenges of feeding a young child and it didn't sound all that challenging. Guilty as charged. Iris sometimes has to be told not to say "blecch" at the table, but I know there are genuine picky eaters out there — kids who would *never* allow bok choy in their dumplings, if they even eat dumplings — and she's not one of them. Right now, her pickiness seems to be in decline. I know this is temporary, but this morning we were reading a Japanese cookbook together and Iris pointed out all kinds of dishes she wanted to try. True, none of them were in the vegetable chapter, but some at least *contained* vegetables. (Her pick for this week is pork *tonkatsu* cubes served on toothpicks, with multiple dipping sauces. This was also her pick last week.)

The other night we were having chicken hash with eggs for dinner. Laurie and I had fried eggs; Iris had scrambled. (I would never make Iris a whole separate dinner, but taking egg orders lets me pretend I'm working at a diner.) Amazingly enough, Iris asked for the pepper grinder, ground some pepper onto her eggs, and ate them all. Laurie and I were both looking on, trying not to say anything, knowing that a single word would break the spell. Two days later, Iris complained that her burger patty was too spicy, and when I admitted I'd put pepper in the meat, she said, "You should NEVER do that again."

What happens at the dinner table isn't something that I, as the cook, get to decide on. It's a compromise hammered out between me, Laurie, and Iris. And even if you do everything I did, you will not end up with Iris, because there's only one of her and you can't have her. That's what I've learned in the past four years.

That, and to guard my lobster claw closely.

* * *

"I'm writing a book about you," I said to Iris. "It's about what you like to eat, and it's called *Hungry Monkey*."

"It should be called *Hungry Mermaid*."

"You can tell my editor that."

"Will the book have jokes?"

"Yes."

"Will it have jokes on every page?"

"I wish."

"It should have this joke. Why did the banana drive the car?"

"I don't know."

"To see Granny and Grandpa Banana. Put that in your book."

recommended reading

For Kids

Iris's mother is a librarian. Her father is a writer. Iris likes books. Soon, no doubt, she'll hit an age where she claims to hate reading, just to torment us, but she's been in love with the printed page for about as long as she's been around.

I remember well the first three books Iris fell in love with. The first was *Owl Babies,* by Martin Waddell, a board book about three baby owls waiting for their mother to come home.

The second was *Jamie's Dinners* by Jamie Oliver, also known as the Naked Chef (I don't have to tell you he's not actually naked, right?). Near the beginning of the book is a two-page photo of Oliver and his posse. "Guy-guy!" said Iris, who was about ten months old and just learning to talk. There was also a page with pictures of kids slurping noodles. "Baby!" Iris cried, applauding. Okay, actually she couldn't say "baby" yet; it came out "daydee." She also learned about corn and burgers from this book.

Letting an Englishman teach your daughter about American food is probably bad parenting in some way, but it's nothing compared to what she learned from Hugh Fearnley-Whittingstall.

Like Oliver, Hugh Fearnley-Whittingstall is a shaggy English guy. He's the star of a BBC series, *Escape to River Cottage,* in which he leaves London for the countryside and buys a small farm. In UK parlance this makes him a "smallholder." It's hard to imagine an American man — actually, any man — using this term.

Iris became enamored of Fearnley-Whittingstall's book *The River Cottage Meat Book,* which was supposed to be *my* birthday present. The cover shows Hugh Fearnley-Whittingstall absconding with a giant rib roast. Inside there are photos of the author's livestock. Iris particularly liked the sheep. "Baa! Baa! Meat!" she'd yell, pointing to the bookshelf. There is also a pictorial of the slaughter of one of Fearnley-Whittingstall's cows. I don't think I showed it to her, but she did enjoy the cuts-of-meat diagrams, especially after I started sprinkling the phrase "chump chops," another British phrase I learned from this book, liberally into conversation.

For the moment, Iris seems to be comfortable with the idea of eating animals. At some point, when she inevitably announces that she has given up meat, I will wave *The River Cottage Meat Book* in front of her and say, "See? This used to be your favorite book." Obviously I will win *that* argument.

After this flirtation with adult books, Iris quickly settled into a picture book routine. Perhaps unsurprisingly, many of her favorites are about food.

First Book of Sushi is in the World Snacks series by Amy Wilson Sanger. It's a board book for age zero and up, but we still read it often, especially at bedtime and especially on days when we've gone out for sushi. The series has clever collage art: the flying fish roe, for example, is made from little beads. *First Book of Sushi* includes the immortal line "Miso in my sippy cup / Tofu in my bowl."

At one point Iris realized, hey, she has a sippy cup. Could I put some miso soup in it? I complied. She took one sip and said, "Miso is too salty." But she still likes the book. And sushi, most of the time.

Other books in the World Snacks series include *Yum Yum Dim Sum, A Little Bit of Soul Food, ¡Hola! Jalapeño,* and *Let's Nosh.* My father, a liberal Jew like everyone else in my family, read the latter to Iris ("Let's nosh on kasha knish!") and said it sounded like Zionist propaganda. I didn't show him *The Matzah That Papa Brought Home* by Fran Manushkin.

The quintessential kid's book about food is *Bread and Jam for Frances* by Russell Hoban. It features one of the best eating scenes in Western literature, the part where Frances's friend Albert eats his lunch with evident satisfaction. Afterward:

> He shut his lunch box, put it back inside his desk, and sighed.
> "I like to have a good lunch," said Albert.

Iris has never asked, like Frances, why French-cut stringless beans are called string beans, but she once tried to convince me that a stomachache is a kind of cake.

Kevin Henkes is best known for his books *Lilly's Purple Plastic Purse* and *Kitten's First Full Moon*. But he also has a series of board books featuring some of his picture book mice and their encounters with sweets. In *Julius's Candy Corn*, Julius the mouse is impatient for the Halloween party to start, so he eats all the candy corn off the top of the cupcakes before his friends arrive. My favorite thing about this book is not actually in the book; it's the one-star Amazon review that went like this:

> Aside from "counting" the candy corn, Julius eats all the candy corn. This is later justified by inferring, "At least he didn't eat the cupcakes." There is no retribution for his eating the candy corn. None of his friends are disappointed that they do not get a candy corn on their cupcake. His mother does not scold him for his malfeasance. So you can't really call it a morality tale.
>
> Education and morality are pretty much the cornerstone of any good children's book. Therefore my conclusion is that there is no purpose to this book.

I assume, because of the word "malfeasance," that this is a joke, which is kind of disappointing, because it would be even funnier if it were serious.

Another favorite of the Henkes books is *Wemberly's Ice-Cream Star*. On a hot day, Wemberly, who is a bit neurotic, gets a star-shaped ice cream bar. But it's drippy and there's none for her stuffed mouse, so Wemberly lets it melt and serves it as soup in two bowls. When I was a kid, my favorite thing to do with ice cream was smash it with the back of my spoon until it melted, so I totally understand the appeal of ice cream star soup.

After perhaps the two hundredth time we read this book, Iris said, "We could make an ice cream star. Could we?" We could. It was pretty easy. I bought a couple of pints of ice cream and cut them into thin slabs, container and all, with a bread knife. Then we cut out stars with a cookie cutter, stuck craft sticks into them, and put them back in the freezer on a cookie sheet. It was a real Martha moment.

We read *The Very Hungry Caterpillar*, Eric Carle's classic tale of an insect punished for his gluttony (salami *and* sausage?) by being imprisoned in a cocoon. The Seattle science museum has a butterfly house where butterflies land on you as you walk around a fake jungle environment. There are plates of food set out for them, mostly oranges and bananas, and the butterflies scrape up bites of fruit with their enormous proboscises. I was disappointed that this exhibit teaches kids that butterflies in the wild eat from some kind of salad bar, because education and morality are pretty much the cornerstone of any good science exhibit.

One of my family's favorite things to eat is sour cherries, so I was delighted to find that there is a whole children's book about them: *Pie in the Sky* by Lois Ehlert. "This tree was here when we moved in," it begins. "Dad says it's a pie tree." And it *is* a pie tree, a Montmorency cherry tree. When I turn to the page where birds are eating the cherries, Iris is always the first to yell, "It's a cherry feast!"

Also in the pests-stripping-a-fruit-tree genre, we've been reading a pop-up book called *The Fuzzy Peach* since Iris was tiny. A peach falls from a tree and is gnawed on by various creatures (ladybug, bird, worm, and squirrel) until nothing remains but the pit, which grows into a new tree festooned with peaches, all of which are being eaten by the descendants of the original animals. Hmm, when I put it that way it sounds kind of depressing.

The notable feature of *The Fuzzy Peach* is that it is the most durable pop-up book of all time. Several of Iris's books bear actual teeth marks from a brief book-biting stage, and many others have missing or taped pages from a less brief book-tearing stage. Not only does *The Fuzzy Peach* have all its pages intact, but the pop-up part still works. I'd like to see one of those Robert Sabuda books survive a baby encounter.

The Fuzzy Peach is actually part of an out-of-print series with titles like *The Green Leaf* and *The Big Cheese*. Naturally we had to order *The Big Cheese*. I was hoping it would be about a cheese shop that keeps expanding to meet customer demand, but it's actually about a mouse that finds a giant piece of cheese and devours it, becoming as large as the original cheese in the process. It was pretty much like the *Seinfeld* episode in which George Costanza brags that he has been eating a block of cheese the size of a car battery.

Children's books about Asian food rock. My obsession with books in this genre began when Iris and I were at Seattle's central library one day and I had to abandon her when I spotted what appeared to be a children's book about *natto*. It turned out it was a children's book about natto. In Japanese.

Natto is a fermented soybean product, but it is not a family-friendly one like tofu or soy sauce. It consists of whole soybeans aged in such a way that, well, there's no polite way to say this. It looks like beans mixed with snot, and it smells like ass. There's an *Iron Chef* episode (the Japanese version, obviously) in which natto is the secret ingredient, and it is absolutely the most TV-MA thing I've ever seen on television: gooey strands of soy mucus stretch all over the place, as if everybody is being attacked by a swamp monster.

In the book, a young boy asks his grandfather how to make natto, and his grandfather shows him, in clinical detail, beginning with the soybean harvest. I am going to warn Iris never to ask my dad about network engineering.

I mentioned the natto book to a Japanophile colleague of mine, Rob Ketcherside, and he was unfazed. "I eat natto for breakfast every day," he said. This makes sense. If you start your day with natto, the rest of the day will be cake in comparison. Rob moved to Tokyo. He never quite fit in here.

I was even more excited on another visit to the central library when I spotted a children's book (in English, this time) about bibimbap, the Korean rice dish from chapter 11. The book, *Bee-bim-bop!* by Linda Sue Park, is about a young girl who helps her mother make dinner. Iris doesn't find this storyline entirely convincing: once I was going out for the night and told her, "Mama's going to make dinner tonight," and Iris replied, "Can she *do* that?" But she loves the rhymes and seeing the girl help, and she loves bibimbap.

Big Jimmy's Kum Kau Chinese Take Out by Ted Lewin is also about a kid who helps out, this time taking orders at a Chinese restaurant in Brooklyn. What I like about *Kum Kau* is its celebration of Chinese American food. The customers order General Tso's shrimp and egg foo young, and I have to get past my "authentic Chinese" snobbery and admit it: those things are good. Plus, there's a surprise ending involving pizza, and the artwork is gorgeous. After reading this book several times in one day when Iris was one, I said to Laurie, "What should we have for dinner?" and this little voice said, "Boo-deligh," which we eventually translated as "Buddha's Delight."

Our favorite food-related children's book series? That's easy: *Irving and Muktuk: Two Bad Bears.*

Irving and Muktuk are two polar bears who sprang from the fertile imagination of Daniel Pinkwater. They will do anything to get their hands on blueberry muffins. Iris's favorite part is when the bears try to break into the muffin warehouse by disguising themselves as giant blueberry muffins; they're caught only when Muktuk drools.

After the first time we read *Irving and Muktuk,* I put Iris down for her nap. "Who loves Iris?" I asked.

"Dada, and Mama, and Grandma, and Pops. And Muktuk."

Later we read *Bad Bears in the Big City,* where our heroes take up residence in Bayonne, New Jersey. They do all the things you would do in Bayonne, New Jersey, like walk around and break into a muffin factory. Then, exhausted, they take refuge in a supermarket. "We became warm and tired," Irving and Muktuk say. "We are lying on frozen peas."

Iris immediately threw herself onto the living room floor. "Iris is lying on frozen peas!"

"Oh, good," I said. "Dada is lying on frozen corn kernels."

"I've got to get out of this kernel place!" she replied.

But nearly every Pinkwater book has a funny food scene. In *Guys from Space,* a kid takes a ride into space with some friendly guys, and they all learn about root beer floats. In *Author's Day,* a familiar author (Bramwell Wink-Porter) visits an elementary school and runs the kindergarten-to-sixth-grade gauntlet, forced to eat a pancake with a piece of crayon in it and a bologna sandwich with extra mayo, on the grounds that this is the favorite meal of the Fuzzy Bunny in a book that Bramwell Wink-Porter did not write.

I'm looking forward to reading to Iris from my favorite Pinkwater book, *The Snarkout Boys and the Avocado of Death,* in which the Snarkout Boys go to a beatnik speakeasy called Beanbender's Beer Garden. Although, now that I think about it, the Snarkout Boys, who are underage, are served beer at Beanbender's. As you know, education and morality . . . sorry, I'll stop now.

And a Few for Grownups

Ellyn Satter's book *Child of Mine* is a patient, firm, and reassuring book about feeding children, the equivalent of Dr. Spock's "you know more than you think you do."

Michel Cohen's *The New Basics* (Collins, 2004) is a great general parenting book. Cohen is extremely laid-back, especially about feeding.

The breastfeeding book we relied on was *The Nursing Mother's Companion* (Harvard Common Press, 2005). I'm sure a lot of people wondered why I was reading this book on the bus.

The review article summarizing the American Academy of Pediatrics' current findings on food allergy prevention, mentioned in chapter 3, is "Effects of Early Nutritional Interventions on the Development of Atopic Disease in Infants and Children: The Role of Maternal Dietary Restriction, Breastfeeding, Timing of Introduction of Complementary Foods, and Hydrolyzed Formulas" (*Pediatrics* 2008, 121, 189–91).

My favorite sushi cookbook is *The Sushi Experience* by Hiroko Shimbo (Knopf, 2006). It does not contain ham, although there is one pork roll. *The Connoisseur's Guide to Sushi* by Dave Lowry (Harvard Common Press, 2005) teaches informed ordering and good behavior at sushi restaurants.

For slow cooking, Beth Hensperger and Julie Kaufmann's *Not Your Mother's Slow Cooker Cookbook* (Harvard Common Press, 2005) is excellent. For pressure cooking, Lorna Sass's *Pressure Perfect* (William Morrow, 2004) and Vickie Smith's *Miss Vickie's Big Book of Pressure Cooker Recipes* (Wiley, 2008) are hard to beat.

The Quick Recipe by Cook's Illustrated is loaded with enough quality muffin recipes to kick-start your muffin shop — including all the muffins I made in chapter 21.

our favorite convenience foods

Rotisserie chicken and organic bagged salad greens. Duh. You buy them. I buy them. People who brag about their great roast chicken and their organic gardens buy them.

Frozen Brussels sprouts. Usually better than fresh, and a fraction of the work (and the price).

Frozen potstickers. If you have access to Safeway, their Select brand chicken and pork potstickers are fabulous, much better than the Ling Lings brand, which Iris and I find too sweet.

Frozen hash brown potatoes. Perfect for making hash.

Frozen ravioli. Pasta Prima Spinach and Mozzarella ravioli, from Costco, is Iris's favorite thing to find in her lunch box.

Frozen blueberries. The smaller wild blueberries are best. Keep them on hand for pancakes and muffins; also, small children often like snacking on frozen things, and the wild blueberries are small enough that even I don't worry about their choking potential.

Peeled garlic cloves. Especially at a Korean grocery, where they're always inexpensive, plump, and fresh.

White miso paste. Cheap, found in supermarkets (near the tofu), and keeps forever. Smear it on a piece of fish before broiling for a classic Japanese preparation, but the power of this soybean paste goes way beyond Japanese food. My favorite way to use it (tip of the hat to the New York chef David Chang) is to mash it together with butter and add it to sautéed vegetables. Miso butter gives anything an umami boost.

Better Than Bouillon. Let's talk about chicken stock. You've heard food writers harangue you about homemade stock. It's so easy, you should do it all the time — just collect chicken bones in the freezer, etc. My kitchen doesn't work this way, and even I don't have time to make stock very often. When I do, I simmer chicken backs and necks with scallions and ginger and use it as the basis for hot and sour soup. The rest of the time, I buy Better Than Bouillon organic chicken base in a jar. It's much cheaper than broth in a can, it lasts forever in the fridge, and if you're making something that requires a small amount of chicken broth (like my Ants on a Tree or Brussels sprout recipes), you'll never know the difference.

Wine in a box. With a small child in the house, it's nice to be able to pour a glass of wine at any time, and not just for the obvious reason. Lots of tasty food is made with wine. Red wine makes a quick pan sauce for steak or the braising liquid for a rich stew. White wine adds flavor and acidity to risotto, pasta sauce, or vegetables. The trick is having it on hand when you need it. (To answer your next question: no, not all of the alcohol cooks off, but the amount you end up consuming is so minimal, it's totally safe to serve food made with wine to children.)

That's where the box comes in. Unlike a bottle, which spoils within a week after opening, a box of wine stays fresh in the refrigerator for *months.* I buy Australian wine in the three-liter size (equivalent to four bottles), and it comes out to about four dollars a bottle.

The quality is acceptable for drinking and thoroughly excellent for cooking: the notion that you have to use real burgundy, or whatever, for cooking is silly. Four-dollar wine is fine. I'd stay away from the five-liter boxes like Franzia, which are sweeter, but even there the results won't be *bad.*

Alternatively, if you don't have refrigerator space to devote to the box, buy the four-packs of little 175-milliliter bottles. These are also very handy for children's slumber parties. Kidding!

Chubs of polenta. I mean the precooked polenta in a Jimmy Dean sausage-shaped plastic package. Iris and I often have this for breakfast, and she laughs every time I call it a chub, which actually is the term for this type of packaging. Slice it a third of an inch thick and fry it according to the grit cakes recipe in chapter 11.

Freeze-dried gnocchi. Sold in plastic pouches in the pasta aisle, these cook quickly and taste quite good. Sometimes you see small "gnocchetti," which are about half the size of regular gnocchi and perfect for small kids.

Chicken breasts. A great way to alienate people is to make snippy comments about boneless, skinless chicken breasts. It's true that I prefer dark-meat chicken most of the time, and chicken skin is delightful, but I really enjoy a good chicken breast. Here's how I cook them.

Remove the tenderloin, if it's attached to the breast, and cook it separately. This is a good piece to serve to kids, because it's the most tender and easy to chew. It also cooks faster, and you can therefore get it into a hungry kid's mouth sooner.

If you have time or feel like getting some aggression out, pounding the chicken breasts between sheets of plastic wrap will help them cook more quickly and evenly, but it's optional. (Iris loves helping out with this part.) Dry the chicken well with a paper towel and sprinkle with salt (and pepper, if you can get away with it). Heat some oil in a skillet (not nonstick) over medium-high until it begins to smoke. Place the chicken in the pan smooth-side down. Cook without disturbing for 3 minutes. Flip the breasts and cook another 3 minutes. Make a nick in the thickest part of the meat and check for doneness; they'll probably need another 1 or 2 minutes at this point.

Now you've got nicely browned chicken breasts, plus a bunch

of tasty brown bits stuck to the bottom of the pan. You can deglaze with a flavorful liquid (broth, wine, beer, cider) or just throw in some sliced mushrooms, which will release water and dissolve the brown bits. I am totally okay with presliced mushrooms. You can see the genesis of Baby Chicken and Mushrooms right here.

acknowledgments

This book began in the minds of Rebekah Denn and Molly Wizenberg. Denn, the food editor of the *Seattle Post-Intelligencer*, essentially dared me in print to write a book. Wizenberg, the author of the blog Orangette and the book *A Homemade Life*, did the same in front of a group of food writers. Rebekah and Molly, is this what you had in mind?

Molly also encouraged me to borrow her agent, Michael Bourret of Dystel & Goderich Literary Management. Michael has plenty of clients more talented than I, but as far as I can tell he works for me full-time.

Terry Durack, Kristin Yamaguchi, Rick Bayless, and Cheryl and Bill Jamison kindly allowed me to reprint their recipes.

The recipes in this book were tested by real home cooks: Wendy Burton, Anita and Cameron Crotty, Susan Ely, Lara Ferroni, Misty Granade, Kathleen McDade, Darsa Morrow, Lynne Sampson, and Becky Selengut. Thank you, recipe testers, for the most humbling experience of my life.

Hungry Monkey was written primarily at Remedy Teas (remedyteas.com) and Joe Bar (joebar.org) in Seattle. Thanks especially to Anthony and A. J. Arnold for opening the best teahouse in Seattle three blocks from my house and letting me camp out there all day with a pot of genmaicha.

Most of the best jokes in this book and none of the really dumb ones were suggested by my manuscript readers: Liza Daly, Dan Schmidt, Dan Shiovitz, Stephen and Misty Granade, Molly Wizenberg, and Shauna James Ahern. Any remaining tyopes are my fault.

Shauna was responsible for getting me and Iris on TV. In fact, the first email I ever got from her had the subject line: "Hey, Matthew, I want to help get you and Iris on TV!" Shauna has an uncanny ability to make absurd and wonderful things happen. She's a busy professional writer, but she seems to spend most of her time helping out other people. I wish I had half her generosity, not to mention energy. Buy her book, *Gluten-Free Girl*.

Steven Shaw and John Thorne took chances on my food writing when I was starting out and have been terribly supportive ever since. Nancy Leson at the *Seattle Times* got me my first-ever paid assignment. Holly Hughes has put me in her *Best Food Writing* anthology four times.

Jenna Johnson, my editor at Houghton Mifflin Harcourt, took a poorly organized manuscript, edited the hell out of it, and showed me how to turn it into a book. Thanks also to Lisa Glover, Alia Habib, Alison Miller, and Melissa Lotfy.

Every word of *Hungry Monkey* was written in Scrivener, a word processor for the Mac written by Keith Blount and available from literatureandlatte.com. Unlike Microsoft Word and its "helpful" suggestions, Scrivener was created by a writer for writers, and it is a joy to use.

Finally, this book and my life would be a big waste of time if not for my extremely high-quality family, Laurie and Iris, and my parents, Richard and Judy Amster, whose many hours of unpaid babysitting made *Hungry Monkey* possible. My mom has been telling me my whole life that I should write a book. Here it is, Mom. Hope you like it.